BORN OUT OF
WENLOCK

*William Penny Brookes and the British origins
of the modern Olympics*

CATHERINE BEALE

BORN OUT OF
WENLOCK

*William Penny Brookes and the British origins
of the modern Olympics*

Catherine Beale

First published in Great Britain in 2011 by The Derby Books Publishing Company Limited, 3 The Parker Centre, Derby, DE21 4SZ.

ISBN 978-1-85983-967-6
Printed and bound by CPI Antony Rowe, Chippenham.

CONTENTS

To two sports lovers in my life:
my husband Edmond, with my love and gratitude, and
my brother, Trevor Owens, with happy memories of being soundly
beaten at cricket in the barn.

FOREWORD
BY
JONATHAN EDWARDS CBE

It would be easy to credit William Penny Brookes with being, like many such men of his generation, a typical Victorian philanthropist. The list of what he was is long and varied. By profession, this family man was a doctor, surgeon and apothocary. He gave up much of his time to civic duties, including that of magistrate for over 40 years. As an entrepreneur he founded both a railway and a gas company and as a philanthropist he established his local National School, and also the Wenlock Agricultural Reading Society with its library and interest groups for the benefit of working men and the local community. Most significantly of all, he set up the Wenlock Olympian Society to organise an annual Games for what he called 'every grade of man'.

But Brookes had a dream, a single idea which burned fiercely inside him: to establish an open Olympic-styled Games where international athletes would compete, and which would have the benefit of creating friendship and unity among all nations.

As both an intellectual and a medical practitioner, Brookes believed that a healthy body was the route to a healthy mind – the Ancient Greek ideal – and his life-long campaign to get Physical Education on schools' curriculum has significance even today. It was a desire to share his work and research on physical education which brought the 81-year-old doctor into contact with a 27-year-old French aristocrat, Baron Pierre de Coubertin in 1890, and it was Brookes's vision and ideas which inspired Coubertin to go on and set up the modern international Olympic Games.

In his address to the Wenlock Olympian Games in 1867 William Penny Brookes wrote:

> A single idea, if it contain the germ of what is useful and good, will awaken kindred thoughts in other breasts; a single institution formed to carry out that idea will lead to the establishment of many similar institutions till the movement becomes a general one.

The importance of his work has remained virtually unrecognised outside sports' associated circles, but gradually, particularly during the last 10 years, his achievements have gained a well-deserved place in Olympic history.

Born Out of Wenlock is packed full of detailed information about the people who contributed to and competed in the Wenlock Olympian Games. Catherine's thorough investigation into the many competitors and contributors has produced intriguing pen sketches into their histories. In among them all, Brookes stands out in her research as a much loved and well-respected Victorian philanthropist – intent on achieving his goals and, even in old age, applying all his energy to improving the lot of the ordinary working man, not just in words, but in deeds.

Brookes was a visionary and generous in his sharing of ideas. Coubertin was also a visionary with the means and contacts to turn ideas into actualities. Inspired by Brookes, Coubertin built on and expanded those ideas and the international Olympic Games were born. The rest is history.

Jonathan Edwards

INTRODUCTION

'The Wenlock people alone have preserved and followed the true Olympian traditions'.
Pierre de Coubertin, 1897

'Où prenez-vous Much Wenlock?'

'Where, you might well ask, is Much Wenlock?'

With these words Baron Pierre de Coubertin opened an article that described his visit, in October 1890, to 'The Olympic Games at Much Wenlock'. Four years later, he founded the International Olympic Committee (IOC), and in 1896 the IOC staged its first Olympic Games in Athens. After a stuttering start, the quadrennial Olympic Games gained traction and became, over the ensuing century, the outstanding international festival of sport. Participation rose from 13 nations and 311 competitors at Athens in 1896, to 197 nations and 10,318 competitors at Atlanta in 1996. Coubertin was President of the IOC from 1896 until 1925. He died in 1937, having established his place in history as the 'Rénovateur' (literally renovator or restorer, but perhaps reviver) of the Games.

'Where,' you might well ask, 'is Much Wenlock's rightful place in modern Olympic history?' The extent to which the Wenlock Olympian Games and their founder William Penny Brookes (1809–1895) inspired Coubertin to revive the Games is the subject of this book. The question has received notice since the Wenlock Olympian Society's late President Norman Wood awoke the Games from 20 years' slumber in 1977. Wenlock has, since then, enjoyed royal visits, received interest from successive British Olympic bid teams, and given its name to one of the London 2012 mascots. Brookes gained an entry in the *Dictionary of National Biography*, and in 1994 the late IOC President, Juan Antonio Samaranch, placed a wreath on his grave, 'to pay tribute and homage to Dr Brookes who really was the founder of the Modern Olympic Games'.

To answer Coubertin's original question literally, Much Wenlock (population in 2009, 2,605) is a gem of a market town in central Shropshire, a county on England's western border with Wales. Coubertin's words, though, were less a question about geography and more an expression of disbelief at the juxtaposition of an agricultural community in a rural backwater with the Olympic Games – one of the most enduring symbols of arguably the greatest civilisation of classical antiquity. Coubertin's article continues (my translation) 'I can sense your discomfort at the coupling of this coarse name with these ancient memories...' It is a prejudice that anyone writing about this subject faces still. Today, though, it is the contrast between the slick, global multi-media event that the Olympic Games have become and the image of Victorian village sports that provides the contrast and provokes disbelief. 'Quirky' is the most common reaction.

As a result of the need to overcome scepticism, as well as having to overturn the depth and breadth of Coubertin's reputation as sole progenitor of the modern Olympic Games, strenuous efforts have had to be made on Wenlock's behalf. And just as Coubertin employed some sleight of hand to dislocate Brookes from the Olympic story, so those making the case for Wenlock have occasionally lost a little in translation, most notably from an oft-quoted phrase of Coubertin's, from the same article: 'si les jeux olympiques que la Grèce moderne n'a pas su ressusciter y revivent aujourd'hui, ce n'est pas à un Hellène qu'on en est redevable, mais bien au Dr W.P. Brookes.'

The promoters of Wenlock have translated this as 'if the olympic games that modern Greece has not been able to resuscitate live on today, it is due not to a Greek, but to Dr W.P. Brookes.' This gives the impression that Coubertin in 1890 was crediting Brookes with the survival of the Olympic Games beyond Greece's shores – painting him as a lone figure keeping the torch alight. In fact, an important 'y' has been dropped to arrive at that interpretation. If included, it reads 'if the olympic games that modern Greece has not been able to resuscitate survive *there* [ie in Much Wenlock] today, it is due not to a Greek, but to Dr W.P. Brookes', a less generous statement.

Whatever the quibbles over emphasis, what is undeniable is that something extraordinary had been happening in Much Wenlock for 40 years before it came to the attention of Pierre de Coubertin. William Penny Brookes, the surgeon of Much Wenlock (plate 1), began holding annual athletic meetings in the town in 1850. ('Penny' was a family name used to distinguish him both from his father, William Brookes, and his contemporary William Philpot Brookes, surgeon at Cheltenham General Hospital.) Brookes went on to stage Britain's first National Olympian Games at the Crystal Palace, London in 1866 and, most importantly, made contact with the Greeks in the 1850s. Over the ensuing decades he repeatedly urged them to revive their ancient games. Coubertin went to Much Wenlock in October 1890 (up to which point he had never publicly uttered the words 'Olympic Games' except in derision) and saw the Games for himself. Less than two years later he had decided to revive international Olympic Games, and within four years he had founded the IOC.

Although, as Coubertin acknowledged, Brookes was the founder, organiser and prime mover of the Wenlock Olympian Games, like all such endeavours, they were a community effort. The new hagiography of Brookes has tended to overlook the involvement of others, and in this account I have tried to temper that by writing the story of the Games and their development, rather than a biography of Brookes. Coubertin described Brookes as no seeker after glory, and it is hoped that he would approve.

Finding Brookes's collaborators has not been easy. The labourers for whom Brookes started his Games were often itinerant, hired in the Wenlock streets at the May fair for 12 months' employment, then free to move on. Wenlock was en route from London to Liverpool or Manchester, and many left, and in some cases emigrated. As the century wore on, the 'flight from the land' of workers into the cities (Birmingham is only 35 miles [56km] from Much Wenlock) ensured that few families are still today where they were in, say, the 1880s.

Paradoxically, another obstacle is the sheer volume of families called for example, Roberts, Davies or Evans in the region. Even some landed families that lent the Games important patronage have disappeared as a result of the problems facing country houses and their estates from the late 19th until the mid-20th century.

This is the main reason for my inclusion at the end of this book of an alphabetical list of competitors during Brookes's lifetime. With the growing interest in genealogy, it is hoped that descendants might come forward to share original material or anecdotes connected with the Games. Sport history is a relatively new discipline. Coubertin wrote in 1897 that 'this great movement doesn't seem, as yet, to have found its historians, but they are sure to come, because its history is most interesting and instructive.' It is hoped that the inclusion of Wenlock, Shropshire and National Olympian Games athletes might help those historians make further connections.

Much Wenlock, fortunately, has changed less than its population. One important aspect of its history which it is important to grasp is that Much Wenlock is the name of the town that stood at the heart of the much larger Wenlock borough. The town grew because of the seventh-century Abbey of St Milburga, (later a monastery) whose ruins (today the property of English Heritage) remain an important draw to visitors. The Abbey owned a colossal 18,000 acres of Shropshire, and those acres determined the geographical size of the borough of Wenlock, when it was first incorporated by royal charter from Edward IV in 1468. The monarch also granted the right to send a representative to Parliament, which was increased to two from the late 15th century.

The small town of Much Wenlock (population in 1821, 2,200) was therefore the administrative centre for the much bigger borough (population in 1821, 17,265) – in fact, by acreage the largest non-county borough in England. As far as its Games were concerned, the Society invited entrants from Wenlock, the borough, not just Much Wenlock the town. The Society founded to organise the Games is therefore the Wenlock Olympian Society, not the Much Wenlock Olympian Society. As a result of this geographical anomaly, to coin a sporting cliché, Wenlock has always punched above its weight.

The town of Much Wenlock would be thoroughly recognisable to Brookes and his colleagues today. This is why this book includes a trail that enlarges upon that which already exists in the town, attempting to connect it to the people and events that this book describes. The main streets have mostly retained their Victorian frontages, and independent shops still predominate. But in the early 21st century, the tanners, maltsters, saddlers, wheelwrights and blacksmiths have gone, though the butcher still thrives and the Talbot, Gaskell Arms, George and Dragon and the Raven Hotel remain where they were. Brookes's house (until recently a bank) has returned to private hands and cannot be visited, but occupies a prominent position on Wilmore Street.

The Linden Field, or Gaskell Field, where the Olympian Games were held, is today slightly larger than Brookes left it, and the trees that he planted have matured. It remains year-round a space for public use, and the former railway line to the east is today popular with dog walkers. The grandstand has disappeared as have the tennis courts, but the bowling green looks exactly as it did, and the cricket pitch lies, as approved at the Society's meeting of 1872, to the south of the bowling green. Overlooking the field is the recently rebuilt secondary school named after Brookes. Part of its rebuild has included, appropriately, the installation of first-class athletics facilities.

Most remarkably, the field is still used annually for the Wenlock Olympian Games over the second weekend in July, which are organised by the Society that Brookes founded (budget in 2010, £13,000). Teams of athletes descend from the Midlands and beyond to compete, and locals give liberally of their time, products, expertise and money as stewards, judges and sponsors, as they have been doing for 160 years, to enable this event to survive. Many of the track and field competitions take place on the new facilities at the school instead of on the field, but children still hurl cricket balls more or less on the home straight of the original turf track. The juxtaposition of first-class facilities with occasionally more home-spun competitions that encourage participation by all, will not disappoint those coming in search of quirks, and they successfully and unselfconsciously extend an arc of continuity from Brookes's Games to the present day.

This account also attempts to set the achievements at Wenlock in the broader context of the development of physical recreation in the 19th century. Seventeen years before Brookes's birth, W.A. Osbaldiston published *The British Sportsman and Nobleman, Gentleman and Farmer's Dictionary of Recreation and Amusement*. It moves from Abate to Zain without passing through 'running', 'athlete' or 'swimming' and certainly without mentioning 'Olympic'. When Brookes began his enterprise, there was very little 'sport' beyond hunting, shooting or fishing.

Along with his dream of Olympic revival, Brookes held dear his long-term aim of securing physical education for every child at elementary (primary) school. That, too, was realised just before his death. Very few are blessed with the necessary combination of skills and character to participate in Olympic Games; but most have participated (or will) in PE at school, and whether it was enjoyed or endured, have reaped the health benefits, and for that we have Brookes, in large measure, to thank. So what led this Shropshire doctor to espouse PE for children and adults of all classes, 'like one crying in the wilderness, at a time when there was universal apathy on the subject' (*Wellington Journal*, May 1909)?

It is less of a surprise that Much Wenlock should be at the forefront of any international movement when it is understood that geographically it lies just south of Ironbridge Gorge in Shropshire. Today, the Gorge is a UNESCO World Heritage site, recognition of its pivotal early role in the Industrial Revolution. Here, iron was first smelted using coke (made from coal) instead of charcoal (from wood) by Abraham Darby, in 1709. The resulting iron was developed by Darby's son in the early 1750s into pig iron suitable for forging into wrought iron, a change which made the Shropshire coalfield (the southern parts of which lay within Wenlock borough) the principal iron-producing area in Britain from then until the 1790s when it began to be eclipsed by other coal-producing regions.

Innovators from all over the country flocked to Coalbrookdale. Among them was John 'Iron-mad' Wilkinson (1728–1808) a leader in iron technology (particularly cast iron). Wilkinson settled at Coalbrookdale, became a Burgess of Wenlock, was instrumental in the building of the Iron Bridge (opened 1790), launched the first iron barge and was even buried in an iron coffin, on his death, the year before Brookes's birth. Further innovations, such as Richard Trevithick's steam railway locomotive and James Watt's steam powered pump were introduced here. Men of science and engineering had therefore been thinking the unthinkable, and then testing it in Shropshire for 100 years by the time that Brookes was born in 1809. Seen in that context, his forward-thinking outlook becomes less unlikely.

Brookes's partner in the medical practice, Allan Mackenzie, made a reference in his obituary of Brookes, to his being 'like Goldsmith', Oliver Goldsmith (1730–1774), who trained as a physician before writing the *Vicar of Wakefield* and *She Stoops to Conquer*. (He also published a *History of Greece,* but it makes no direct reference to the Olympic Games.) One of Goldsmith's poems, *The Deserted Village* conveys nostalgia for a lost English idyll of village life before nature's blessings were exchanged for the follies of luxury and 'the rage of gain'.

'…all the village train from labour free
Led up their sports beneath the spreading tree,…
And slights of art and feats of strength went round.
And still as each repeated pleasure tired,
Succeeding sports the mirthful band inspired…
These were thy charms, sweet village; sports like these…
These were thy charms – But all these charms are fled.
Sweet smiling village, loveliest of the lawn,
Thy sports are fled, and all thy charms withdrawn.'

This was written in response to the clearance of a village and farms to create the parkland of a country house. However, in rural Shropshire, where the effects of industry were early apparent, it took on a broader meaning. As men's lives began to be ruled not by the agricultural calendar but by the manufactory bell, the sense of a lost, more innocent time, less circumscribed by working hours, deepened. As Barrie Trinder, Shropshire's leading industrial historian has shown, until the 1840s it was customary for blast furnacemen to work seven 12-hour shifts a week. The physical, mental and moral effects on the workforce of the new industrial processes were evident here earlier than in the rest of the country. Therein lies another clue to Brookes's foundation of Olympian Games.

Goldsmith's poem was a favourite in the Brookes household. Brookes quotes almost directly from it, for example describing the poor man's best possessions as 'innocence and health'. He more than once paraphrases Goldsmith's fear that 'a bold peasantry, their country's pride, When once destroyed, can never be supplied'. His brother Andrew in writing to their sister Anne in London before Christmas 1872, when one of her sons, a curate, was considering marriage, cautioned that 'the time is gone by for Parsons to be *passing rich on forty pounds a year*', the italicised phrase taken directly from *The Deserted Village*.

Nostalgia alone, though, could not inspire a man to spend his life striving, as Brookes did, to bring physical recreation to all. Unfortunately, Brookes left us no written account of his motivations, but from the numerous speeches that he delivered at the opening of the Wenlock Olympian and other Games, reported in the press, and from the accounts of contemporaries that knew him, we can piece together several elements that shaped his resolve. Many of them will become clear but a few should be mentioned here, as they predate this account. They include his parents, his profession, and his politics.

Some of the philosophy with which Brookes's parents inculcated him survives in his mother Mary's letters. (Mary Brookes [née Doughty, of Worcester 1776–1869] remained at Wilmore Street in her widowhood.) In 1857 she wrote, 'Our time here is short even at the longest & if we strive to do our duty we shall quit this world more happily than if we surely lived for ourselves alone, & laid up riches for others who follow after us.' On another occasion she gave thanks 'that not one of my children are selfish in disposition. I do think nothing more sinful than not using Gods gifts for the benefit of others as well as ourselves.'

Brookes's father, William Brookes (1776–1830), was the surgeon apothecary in Wenlock before him, the profession from which the 'general practitioner' would emerge by the 1850s (the 1851 census describes William Penny Brookes as a surgeon, 'Practising generally'). All three Brookes sons entered the medical profession. After William Penny, John (1811–1835) practised in Madeley within Wenlock borough but was killed after falling from his horse, just a couple of years into practice. Andrew (1813–1894) two years younger than John, worked initially with his eldest brother at Wenlock before moving to nearby Cressage in around 1844 and to Shrewsbury in 1860.

William Brookes senior is glimpsed in his wife's letters. She wrote to her daughter, Anne Wilkinson (1820–1900) in London, that William Brookes senior was 'so kind a person...for although whilst living he had many enemies – when dead, one of the bitterest he had, shed tears at his grave – I am often delighted now by hearing the poor speak about him.' This suggests that Brookes senior was a friend of the poor, and unafraid of upsetting others when necessary, both qualities that he bequeathed to his eldest son.

William Penny Brookes was apprenticed to his father on 12 August 1824, the eve of his 15th birthday. Brookes, therefore, spent five intensely formative years travelling round Wenlock visiting patients with his father, absorbing his views during the long rides between consultations, dismounting to gather botanical samples as they went, acquiring his father's philosophy, being influenced by the medical thought of the previous generation, witnessing with his own eyes the living conditions and physical state of Wenlock's inhabitants, and learning his father's view of the reasons for that.

Among Shropshire's doctors of Brookes senior's generation were the father of Charles Darwin, Robert Darwin of Shrewsbury, and William Withering of Wellington, Shropshire, (1741–1799). Withering first recognised the medicinal properties of digitalis, the foxglove, was a co-founder of Birmingham General Hospital, a member of the Lunar Society, a friend of radical Joseph Priestley, and an expert botanist. Of most influence on William Penny Brookes's work though, was Thomas Beddoes (1760–1808) of Shifnal. Beddoes is today remembered for his experimental hospital in Bristol where he studied in particular, the effects on the body of nitrous oxide (laughing gas), with his apprentice, the chemist Humphrey Davy.

Beddoes died the year before William Penny Brookes's birth, but his writing must have been brought to Brookes's attention by his father. In 1792, Beddoes wrote *The History of Isaac Jenkins*, an illustration of the evils of drunkenness, which sold over 40,000 copies. This was highly pertinent to the cases that Brookes was visiting with his father, as Much Wenlock had an unenviable reputation for drunkenness. In 1859 Brookes warned the men at his Olympian Games 'against the fearful consequences of intemperance'. Twenty years later, Brookes congratulated the competitors for 'taking away from Wenlock the reproach of drunkenness by which it was formerly characterised'. Another decade and he could reflect that 'Many years ago Wenlock was one of the most drunken places in the county, but now it had become one of the most sober'.

Another of Beddoes's earliest works considered the 'causes, early signs, and prevention of pulmonary consumption' a widespread killer. In Shrewsbury, in 1790–99, 'above one death in four' was caused by consumption. Beddoes observed that workers inhaling particles were most susceptible and considered exercise advantageous. Beddoes blamed new manufacturing systems for destroying the strength of workers 'cooped up for long hours in cramped, polluted workshops, and exposed to noxious fumes, heat and dust.' In *Hygeïa* (1802–03), Beddoes asserted that consumption would affect worst those with 'too great narrowness of the chest,' and those with 'the want of a free sweep in the ribs'. Beddoes privileged the preservation of health over its recovery once lost, and stressed the importance of diet and exercise. He suggested that some of the old sports might be revived. He thus helped revitalise medicine 'as an engine of social improvement'. His ideal doctor would be a 'humanist physician' pursuing national improvement – almost a definition of William Penny Brookes's career.

Finally noteworthy for an influence on Brookes, is that in *Hygeïa* Beddoes compared Britain in his post-Enlightenment times with classical Athens. The latter was widely seen to have squandered her greatness on becoming softened by a sedentary, urban existence. As Scots physician George Cheyne had expressed it 'while they lived in their Simplicity and Virtue [the Athenians] were Healthy, Strong and Valiant: But afterwards…they sunk into Effeminacy, Luxury, and Diseases, and began to study Physick, to remedy those Evils which their Luxury and Laziness had brought upon them'.

William Brookes also bequeathed to his sons his politics. Both William Penny Brookes and his brother Andrew Good Brookes supported the Whig (later the Liberal) cause, at a time when, politically 'to be a Liberal, in Wenlock was to be suspected of all manner of wicked designs, to be watched and hunted like a mad dog, to have the means of living taken away, and to be crushed like a snail in its shell, or driven from the town.' Between the first and second Reform Acts (1832–67) Wenlock's two MPs were unshakably Tory. From 1835 until 1847 all 12 of Shropshire's MPs were Tory – known as the 'Twelve Apostles'. As a young Whig in Shropshire, Brookes was certainly influenced by the Whig MP for Shrewsbury from 1826, Robert Aglionby Slaney (1791–1862) of Hatton Grange, Shifnal. The Slaneys owned mines and ironworks in Shropshire which they leased to the Darby family, so a share of their income was produced by the new workers in Shropshire's industrial coalfield.

Slaney was concerned by the conditions of the workers in industrial towns as much and perhaps more than any other contemporary politician, yet he has received scant recognition and has been described as 'one of the most neglected social reformers of his period'. He would play a leading role in the foundation of the Education Department (1839), and would chair the influential 1840 Select Committee on the Health of Towns which would propose improvements in urban dwellings, sewerage and drainage, public amenities such as cemeteries, public baths and parks, and the creation of local boards of health in towns.

Brookes appears to have been profoundly influenced by Slaney's early writing on political economy, his 1824 *Essay on the Beneficial Direction of Rural Expenditure*. This reads almost as a manifesto for Brookes's work in Wenlock, and Slaney was an early donor to Brookes's Olympian endeavours. He recommends the foundation of libraries, the planting of trees, the improvement of farm cottages, buildings and roads (Brookes was to become the Borough's Commissioner for Roads – he travelled them more than most), 'clearing a water-course; building a market, or school-house...sinking a well, or erecting a pump'.

Of most relevance to Brookes's formation of the Wenlock Olympian Society, Slaney wrote that 'Health is the poor man's only possession;...whatever tends to preserve or restore it must be of infinite advantage to him...' He believed that the poorer classes' tendency to drink arose 'from their having no place of exercise or amusement on their holiday; for at cricket matches this is seldom the case...Music should be provided to enliven the scene, and some kind of rural sport should be introduced. Dancing, prison bars, foot-ball, quoits, cricket, &c. and a prize be given to the winning party...Stalls and booths may be erected for the display and sale of different articles...The meeting should break up at an early hour, that all may return home whilst it is light.'

Slaney devoted one chapter to places of amusement for the labourers. 'A few years ago, the peasantry used to spend their holiday in some athletic sport. The victory obtained by their parish or hundred, served them for boast for the next half-year...At present, owing to the inclosure of open lands and commons, the poor have no place in which they may amuse themselves in summer evenings, when the labour of the day is over, or when a holiday occurs.

'The consequence is, the peasant either sits sullenly at home, trespasses on the woods and fields of others, or goes to the public house, where he loses his money, and spends his time in gambling and drinking...they are driven to country wakes, and ale-house dances, where, being exempted from that decent control which publicity, daylight, and the occasional presence of their masters occasion, it is not surprising they commit excesses.'

To drive home his point, Slaney quoted John Sumner, the future Archbishop of Canterbury's *Treatise on the Records of Creation*: 'The love of ease is the great incentive to industry; relaxation is certainly advantageous, and probably necessary...; the ancients sought it in their games and spectacles'. Throughout this work, Slaney referred to Joseph Strutt's *Sports and Pastimes*, published in 1810. This history of English recreation was a favourite of Brookes's. He gave it as a prize at the Wenlock Olympian Games.

Slaney's conclusion is worth quoting in full, as it reads like a description of the Wenlock Olympian Society's Games field, then and now:

'Let us endeavour then to give to the poor...a place of exercise, where they may amuse themselves at leisure hours without injury to their neighbours. For this purpose a piece of level ground, from two to five acres in extent, should be prepared, laid down with grass and clover, and dedicated to the use of the labouring classes, of the hamlet or parish; if situated near the school it would serve as a play-ground for the children, and in summer evenings would entice many of the men from drinking. As they become more expert in any exercise they used, emulation would increase, and matches between their own and neighbouring parishes ensue…A square form is neither picturesque nor convenient; a few trees on the east and north sides might be planted so as to give shelter and ornament; it should of course be open to the south and west sun: some neighbouring farmer would probably undertake to keep it in order, on consideration of being permitted to graze it with his sheep; and a few stone benches and a shed would add to the comfort of the inhabitants.'

The main projects that Brookes undertook in Much Wenlock were sewage disposal, a clean water supply, gas lighting, the building of the school, the improvement of roads, the bringing of the railway, the restoration of the Guildhall, the renovation of the church, the provision of a reading room, and the recreation of the population. Brookes was doing, in Wenlock, what others were doing on the national scale in the metropolis and other large cities. Brookes explained that he did what he could within the sphere in which the Almighty had chosen to place him. When laying a foundation stone for a railway bridge in Much Wenlock in 1862, Brookes quoted the scriptural maxim, 'Whatsoever thy hand findeth to do, do it with thy might.'

Early 19th-century Britain was acutely exercised by trying to avoid the kind of revolution that had overturned France in 1789. Brookes was in Paris studying in late July 1830, when the city suffered another revolutionary convulsion. A friend of Brookes's and fellow medical student, called Foulkes, was shot dead while looking out of a window at Lawson's Hotel on the rue St Honoré. Some tiles had been flung from the neighbouring house on to the troops below and General Coutard ordered the soldiers to fire, which they did at the windows of the hotel. 'Mr Foulkes received a ball from a pistol in the forehead, and he instantly fell dead at the feet of his friends'. This experience must have sharpened further Brookes's liberal sympathies.

Along with his parents and politics, Brookes's profession was unquestionably the greatest influence on his life's work. His apprenticeship served, Brookes went to study at St Thomas's Hospital in London (September 1829–May 1830), spent three to four months in Paris (until the end of August 1830), and almost six months in Padua, Italy (until around the end of February 1831). Brookes took his examination at the Society of Apothecaries on 3 March 1831, and proceeded home at once to begin 60 years of medical practice in Much Wenlock. His father had died of typhoid on 23 June 1830 (three days before King George IV) while Brookes was in Paris.

This was a fairly typical training for an aspiring surgeon of Brookes's day. The qualifications required for Brookes's practice were the licence of the Society of Apothecaries, and membership of the Royal College of Surgeons (known as 'hall and college'). The time at the London hospital (usually six to 18 months) was a chance to hear the latest theories and acquire a framework for the cases seen during the previous five years. St Thomas's had just split from Guy's and had entered a period of decline when Brookes attended. He took himself also to the private school of Edward Grainger in Webb Street, where he studied theoretical anatomy and physiology – the proper function of the body and its organs, which was to be the great field of study in 19th-century medicine. Not until the 1832 Anatomy Act was passed though, did a reliable supply of bodies become available. There is a good chance that any cadavers that Brookes dissected were exhumed by the grave-robbing Resurrectionists. On the continent, matters were very different, and this provided much of the impetus for students (about 200 of them in Paris in 1828) to travel abroad.

Paris, post-revolution, had restructured its medical profession. Teaching was by the highly enlightened method of 'walking the Paris hospitals' (of which there were seven general and five specialist). By accompanying surgeons on their rounds, Brookes could observe leading men treating a wide range of cases. After the rounds, there was often an informal lecture covering the cases seen, with discussion of diagnosis, prognosis and the likely causes of the illness. There would also be opportunities to witness surgery, and where relevant, an autopsy. Dentistry, diseases of the eye, and courses on bandaging could also be attended. In addition, midwifery by men, which would constitute a large part of provincial practice, was a derided profession in Britain, but was carefully taught in Paris, where there were opportunities to see and examine pregnant patients.

The great medical innovation (showing just how little doctors of Brookes's day had to work with) was what *The Times* described in December 1824 as 'a wonderful instrument called the stethoscope', invented by René Laennec of the Necker Hospital, who had died in 1826, just before Brookes went to Paris. With pleurisy, tuberculosis, pneumonia and emphysema taking so many lives, the skill of auscultation (diagnosis by listening through the chest wall) was immensely valuable. Laennec's discovery had been made one day when, embarrassed to put his ear directly to the *embonpoint* of a young lady, he had rolled up a sheaf of papers and listened through that. The sound was much clearer. Thus the early stethoscope, resembling an ear trumpet, was invented. By the time that Brookes reached Paris, 14 years later, diagnosis there using this instrument was highly advanced, and the benefit of a healthy chest clear.

Brookes was in Paris when Guillaume Dupuytren, the great French anatomist was at the height of his powers as head-surgeon at the immense Hôtel-Dieu hospital, opposite Notre Dame Cathedral. Also still working was the great military surgeon, Dominique-Jean Larrey (1766–1842), who had been surgeon-in-chief to Napoleon's armies until injured and captured at Waterloo. In this role, he had organised more mobile and efficient field hospitals and had prioritised cases, regardless of rank or nationality, according to surgical priority. His system significantly reduced death rates. Larrey's compassion won the admiration alike of Napoleon and Wellington. Brookes was later to refer to the work of this remarkable man, and it seems highly likely that while in Paris he would have walked over to Les Invalides to see Larrey operate.

The bodies of those who died at Hôtel-Dieu were taken to vast dissection rooms, behind La Pitié hospital, near the Jardin des Plantes. Anyone, after paying the appropriate sum, had the opportunity to dissect here. Evidence of the lasting influence of this on Brookes's promotion of sport came in a speech of his of 1866. 'If others only knew, as medical men do, the wonders revealed by an examination of the structure of the human body…[athletic] societies like these, which have for their object the preservation of this noble structure from debility and premature decay, would not be lightly estimated'. In 1872, he asserted 'Were a knowledge of the structure of the human body more general, it would be more valued and better cared for'.

Brookes left us one reference to the influence that his training in Paris had on his encouragement of exercise for health. At a meeting of Hadley Athletic Society in 1882, Brookes said that 'he was first attracted to physical exercise in 1830, by taking up a book at a small inn on his way to Paris, which dealt with the subject of weavers, who died out in the third generation…caused by long confinement and want of out-door recreation and exercise. The book made a great impression upon his mind, and since then he had taken a greater interest in the recreation of the working class.' The developments at Coalbrookdale helped Brookes to realise the importance of occupation on health. In the year Brookes returned to England, Charles Turner Thackrah, a doctor in Leeds, demonstrated that the local flax and cotton workers were suffering premature mortality because of their working conditions, and it was a field rising in importance.

From Paris, Brookes went on through Europe to study at Padua, effectively the university of Venice, founded in 1222. Padua's medical school had been the great European centre of Renaissance medicine, at its height in the 16th century. Notable English medics who had preceded Brookes under the Lion of St Mark and the inscription 'Gymnasium omnium Disciplinarium' into the university Palazzo, included Thomas Linacre, court Physician to Henry VIII who founded the Royal College of Physicians, and William Harvey (1578–1657) who, by careful observation, discovered that blood was pumped round the circulatory system by the heart.

Of most relevance to Brookes's Olympic future was the fact that there were close links between Padua and Greece owing to Venice's former possession of several Greek territories, including the Ionian islands and Crete. By the time that Brookes arrived in Padua in 1830, Venice had lost her empire, but Greece was negotiating the recovery of territories from the Ottoman empire after being engaged in an armed struggle from 1821–28. The Greeks received immense sympathy from western Europe, where classical Greece had exerted such a strong influence since the 18th-century Enlightenment. Most notably in England, Greece's struggle had inspired Lord Byron. After he left England for good in 1816, Byron took up the cause and died from a fever at Messolonghi in 1824. The modern history of Greece became, in the mind of keen supporters, an extension of its ancient history, and it was hoped that independence would bring a rebirth of the Golden Hellenic Age. Such supporters were known as Philhellenes, a label that Coubertin, among others, was to apply to William Penny Brookes.

Having witnessed revolution in Paris, Brookes found himself in Padua studying alongside Greece's youth, learning of their aspirations for a new nation. By 1830, the independence of some southern regions of Greece, including the Peloponnese (then called the Morea), had been agreed, although a new monarch would not be settled until 1832. The Peloponnese incorporated ancient Elis which included the site of the Olympic Games (one of four including the Nemean, Pythian and Isthmian Games). These trials of strength between the city states of the Hellenic peninsula, may date from the ninth century BC, but the first recorded Games date from 776BC. For the duration, peace reigned, thousands of men (only) came to watch, artists exhibited, poets recited and scholars and teachers debated. A herald introduced the events, and victors were crowned with olive. The events included running, jumping, discus, javelin, wrestling, pentathlon (from around 708BC), boxing, pankration (a brawl in which strangling seems to have been permitted) and chariot and horse racing.

In 1829, nearly 1,500 years after the Games were abolished, for six weeks from 10 May, the French systematically excavated the site, including the temple of Zeus, whose statue had been one of the seven wonders of the ancient world. Archaeology can rarely have exerted such power. The uncovering of Greece's ancient site evoked her past glories, just as the new nation was rising. The Greek Senate gave several architectural fragments from the temple of Zeus to the French in 1830, and they were transported to the Louvre in Paris where they might have been seen by the young doctor abroad. Therefore, Brookes's foreign training gave him much more than medical knowledge, including an international outlook and a sense of the relevance of even ancient history to the modern world.

When writing of anyone as remarkable as William Penny Brookes, the subject can become burdened by their own goodness. This is a particular risk where the subject has selected the material to be used. The Society's surviving sources mainly consist of its Minute Books, into which Brookes pasted the Games Programmes, newspaper reports of Games days, supportive letters from significant public figures, photographs where appropriate, and any other material that he thought relevant. What is clear from the newspaper content is that at times Brookes was probably as effective a spin doctor as he was a medical one. He certainly recognised the power of the newspapers to convey a message.

For a more rounded account, other sources have been consulted, particularly surviving newspapers (for items that failed to make Brookes's cut) and archival diaries and letters. Unfortunately, it appears that no large body of personal material has survived from which to attempt to draw a broader portrait. What does come through from other sources, which balances the picture a little, is a sense that Brookes, in his later years, when he was known as 'the King of Wenlock', had begun to irk younger men with his unbending demands in meetings, and attempts to steam-roll things through.

This is glimpsed at a meeting reported in the *Shrewsbury Chronicle* of Friday 8 May 1891. Wenlock Burial Board, was about to have the new cemetery consecrated by the Bishop of Hereford. Brookes wanted to buy shrubs and plants, but the vicar and others felt that no more should be spent. Brookes declared that he would go himself to Wellington (Shropshire) and get five more shrubs and see they were properly put in, if the meeting would sanction it. Dr Hart, the other doctor in the town, rescued the meeting by seconding Brookes's proposal only on condition that 'the Board were never again asked by him to spend more money in planting trees or shrubs.' Brookes got his way. It is a small example, and Brookes had only the good of Wenlock in mind, but it is eloquent of a change of guard. Similarly, one also cannot help but wonder whether in an otherwise overwhelmingly fond obituary, his medical partner Allan Mackenzie's observation that Brookes 'could tell hundreds of anecdotes to illustrate the changes which had occurred in his lifetime' does not have an underlying note of exhaustion.

There is one portrait, though, that rings particularly true. Although not identified, I believe it to be of Brookes as Wenlock's doctor in his 50s or 60s. It is by the Revd Charles Great Rex, who married Brookes's youngest daughter Isabella on 6 October 1863. Great Rex was curate at Much Wenlock before becoming vicar of Halberton near Tiverton in Devon. He returned to Hope Bagot, Ludlow, and went afterwards to Montgomery, just over the Welsh border. During his time in Wenlock, Great Rex supplied odes for the Wenlock Olympian Games, and later wrote short stories under the pseudonyms Abel Log, and, intriguingly 'Lindon Meadows', a barely-veiled play on the name of Wenlock Games's Linden Field.

As Lindon Meadows, Great Rex wrote *College Recollections and Church Experiences*, dedicated to Isabella. In 'The Ride Along the Ridge' (Wenlock Edge) he is called out to baptise a baby 'took with fits, shocking' after 11 o'clock at night, somewhere near Major's Leap, a precipice over which the Royalist Major Smallman allegedly rode on his horse to evade capture during the Civil War. While the young lad who raised the alarm goes to get the doctor, Meadows sets out in the darkness on foot, assuming the boy would tell the doctor that he was on the road. However, the doctor's horse is startled by the curate. Rivers [surely Brookes] shoots at the stranger, but luckily his blunderbuss misfires. Meadows makes himself known before the doctor can fire again.

'"Bless me! I beg your pardon," cried the doctor…; "I took you for a highwayman; I never knew my blunderbuss miss fire before."

"Pray don't trouble yourself to apologize for that," I said, seating myself comfortably by his side (for we were already acquainted); "I was in hopes our young friend who is hanging on behind would not forget to tell you that I was expecting to be picked up."

"He never said one syllable about it," said Rivers, turning round and giving the lad's ear a pinch that brought the tears to his eyes; "and a very pretty mistake I was nearly making in consequence!" Here the doctor, asking me to hold the reins a moment, took out his match-box, lighted a cigar, put on his glove again, and then, relieving me of my charge, began one of his entertaining stories – about a mad patient who fancied himself a tea-kettle, and was obliged to be watched lest he should place himself upon the fire.'

They drive on until Rivers pulls up suddenly, recalling that a landslip had recently occurred at Major's Leap, taking the railings with it. Suspecting they had had a narrow escape, they go on to the farmhouse, attend to little Isaac, borrow a lantern to see just how close they had been to the edge, and set off home.

'When we had reached the place where the side of the road had fallen, I took the lantern in my hand, got carefully down from the gig, and measured the distance between the mark left by our passing wheel and the edge of the abyss.

"What do you make of it?" said Rivers, who, being short-sighted, did not trouble himself to alight; "*I* say, a foot, and perhaps less."

"What think you of six inches? Not a hair's breadth more, I assure you."

"God be praised!" cried he, wiping his forehead; "this is enough to give a man some serious thoughts."

…Nor did I ever visit that part of my parish again without pausing for a few moments to gaze over the brink of the dangerous gulf into which the doctor and I had so narrow an escape of being helplessly precipitated.'

In modern athletics, 6in (15cm) is itself a 'gulf' that might as well be 100ft. It is intriguing to consider that such might have been the margin that preserved William Penny Brookes to meet Pierre de Coubertin. International athletic competition would have come to life without their encounter. But, as will be seen, it might have taken a very different form had Coubertin not received a packet of papers and photographs from Shropshire, and asked himself 'Where is Much Wenlock'?

CHAPTER 1

He loved chivalrye,
Trouthe and honour, freedom and curteisye
Canterbury Tales, Geoffrey Chaucer

The peal of bells reached the ears of William Penny Brookes on the clear air of an autumnal morning, as he sealed and stamped the last notes for the post before he set out. He hesitated, and looked across at Holy Trinity. How ironic that the church bells should hail a day about which he had met opposition from the clergy. Well, 22 October had arrived, and events must take their course. Gathering a crowd of the working classes together in 1850, just two years after revolution had raged through Europe and Chartists had rioted throughout England, was a risk, he must acknowledge. But what he was doing was essential. He must trust the men of Wenlock, and cleave to his faith.

As he opened the door to the hall, he found Jane and the children lined up where his patients usually waited. What would become of them if the day were a disaster and it damaged his practice? Mary, Adeline and Isabella looked fit to burst, their neat curls dancing at the prospect of going up to the racecourse later, while John and Willie were feigning indifference at being allowed to go in the procession with their father. Mama and his sister Maria had descended from their rooms at the top of the house to see him off. His mother's smile seemed to reassure him 'you have put the poor first; your father would approve'.

Once his coat and hat were on, the door was opened, and the bells' joy somersaulted across the threshold with the morning sunlight. He squinted across to the churchyard where, in his own youth, the townsfolk had enjoyed their fairs and church wakes, accompanied by every kind of drunken intemperance – wrestling, quarrelling, fighting (and worse) – on the very turf that covered the remains of their departed relatives. It had been easy to condemn, but until now, nothing had been offered instead. Looking the other way towards Barrow Street, he saw the first knot of his fledgling class beginning to form outside the Guildhall (plate 2). There was no turning back now.

John Elmer, a master painter by trade and their President, and young Edwin Yardley, the cooper and Treasurer, each proffered a hand as Brookes approached. A 'fair morning' was the verdict. Stowed under the half-timbered hall were the cricket stumps and bat, the football, the rope for the high jump and the banners. Between half past nine and 10, the Wenlock band rolled up piecemeal, and blacksmith William Yates appeared with a set of quoits. The remaining committee members, shoemaker Francis Richards, Thomas Lawley the printer, Richard Franks the Lancashire builder and joiner, and Edward Hinton, the agent to the Wenlock estate of landowner Sir Watkins Williams Wynn, converged from Spital and Barrow Streets. Brookes was grateful for the show of support, particularly from Hinton whose influence spread wide. He felt nervously for the notes for his speech, but was immediately distracted by the welcome sight of nearly 30 footballers shambling towards him.

As 10 o'clock drew nigh, Brookes and Yardley began to form up the procession three abreast, first the band and flag-bearers, then the competitors aged five to 25, Brookes twitching them into some kind of order with occasional inquiries about the health of mother or the new baby. Finally, the committee brought up the rear, having shared out between them the implements needed for the games. Brookes and Yardley settled themselves at the head of the procession at exactly 10am, and as the chimes died away, the band struck up.

From the Guildhall the little procession began to walk up Spital Street, past Barnett's the butchers, and Trevor's the grocer (plate 3). At the noise and spectacle, passers-by turned on their heel to gawp, and others were beckoned from the depths of the ironmonger's and the smithy to 'come, see'. Every stray dog was soon running alongside, some barking at the band. Brookes quietly offered up thanks that market day was yesterday and the cattle fair five days ago, so he was unlikely to meet a flock of sheep, and the oxen were now being dispersed by drovers all over the region. That was not to say that they had not left their mark, though, and adhesions to the boots were inevitable.

On past Boycott the baker, and Webb the saddler, they advanced on to the High Street. Brookes reflected how glad he was that he had caused the old watercourse that ran up the street – well-named as 'Schittebrok' since the 14th century – to be covered in. The open sewer, filled with the effluvium of the tannery, skinner's, abattoir, domestic dwellings and town's many farmyards had been a hazard, but the ability to process up the street was an unforeseen benefit. Word of their approach raced ahead, and soon curious onlookers were pointing and gesturing at the novel attraction. Mrs Woof and Miss Bryan stood on their doorstep wiping their hands on their apron, and a waggon pulled up to let them pass, while the driver pushed back his cap and gave them a 'side'ards' look. George Ross, the Edinburgh-born policeman called out that he would be up later, while others gestured to the doctor. Brookes acknowledged them with a touch of his hat, stuck out his chin, and pressed on. Some fell in behind, and followed the band.

On gaining the Wynnstay Arms, the doctor led the procession left on to the Bridgnorth road, and up the bank to the racecourse, where their games were to take place. Beyond the town and relieved to have that part behind him, Brookes, like a latter-day Pied Piper, had a few moments to reflect on how a 41-year-old surgeon had come to be leading such a rag-tag and bobtail mob to the racecourse. The Olympian Class had been his idea, one of several classes including natural history and botany that had developed from the Wenlock Agricultural Reading Society (WARS) – a sort of mechanics' institute for educating adults in Wenlock borough. Brookes had been the driving force of this institution, founded nine years earlier in 1841.

WARS had begun as a library to bring the latest agricultural innovations to farmers – mostly tenants of the local landowners, the Foresters, Sutherlands, Wynns or Lords Wenlock – at a time when the supply and price of food to the growing industrial districts was highly sensitive. Rioting over the price of wheat, which fed through into the workers' staple food, bread, had become alarmingly frequent. Debate had raged about the Corn Laws (which protected the price farmers got for their wheat) until in 1846 they had been repealed, a victory for impoverished factory workers, but a move that meant that in theory corn from abroad could now enter the country free of charge. Farmers were going to have to compete, and their farming practices to improve.

Many influential figures, including the Duke of Wellington, Benjamin Disraeli and the Duke of Sutherland were approached by Brookes to help with WARS library and responded with books on agriculture, or financial donations. Many women in Wenlock gave to the cause, which was gratefully noted, and although 'works of light and trifling character, as novels, romances etc.' (evidently assumed to be the ladies' choice of reading) were forbidden, their needs were met with 'many histories and biographies'. The library was established in the home of Thomas Lawley, next door to Brookes's house, until it outgrew its accommodation. By 1849 it had 1,084 volumes.

With WARS's lending library up, running, popular and topical, Brookes had broadened its scope to lessons in natural history and botany, Wenlock Edge, the escarpment running south west from the town, being a unique limestone outcrop containing extraordinary fossils. Eventually art classes and music (the Philharmonic class) would be added. All of this, however, attracted the middle classes of Wenlock, the families of the solicitors, bankers, grocers, the clergy and wealthier farmers. Brookes felt strongly that something must be done through WARS to benefit the labourers. What was there for their entertainment?

The agricultural calendar held several occasions for fun and games – the hiring fair at which farm workers were engaged on May Day, harvest home, Whitsun, Easter and Christmas, besides the fair in June and the town's wakes, usually in August. All of these occasions, though, were marked by drunkenness and brawls, with damage done to the person and to family life, as Brookes, the doctor, knew only too well. The other working-class entertainments, like cock-fighting and bull-baiting, though repellent, had provided amusement, but the Cruelty to Animals Act of 1835 had made them illegal. The ale-house was now the labourers' only resort. So deep-seated was drunkenness, that when some of the new Teetotallers from Broseley had brought their mission to Much Wenlock in 1843, the windows of their meeting place were broken, they were subjected to rough music, and drummed out of town.

To be an agricultural labourer in 1850 was, in most cases, to be a pauper, living on nine or 10 shillings a week when there was work, and nothing when there was none – an income determined by the climate. Home was a one up one down cottage with an earth floor, damp walls, a leaking roof and no sanitation. The working hours were long, clad in heavy clothes, fuelled by bread, cheese and potatoes. It required a strong constitution to throw off the almost inevitable chest and lung conditions (aggravated by threshing or milling corn) and rheumatism resulting from working in the wet and cold. Brookes knew that the agricultural worker's lot would be improved by better living conditions and higher wages, but these would take a long time to effect. A government inquiry in 1869 would conclude that the labourers' cottages in Shropshire were worse than in any other county bar Dorset. What could best be supplied to the working classes of Wenlock in 1850 was improved health to try to stave off the effects of their conditions.

Brookes had the idea of creating a class of WARS 'for the promotion of the moral, physical and intellectual improvement of the Inhabitants of the Town & Neighbourhood of Wenlock, and especially of the Working Classes by the encouragement of outdoor recreation and by the award of prizes annually at public meetings for skill in Athletic exercises and proficiency in intellectual and industrial attainments.' The annual meeting would have to be entertaining, so that competitors would be engaged and onlookers amused, yet at the same time encourage health and vigour. They would need money to offer as prizes for the competitions and to acquire the necessary equipment, to be raised from subscribers to the class and from local patrons that might benefit from a fitter working class – the local farmers and landowners, as well as local furnace and works owners. To secure their support, they would need to be sure that the class was run with the utmost decorum – not easy in a town renowned in Shropshire for its drunkenness.

The veneer of respectability might be supplied by invoking the games of ancient Greece, a nation close to Brookes's heart as the birthplace of modern medicine, and for its struggle while he had been in Padua, for independence from the Ottoman Empire, a cause lent glamour by the late Lord Byron. The ancient Greeks had been the most civilised people on earth. Thus, only one name had suggested itself to Brookes for his new endeavour – the Olympian Class of the Wenlock Agricultural Reading Society.

The ancient games, though seemed remote, as barely 100 people straggled up the bank on to the racecourse and gathered into a square in front of the grandstand. The band fell silent. John Elmer bid them good day, and read out the terms of their entertainment. There were three umpires and their decision was final. 'Any person guilty of drunkenness, or using profane or improper language, or otherwise misbehaving himself' would be liable to a one to five shilling fine. Elmer also listed the prizes for the two days' events: quoits, cricket, football, juvenile footraces for boys under seven and 14 years, two footraces for adults, leaping in height and leaping in distance (high jump and long jump).

The choice of competitions was influenced by the games formerly held at the church wakes. The fund-raising wakes had been held throughout England usually starting on the Sunday after the saint's day of the local church, and continuing for several days. Over the centuries, they had evolved into something akin to a secular carnival, at which pleasure-seeking for the working classes predominated. Rustic sports included donkey racing, wheelbarrow races (blindfolded), a women's race for a smock, hot tasty-pudding eating, grinning through a horse collar, chasing a greased pig, running in sacks, smoking pipes of tobacco, and sometimes bull-baiting, cock-fighting or badger-baiting in a local pub yard. The revellers were fuelled by stalls selling gingerbread, nuts, fruit, and alcohol, and a fiddler might play for dancers. Scattered family would gather, so providing a chance for social ties to be reaffirmed.

Athletic races had also formed a part of the wakes, pubs often providing the prizes. At these first games, Brookes chose to perpetuate only the athletic elements of the former wakes, although some of the rustic sports would be revived in subsequent years. After Elmer had spoken, Brookes stepped forward and delivered a speech designed to cement an alliance between himself and the working-class men of Wenlock, the men for whom he was risking failure and ridicule.

'It was often said by those opposed to public games that the working men of England could not meet for amusement without drunkenness, rioting, and the destruction of property'. Brookes felt sure that the men of Wenlock would prove this 'ungenerous and untrue...I have such reliance on your good conduct that when a police officer asked me whether his services would be required, I unhesitatingly answered 'No, but the members of the society would be happy to see you as a spectator if you would come in plain clothes.' Cheers rose, and Brookes expanded his theme. He tacitly demanded their cooperation by reminding them that their betters had paid for their entertainment, and that 'as Mr Edward Crowther has gratuitously allowed us the use of his fields on this occasion I feel assured that you will evince your gratitude for his kindness by doing no injury to his fences or other property'.

The group broke up and positions were taken for the first sport of the day – a cricket match between teams led by Edwin Yardley and Thomas Jones (a wood carver from Sheinton Street). The 22 shillings prize money for the highest score went to Yardley's triumphant XI, Thomas Yates, the Spital Street hairdresser, being their top-scoring batsman. Between the innings, the boys' footraces were run. In the under-sevens, both the Brookes boys, John and William, ran. Unfortunately, although John was beaten by just 'a few inches', neither could out-run George Thomas of the White Horse, who carried off the two shillings and sixpence winnings, and was crowned with laurels.

The second innings of cricket was followed by an hour's 14-a-side football. Football had been played for centuries, usually along the main road through towns, particularly on Shrove Tuesday. Goals were not necessarily involved, some target at either end of the agreed 'pitch' being instead aimed at. Two years earlier, Cambridge University had drawn up a form of rules, but it is doubtful that they had reached Wenlock. Of the match, the newspaper reported, 'The fluctuations in the chances of the game, the frequent tumbles of the contending parties, and the boundings of the ball after a kick from some sturdy player, seemed to afford great amusement to a large concourse of spectators.'

The first Wenlock Olympian Games were spread over two days, and it is not clear how the events were split. However, as they were held on the shortening days of 22 and 23 October, probably only cricket, the footraces and football were held on the first day. The next day, then, the under-14 boys raced, and Henry Lawley, the 11-year-old son of the stationer, WARS librarian and postmaster, emerged victorious. After this, the quoits began. Richard Felton won, a 23-year-old ostler, lodging in the High Street, who was presumably familiar with the aerodynamic properties of the horse shoe. The pins were removed for the leaping in height and leaping in distance. The high jump was won by Edward Poyner a butcher's son from Beckbury east of Much Wenlock, who bore out the saying 'as fit as a butcher's dog', by being victorious again in the 50 yards hopping race. Winning long-jumper was John Bright, the general servant at Thomas Yates the hairdresser's.

During the afternoon, to Brookes's delight, Lord John Manners (1818–1906, the future seventh Duke of Rutland) appeared on the course, among a party from the local 'big house', Willey Hall, the home of John, second Baron Forester (1801–1874). The men were first cousins, Lord Forester's mother, Lady Katherine Manners, being a sister of the fifth Duke of Rutland. Lord John Manners was a member of the Young England movement (born on the playing fields of Eton and Cambridge) that had reacted against growing industrialisation by looking back to a paternalistic feudal past. Seven years earlier Manners had published *A Plea for National Holy Days* calling for rest days to brighten working-class lives. An afternoon of 'merrie' sports in a Shropshire field was perfectly to his taste. The band, catching sight of the eminent guests, struck up and set off across the racecourse to march them in. Manners was given three cheers as 'The Labourer's friend, and the advocate of the good old English games.' He offered a £1 prize for anything the committee thought fit. The ensuing foot race was won by John Hickman, servant at the Wenlock Academy on Barrow Street.

With the games concluded, the procession formed up four abreast to march back to town. The band went in front and young Henry Lawley and George Thomas were borne aloft, trying not to lose their laurel crowns. The downhill slope into Much Wenlock was a mercy for tired and bruised legs. The procession stopped outside the Guildhall where Brookes, as founder of the Olympian Class was given three cheers. In response, Brookes offered his thanks to Edwin Yardley, who, as Treasurer, had worked hard to manage the event's finances (total turnover, £10 15s). Edward Crowther, local farmer of 300 acres, living at The Bank, was also cheered before the procession broke up, and in response offered the use of his field the following year.

Brookes walked the few yards from the Guildhall to the steps of his home with his thoughts already moving beyond relief to future arrangements. There were letters of thanks to be sent, particularly to Lord John Manners and the Willey party – such a public show of support would be invaluable to his cause, and a bulwark against detractors. Yardley had indicated that receipts meant that next year's prizes might be doubled in value. Other sports might be added, like archery or leaping over hurdles, and what about challenging other villages? As he approached his steps, his eye fell on the Lawleys' house, next door but one. What a look on young Henry's face as he was crowned! And his own dear boys – how well they had acquitted themselves. As Brookes scraped his boots before going inside from the gathering darkness, not even he, with his zeal to drive drunkenness and sickness from his Shropshire community, can have imagined what he had started.

* * * * *

After the initial Games of 1850 proved successful, the amount raised by subscriptions to the class the following year more than doubled, from £10 to £23. Suggestions were offered for its further success, such as that by R.A. Slaney of holding a dance at the end of the day – dancing being a recreation suitable for women. Cricket, football, leaping in height and distance, an adults' footrace and quoits were retained, as were the under-seven and under-14 boys' races, with an under-10s' race added. New attractions included archery – indifferently competed for except for Richard Felton, victor of the quoits in 1850 (and again in 1851), who won in great style by hitting the bull's eye. New, too, was a half-mile hurdle race, which 'excited much interest', the seven hurdles being more usually employed for sheep pens.

The procession to the racecourse was repeated, sent off, in 1851, with a cannon as well as bells. The procession had increased in size and at its head was a standard carried by two men 'consisting of flowers, intermingled with laurel boughs, branches of wheat, barley and oats, gracefully entwined with blossoms of the hop-bine, and the whole surmounted by a crown of flowers'. Little boys bore crowns of olive, and others, bows and arrows, like so many mischievous little Eros. Edward Crowther lent the racecourse field, both for practising in advance, and for the Games, and was rewarded with a rendition of 'The fine old English gentleman'.

Brookes made another speech saying that he considered athletic exercise 'conducive, if not indispensable to the growth, health and activity of the body, as well as to cheerfulness and strength of mind'. For the first time he called for the incorporation of Physical Education into the schools' curriculum. Brookes, who sat on the Management Board of the school, said that he felt it never more important than in the current age of 'excessive mental competition, when the young were too often urged to continue intellectual exertion, which undermined the bodily health and ultimately impaired the faculties of the mind'.

The renown of the Wenlock Games had already spread. Two competitors came from Birmingham in 1851, Woodhouse and Mainwaring, and two more, A. Badger and W. Taylor from Wolverhampton (the former a 22-year-old shoemaker from Montrose Street). The athletes in the new hurdle race were marvelled at, and 'the activity with which they cleared these awkward and unyielding fences called forth general admiration from a large concourse of spectators…One man fell, but he was speedily on his legs again'. Edward Poyner won the hurdles just as he had the high and long jump the previous year (and the high jump again in 1851) being 'decidedly the best leaper, bounding over the hurdles with the agility of a stag'.

The outstanding competitor of the mid 1850s was David Padmore – a name comically reminiscent of the running footmen, who were literally the forerunners of the professional athletes of the time, known as pedestrians or peds. Footmen of the 18th century had been employed by the wealthy for their strength (useful for putting their liveried shoulders to the wheel of coaches stuck in the ruts of Britain's appalling roads) or for their fleetness of foot, as they were sent ahead to warn inns of approaching clients, or country houses of the master's return. In time, the aristocracy wagered bets on their footman outrunning the servants of their friends.

Padmore, a Wolverhampton boy, was far removed from the marbled halls of country houses. This 'tinman journeyman' (a journeyman having completed his apprenticeship, but not submitted a master piece for approval by his guild to become a master of his craft) was the son of an agricultural labourer and a bonnet worker, living, appropriately, in Salop Street, Wolverhampton (Salop is a former name for the county of Shropshire). Something in Padmore made him not only a great runner, but a great jumper. At the 1854 Games he won both the leaping in height and the leaping in distance. In the one-mile open hurdle race, he was pitted against Badger and Poyner, 'who were well matched, and whose fleetness and agility were loudly applauded by the spectators'. Padmore emerged victorious, beating Poyner into second. The 200 yards sprint, a 'best of heats' competition 'was a well matched race'. The first heat was won by Badger of Wolverhampton, but the second and third (the final) by William Birbeck of Coalport. The football was enjoyed over two days despite the 'collisions, kicks and tumbles, the usual accompaniments of this shin-bruising game, the favourite sport of school-boys'.

Most memorable in 1851 was a running race, a throwback to the wakes, between 'old women' for a pound of tea, 'woman's much-loved herb'. The winner was Mary Speak (aged 45) the wife of a labourer from Pouk Lane, who ran a household of 11. She beat Anne Meredith, described, appropriately, as a 'char woman' (and common law wife of a joiner on Mardol Lane) who was also 'rewarded for her exertions by a smaller prize out of the same canister'. The ladies (at this time before 'drawers' were commonly worn) were judged to have 'acquitted themselves remarkably well, considering the disadvantage under which they laboured in not being provided with the 'Bloomer costume,' attired in which they would have run capitally'.

Although the Wenlock Olympian Games were first held at the racecourse, which naturally suggested itself, it was not to be their permanent home. Games were held there in 1850–51, 1853 and 1855–57 only. In 1852 (the year the Games became a one-day event) and 1854, a new venue was tried, a meadow north-east of the town, near the seventh-century Wenlock Abbey. The seven-acre plot was let by landowners the Wynn family (and from 1858 by James Milnes Gaskell who bought the Wenlock estate from his wife's family) to their tenant, Benjamin Ainsworth of Beggarhill Brook Farm, who made it available to the Society. It was a natural amphitheatre having a sloping bank at the north-eastern end. On top of the bank stood a redundant windmill, burnt-out after a lightning strike in 1850, which gave its name to Windmill Field. The site was more sheltered and intimate than the racecourse, and deemed to be 'certainly an improvement'. From 1858 it became the permanent home of the Wenlock Olympian Games.

The old windmill made a picturesque backdrop to the Games, standing sentinel on the hill. Through half-closed eyes, one might believe it a tower of distant Camelot, as described by the new Poet Laureate (from 1850) Alfred Tennyson in his *Lady of Shalott* (1833). In 1859 a flag was flying from the top, and a signal gun was fired three times from it when a photograph of the Games was taken in 1860, 'the first to announce that preparations are being made; at the second, it is requested that all parties remain perfectly still; the third gun will be fired on the completion of the photograph.'

Windmill Hill was perennially popular with newspaper reporters, who could never resist painting a verbal picture of it 'prettily-dotted' with knots of spectators gazing down at the games below, 'lazily lying' or 'presenting an appearance such as is only to be seen at the world's pic-nic – the Derby, Ascot, or Goodwood'. In other years, like 1867, 'hardly a bit of green was visible', so tightly was it packed with the crowds. After a wet start in 1873, people gradually appeared on it, 'like spontaneous mushrooms'. In 1859, Gaskell fitted up the tower as a viewing platform, 'from the summit of which an excellent view may be obtained of the Games and the surrounding country'. He also had 'Seats for accommodation of a large number of spectators' set out 'on the adjoining hill', making a 'picturesque' scene.

The mediaeval air was reinforced at the first Windmill Field games of 1852 by the inclusion in the procession of floral shields of white, scarlet, yellow and crimson dahlias, with small bunches of wheat affixed to look like sheaves. On the back they were inscribed 'Success to the Olympic Games' – the first time that the Wenlock games were specifically described in this way. On 10 January that year in Berlin, Ernst Curtius the German archaeologist (who would eventually carry out full excavations at Olympia in the 1870s and 1880s) made a widely reported speech about the ancient Olympic Games, which might have influenced this. The dahlia shield was surmounted by a hand brandishing a crown of bay with the motto 'Who wins shall wear', the emblem and Latin motto of the Olympian class, 'palmam qui meruit ferat'. This was the work of John Roberts, a tailor and the Police Constable of Much Wenlock, who lived in Sheinton Street, and was responsible for the procession.

At those first Windmill Field Games in 1852, 15 events were held, including football and cricket, quoits, leaping in height and in distance, throwing the stone (15lb), hurdles, a wheelbarrow race, footraces, archery and a jingling match, which reinforced the mediaeval theme. The influences for this mediaevalism are several, not least the contemporary gothic revival movement in architecture, art and literature, which was succeeding the neoclassical style (felt by some to be connected with republicanism) that had reigned supreme since the 18th century. Hence the choice of Sir Charles Barry's gothic designs for the Houses of Parliament begun in 1840. The supremely influential John Ruskin, too, promoted the gothic ideal of architecture as found in Venice. The gothic revival was a response of the romantic soul to the brutal new mechanical times, shortly to become evident too in the pre-Raphaelite movement. Its founder William Morris was to publish his first volume of poetry *The Defence of Guenevere* in 1858, five years after these games.

The mediaeval theme was present, too, in the prize that Brookes offered to the winner of the archery in 1853. William James, another Wenlock surgeon and a close friend of Brookes, won a copy of Joseph Strutt's *Sports and Pastimes*, to which Brookes would also refer in his speech at the 1858 games. This book, one of the only ones on the subject at this time, greatly influenced Brookes's choice of sports in the Wenlock Games. Strutt held up the mediaeval knight as the most-rounded sportsman. Besides being accomplished physically, he had also, said Strutt, to be 'endowed with beauty, strength and agility of body; skilled in music, dance gracefully, run with swiftness, excel in wrestling, ride well', have urbanity of manners, truthfulness and invincible courage.

Strutt included an account of the games organised annually from the early 17th century on a hill above Chipping Campden in the Cotswolds, Gloucestershire by Robert Dover. They are known today, (having been revived in 1951) as they were originally as 'Olympick Games', but were not specifically named as such in Strutt's account. Strutt did use the phrase 'Olympic Games' in his book, but only in the context of the history of wrestling, which, he wrote, was 'highly esteemed by the ancients' (but which was not included by Brookes at Wenlock). Dover's Olympick Games may have influenced Brookes (though he never mentions them) although they had become more akin to church wakes and died out, largely because of the enclosure of their site, in 1852. Dover's games had included wrestling, hammer and bar throwing, sword play, running, leaping, handstands, horse-racing, hunting, coursing, dancing and possibly a turf maze. Also mentioned by Strutt, and therefore another candidate for influencing Brookes was the July Carnival at Halgaver near Bodmin, Cornwall, although Brookes never mentions this either.

Of most probable influence on Brookes were the athletic games begun at Necton in Norfolk in 1817 by Major Mason, called the Necton Guild, described as being 'beyond all question, the first English athletic club to come into being'. The wakes at Necton had given way to a pure sports meeting – no stalls, stands, or entertainment booths being permitted. The Necton Guild included wrestling, footraces, jingling, jumping in sacks, blindfold wheelbarrow-races, spinning, whistling, grinning, and jumping matches. They lasted until 1826. John Elmer was born at Fritton in Norfolk. This, combined with their similarity to the early Wenlock Games, and Elmer's being the first President, suggests that Elmer (born in 1810) with memories or anecdotal tales of the Necton Guild, encouraged Brookes in his endeavour.

In the 1850s, the traditional country sports included at Wenlock, besides archery and quoits, were a wheelbarrow race (won in 1852 by the police constable John Roberts) run blindfold in 1854, and jingling (won in 1852 by William Skett, a journeyman tanner), both of which were included by Strutt in a section about the history of church wakes and fairs. In 1855, the blindfold wheelbarrow race at Wenlock 'afforded much amusement owing to the tortuous circuit by which many of the blindfolded candidates approached the goal. The winner was John Skett, who completed his performance by a somersault into the hedge at the end of the field'.

The jingling match drew press attention. The reporter described 'a large roped ring, in which 20 blindfolded competitors for the prizes made many ineffectual attempts to catch the jingler, who, by ringing a small bell, attracted them successively to various parts of the ring, and slipped aside adroitly as they approached him, to the great merriment of the spectators.' Henry Lawley finally grasped the bellman, and won. In 1856, the committee restricted the jingling to 10, and 'Jumping in Bags' was added – another of Strutt's inclusions. He specified that everything but the head had to be inside the bag.

In 1857 the Games included jumping in bags, climbing the pole (no entrants, so the prize, a hat, 'remained in all the glory of gloss and ribbons') and a half-mile donkey race. The entrants for the donkey race formed an attractive addition to the procession, '12 sturdy donkeys' being 'ridden by as many adolescent bipeds in picturesque costume'. The donkey race 'was most laughable, and the old saying that 'persuasion is better than force,' was exemplified in one or two cases where the ambitious for assinine distinction commenced using the cudgel when they began to fear losing the race.'

The donkey race was repeated only once in 1858, limited to six entrants, and with the specification that 'no spurs' were to be worn. The novelties of 1858 included a 'wooden-leg race' and 'Great fun was caused towards the close of the day by a pig race. The pig was started in the middle of the field, and led its pursuers over hedge and ditch right into the town, where it took ground in the cellar of Mr Blakeways's house [the local solicitor who lived at the Bull Ring] and where it was captured by a man named William Hill.'

In 1858 came the greatest mediaeval innovation at the Wenlock games, which was unique, and which Brookes was to include in all his Games, tilting at the ring (plate 5). Strutt explained that 'The excellency of the pastime was to ride at full speed, and thrust the point of the lance through the ring.' The ring, said Strutt, quoting Pluvinel in the *Art de monter à cheval*, of 1628, ought to be placed, 'somewhat higher than the left eyebrow of the practitioner, when sitting upon his horse'. As to the form of the competition, '3 courses were allowed to each candidate; 'and he who thrust the point of his lance through it the oftenest, or…struck it the most frequently, was the victor.'

When it was decided at the meeting of 8 July 1858 to introduce tilting at the ring, the committee resolved to ask Thomas Edwards the wheelwright on the High Street, to make 'the requisite apparatus for a Tilting match' (cost for 'the Tilting post, Spears and Ring', 22 shillings). Brookes must have descended upon Edwards brandishing his copy of Strutt. For all the quirkiness of this arcane sport, it required extraordinary horsemanship to succeed. The ring was suspended from a wire attached to a crossbeam above the riders' heads. Participants, holding a lance 10ft in length, had to gallop (at full tilt) towards the ring (no mean feat in itself), and on approaching the bar, raise the point of the lance and put it through the tiny ring, which was *less than one inch* in diameter.

Wenlock, at the heart of the Wheatland Hunt country (Lord Forester's ancestor had famously employed the legendary Tom Moody as his whipper-in) had several horsemen ready to accept the new challenge of tilting at the Windmill Field. William Gregory, the postman Mr Bowdler, and Thomas Jukes of Coates Farm, came forward. The newspaper noted that the tilting 'caused the greatest diversion', the participants showing 'great steadiness of eye and hand in carrying off the ring'. William Gregory won, with Thomas Jukes second. Prior to this, Jukes had won the under-14 running race in 1854, and had been third in the donkey race in 1857.

William Penny Brookes had something of the showman, which helped these early games to survive. There is no doubt that the more traditional events and the pace of the tilting were crowd-pleasers, and made the games popular. He also sensed that they would capture the attention of the newspapers, and Brookes knew how to use the coverage to advantage. For make no mistake, beneath the fun and games were lurking issues quite literally, of life and death, and not just that of the individual taking part.

Social cohesion was vital to national survival if Britain was not to be torn apart by revolution such as Brookes had witnessed as a student in Paris in 1830. As early as 1852 *Eddowes's Journal* was wishing at the end of its Games report that other towns would emulate Wenlock, 'as we feel convinced that innocent recreations of this description are desirable for all classes, and have a tendency to maintain that good feeling between high and low, rich and poor, which, happily for us, is the national characteristic of Old England, and would be found its greatest bulwark in the hour of trial.' Here, then, are games as an insurance against revolution – politics has never been entirely absent from sport.

Brookes was a wily political operator – he had to be as a Whig/Liberal in Shropshire – and while he spoke of the happiness of the classes in Britain in 1854 at Windmill Meadow, he laced his words with warning. While glad of the growing opinion that recreation was necessary for the working classes and that public holidays should be legally appointed for the purpose, he noted that some were opposed to them. They believed that the daily walk to and fro' work was exercise enough.

'I would tell these objectors to the humble amusements of the poor that it is their interest, in a sanitary point of view, to encourage and support public games…the secret poison that comes wafted in the air generally first takes effect on systems debilitated – by whatever cause, excessive fatigue among others – and thus acquires a contagious virulence to which the strongest constitutions fall an easy prey.'

Brookes's games grew annually in popularity. His wisdom in moving away from traditional wakes sports is shown by reaction to the 'rustic sports in the castle green' at Ludlow (which besides had an annual Shrove Tuesday tug of war) to celebrate the opening of the Shrewsbury to Hereford railway in 1852. Ludlow's games included jingling, jumping in sacks, climbing a greasy pole, eating treacled loaves, and chimney sweeps dipping their faces in a tub of flour for shillings. Young American Anna Maria Fay of Savannah, Georgia, staying for a year at nearby Moor Park, said that they delighted 'the riff-raff', but they were condemned by the Methodist minister as 'degrading and demoralizing'. The Methodists were vociferous again in 1856 at Wellington for similar celebrations to mark the end of the Crimean War, when the games included diving for live eels. The minister there called them a 'revival of barbarism'. The church was quick to condemn, but made no attempt to provide any alternative. Indeed, the Lord's Day Observance Society was attempting to restrict Sunday activities. When were folk to amuse themselves?

At Much Wenlock, in 1855, it was noted that 'the attendance of spectators from the town and country round, far exceeded in the afternoon that of previous years; the long lines of well-dressed females, who were seated on the rising banks commanding good views of the games, and the flags floating in front of the booth, imparting to the scene a very animated and interesting effect.' The growth of the crowds this year was confirmed by Brookes's speech at the Corn Market after the 1855 Games. Social cohesion was another theme to which he referred. 'In the present day, when nearly every spot of ground in the vicinity of a town is enclosed…the poor would lose much recreation were the occupiers of land not to act with that consideration and kindness which Mr Crowther has evinced.' He thanked the Olympian Class's subscribers for helping 'in the improvement and innocent amusements of those in a humbler sphere of life.'

By this, the sixth Games at Wenlock, Brookes was expanding his work from the purely physical to intellectual improvement. On the Friday after the Games, the public was invited to 'a very interesting exhibition of beautifully preserved specimens of the wild plants and flowers growing round Wenlock.' However, only 300 out of 600 specimens collected in the year by WARS members could be shown 'for want of space'. In 1852, Brookes had raised £2,000 to build a Corn Market on Spital Street, erected in 1853 by Messrs Nevett of Ironbridge to plans by the Shrewsbury architect Samuel Pountney Smith. Above the open arcade for the market was housed the WARS library and reading room. The building's Latin motto, from Virgil's *Georgics* was 'Facere laetas segetes' – to produce joyful harvests. Already, three years on, an office and museum extension, 30ft by 15, was proposed.

It brought Brookes an early harvest of his Olympian endeavours. The working men of Wenlock felt able to approach him in October 1855 with a petition signed by 50 of them asking for permission to use one of the proposed new rooms as a reading room. It was decided that the ground-floor office should supply. By 1856, 37 labourers had joined. Thus, 17 years before a national union for agricultural labourers would be formed, the labourers in Much Wenlock were, thanks to William Penny Brookes, finding the confidence to ask for improvements to their lot. This was no small matter, as in 1833 the Tolpuddle Martyrs had been transported to Australia for daring to form a collective union to seek improvements to their working lives. The 1857 games report noted that it was 'well-known' that Brookes took 'a very great interest in the welfare of the labouring population of Wenlock and its neighbourhood'.

To raise the necessary funds for the extension, a 'Grand Fancy Bazaar' was proposed for October 1856. The Wenlock ladies came into their own. Lady patrons donated many of the goods, and the organising committee of 11 women included four from the Brookes family. Brookes's sister-in-law Eliza, married to his brother Andrew had a stall, helped by Brookes's daughters. Brookes's own wife, Jane, had stall number five, with Brookes's sister, Anne. Anne had been drafted in from London, where she was married to Thomas Wilkinson (who owned Botolph Wharf near London Bridge on the River Thames) and lived in Hackney (a host borough of the London 2012 Olympic Games). Mrs James, wife of the surgeon, had another stall. Eleanor Adney, wife of the Sheinton Street tanner, had a stall too, as did Mrs Blakeway, in whose cellar the pig would take refuge in 1858. Finally, the vicar's wife and daughters, Jane Wayne, Mary and Sophia, who lived at the top of the High Street, had a stall at the 'upper end of the room'.

The patrons, including Lady Wenlock, were generous. The six stalls 'contained every description of fancy ware and knick-knackery'. Jane Brookes's stall displayed 'a great variety of *recherche* articles', many of great value. The most noticeable specimen of needlework was 'a fire screen of large dimensions'. Mary and Adeline Brookes's stall included a Bedouin cloak 'purchased by Mrs. Gaskell', 'cricket implements' from Page Brothers and from Cheek of London, perfumery and scented soaps from Eugene Rimmell, music from Alfred Novello, and, from Sangsters of London, Persian parasols, 'made without seam', besides other gifts from Chance Brothers of Birmingham (who had supplied the glass for the Crystal Palace). The daughters from the local hostelries, Miss Hartland from the Raven (plate 7) and Miss Wheeler of the Falcon, were, appropriately in charge of refreshments, among whose donors was R.A. Slaney, of Wellington.

Brookes coupled this event with the lighting, by gas, of the Corn Market. The bringing of gas lighting was another of his endeavours, completed by 1856 after overcoming objections about the smallness of the population and the cost of bringing coal (needed to make the gas). Brookes was chairman of the Wenlock Gas Company. A works site at the racecourse end of Barrow Street was bought in 1857, and managed by Walter Horton. The installation of lighting was a great boon to the inhabitants (not least a middle-aged doctor called out in the dead of night). Until then, Much Wenlock had been 'one of the few belated towns without gas. A few miserable oil lamps were dotted about the streets, and together with sputtering tallow candles were seen in the shops'.

Now Brookes illuminated the front of the Market 'by three stars and the initials VR in gas jets' – a marvel indeed for the dark late-October evenings. As one newspaper mocked, the illuminations 'did not fail to excite the wonder of that portion of the inhabitants that had never travelled beyond the length of the shadow of their native hills. One wondered the lights did not want snuffing, and another was equally astonished they burnt so long…congratulations upon the advance "Old Wenlock" was making were frequently exchanged'.

All of Brookes's efforts 'for many weeks – aye months,' including an 'enormous' amount of correspondence, paid off. About 800 people visited the bazaar on the first day, including local landowners the Foresters, the Gaskells, the Bensons of Lutwyche, and the Mores of Linley Hall. The bells rang 'their enlivening strains', music was supplied all afternoon by the Dorrington band, 'and the town of Wenlock wore a gay and animated appearance'. The bazaar realised £475 and, after the raffle of unsold items, £500. The Society was still £50 short, but the Duke of Cleveland (whose Raby estate owned land close to Wenlock) sent £10 more, and the Mayor of Wenlock, William Nicholas of Broseley £5.

Displayed beneath the building, for the three days of the bazaar, were Williams of Bedford's diagonal harrows, and Howard of Bedford's champion plough, alongside 'various samples of inodorous manure for flowers and shrubs in the drawing-room and greenhouse', supplied by Fisher and Sheppard of Ironbridge. Brookes hoped these might detain the menfolk while the ladies shopped upstairs. The ladies, too, had an opportunity to see the latest domestic technology, 'an American floating-ball washing machine…[supplied by B. Moore & Co. of 133 High Holborn, London] which seemed to excite considerable interest…From the opinion of several ladies, who appeared to appreciate the merits of the machine, it would seem that…in addition to the great saving in the cost and labour of washing, the machine did not tear the clothes even so much as hand washing.'

Brookes was keen to encourage, sustain and acknowledge the participation of women and girls, albeit within the limits of contemporary constraints. Just as the sports were designed to make the men 'fit for purpose' in their role as physical labourers, so events useful and appropriate to women's station in life were added. At the 1852 Games, the under-14 'neatest and quickest sewing' won Sarah Rowley a book worth three shillings and sixpence, and Mary Seabry and Margaret Hill, second and third, lengths of calico fabric. Similarly Ann Nicklin won the ladies' quickest and best knitting and she, Mary Skutt and Ann James won fabric for gowns. From 1851, Games day was rounded off with dancing, either on the field, or, for example in 1852, at the Assembly Room of the Raven Hotel, kindly lent by proprietor Robert Hartland, when 'dancing was kept up with great spirit and order till 12 o'clock'.

Brookes explained in 1854 that when a student, he had enjoyed attending dances in Paris and 'the neighbouring villages', and was 'much struck with the order and decorum which prevailed. I never witnessed a single instance of intoxication or impropriety of any kind – not a single instance of disrespect or want of courtesy to the female sex; and I have always since entertained the opinion, which subsequent observation has confirmed, that out-door amusements in the presence of females, and where both sexes mingle in the dance, have a tendency to soften the manners of the men and lead them to treat the gentler sex with that polite and respectful attention to which it is entitled.'

Brookes built on these slim foundations by extending the children's competitions to include intellectual elements, in a more self-conscious echo of the Greek games. Arithmetic and writing for boys under 14 was included, and recitation for boys and girls under 14. In 1854 this produced a truly extraordinary effort from one of the girls. The judges, the curate, Revd Mr Heywood, and local solicitors, George Burd and Roger Blakeway, met in the reading room. They must have been astonished to hear Sarah James recite 374 lines of poetry without a single mistake. Sarah Pearce and Elizabeth Mason, coming second and third, recited 226 and 156 lines respectively with only one mistake each. Sarah James also won the writing competition.

In 1857 there was knitting for women, and knitting and sewing for the girls as before, with arithmetic for the boys. In addition, reading, spelling, English History, Bible History and drawing competitions were included for both the boys and girls, the winners of the last receiving 12 months' membership of the Wenlock School of Art (which had grown out of the art classes at WARS) plus three shillings to buy drawing materials. Collectively, these were called the 'prizes for industrial and intellectual attainments'. William Weale, aged 13 was the star in 1857, being second in maths and in writing, and winning Bible History and English History for boys. The Miles sisters, Anne and Jane won the reading, Bible History and English History. Mary Titley and Lucy Hughes won prizes in the sewing and knitting in both 1857 and 1858. The boys' drawing prize in 1858 (as well as the English History prize) went, appropriately, to Thomas Edwards, son of the wheelwright who had that year supplied the new tilting equipment.

The end of the first decade, 1859, was a major landmark for the Wenlock Olympian Games. This was reflected in the expenditure. From 1851–56 annual expenditure on the Games rose little. In 1857 and 1858 it moved through the £30 ceiling but from 1858 to 1859 it tripled to £96 5s 2d, including £42 11s for the silver tilting cup, money and book prizes (nearly 10 times the first year). The 10th games were celebrated with much more hoopla than usual. 'Never, probably, in the history of Wenlock has such a pageant been witnessed as that which took place on Wednesday last…' began the newspaper report. '"Welcome to Wenlock" was the motto in chief of the day, and nobody there could feel any doubt upon the veracity of that assurance.' Banners were strung across the streets from the Wynnstay Arms and the Fox. The Britannia's, painted by Mr Tanswell, wished 'Long life and prosperity to our worthy townsman, W.P. Brookes, Esq., the promoter of the Olympian games' and Robert Hartland's banner, between the Raven on Barrow Street and Mr Share's house opposite said 'Welcome to Wenlock's Merry Sports'. A deputation of the Mayor and 50 men descended from Bridgnorth and lunched at the Wynnstay, before following the procession in an omnibus.

Not only the budget but also the crowds exceeded all that had gone before, having climbed from scarcely 100 to 2,000. This was partly because of the discovery nearby, in February, of the

Roman city of Viriconium, (Wroxeter), whose main feature was the vast wall of an exercise hall next to the baths. Thanks to coverage in the *Gentleman's Magazine* and the *Illustrated London News*, the excavation of the fourth-largest Roman city in Britain was drawing enormous crowds by April, including Charles Dickens. The Wenlock Games must have benefited from the virulent outbreak of Viriconium fever. In 1861, a prize was awarded for a poem about the city co-judged by Dr Kennedy, headmaster of Shrewsbury School.

In his 1859 speech, Brookes warned as ever against 'the fearful consequences of intemperance'. Beyond that, with the recent war in the Crimea (1853–56) fresh in people's minds, as well as the Indian Mutiny (1857) and the threat of invasion from France (that had prompted in 1859 the formation of the Rifle Volunteers), Brookes commended their games in military rather than health terms. 'You are training up a hardy, active, resolute race', he told them, 'well-qualified, physically, for the great battle of civil life; and able, as well as ready, to bear arms, should need be – which God forbid – in the defence of their country…it is by the early training of our youth in athletic exercises, that we shall lay the best foundation for military excellence'.

The programme of events had been tightened up, too. Cricket had been dropped, probably because of time constraints and because it needed little encouragement to be played outside Games days. Football would do likewise (and for similar reasons) by the mid-1860s. By 1859, jingling, hopping, blindfolded wheelbarrows, wooden legs, races for tea, donkeys, pigs, and sacks had all gone the same way. Instead, there were a more lithe 18 athletic events that year. They included (for various ages, and some restricted to the parish) quoits, high jump, 200 yard foot races, spear throwing and javelin, archery, a wheel race, tilting, hurdles, and a half-mile foot race. Besides these, the intellectual events included an essay on Physical Recreation (for a considerable £5 donated by Jasper More of Linley, won by Mr Sharpe, the chemist of Madeley), a poem on the Wenlock Olympian Games (won by Miss Davies) and for the under-15s knitting, sewing, English history, drawing, arithmetic and writing.

The tilting pageantry was taken up a notch, too, with the introduction of a herald at the head of the procession to the field, who proclaimed the tilting just before it began. About 30 runs at the ring were made before Joel Ainsworth, aged 17, a farmer's son from Upper Spoonhill, emerged as the winner. He approached Lady Forester as the band played *See, the Conquering Hero Comes!* to receive his olive crown and silver cup, and knelt as the crowd cheered. This must have become a particularly poignant memory after Ainsworth died in 1861, aged 19.

There was even something new in the reporting of the event in 1859 – the first really journalistic account of a race, the one-mile hurdles. 'In this race, three started. Their names were William Roberts (who was successful last year), Samuel Oare, and Edward Thomas. The betting was in favour of Roberts, who was taken against the field at starting. The lot got off well together. The hurdles – four – were all cleared well throughout. The racers kept within a couple of yards of each other round the course. On clearing the last hurdle, Roberts, who had reserved himself, put out, and showed up in front, cleverly passing his competitors, and out-distancing the one (Oare), by a yard and a half; and the second (Thomas), by three yards and a half.'

Pony tilting was also introduced in 1859, to prepare the next generation of competitors. To close the event, there was 'an ascent of Mr Dutton's balloon, with a brilliant display of fireworks attached.' Miss Davies's ode on the Games made overt reference to ancient Greece:

'The games of classic Greece are now
Revived; round fair Salopia's brow
Fame binds her olive wreath; 'tis ours
To raise once more those vanished hours
Which fled in fair Olympia's grove,'

Besides all this, which contributed to a sense of coming of age for the Wenlock endeavour, Brookes's cause had received unexpected support in 1858 at the Shrewsbury summer assizes. In his customary speech before the proceedings, the judge Mr Justice Byles told the Grand Jury and public that he had just come from Worcester where a new working man's club was offering chess, draughts, dominoes and occasional lectures to the city's working men. Byles felt that this was appropriate for winter, but 'hardly fitted' for the long summer evenings. 'I do not believe,' he said 'a more useful thing can be done in any large town…at a comparatively small expense – than to encourage and assist the youth of the country in out-of-door exercises and recreations which improve the health, increase the stature, mature the courage, and fire the pluck of our youth, on which God knows, the very existence of the country depends.'

The extent to which Wenlock's Games had tapped into the spirit of the age was further demonstrated by the extraordinary success, when published in 1857, of *Tom Brown's Schooldays* by Thomas Hughes QC. This novel, about the physical exploits of a public schoolboy at Thomas Arnold's Rugby School, sold 11,000 copies in its first year, and inspired not only the future Baron Pierre de Coubertin, but young men up and down Britain. Tom Brown became the embodiment of a movement known as muscular Christianity, which attempted to bring order to the rapidly-changing world by establishing a wholesome model for young men in Victorian patriarchal society.

The main exponents (willingly or unwillingly) of muscular Christianity (a phrase coined in an 1857 review) were Charles Kingsley (who donated *Westward Ho!* to WARS library in 1859), Thomas Hughes and F.D. Maurice, in whose novels manliness was synonymous with strength, both physical and moral. From Jean-Jacques Rousseau, through Thomas Carlyle to the muscular Christians, there was a consistent sense that brute strength was nothing without social utility. In this, there was much in common, as Carlyle in particular appreciated, with the chivalric ideal, as espoused by Brookes. Man had a duty to use physical superiority to protect the weaker in society.

At the same time, muscular Christians suggested that male physical prowess and sexuality were to be enjoyed, since human nature was God-given, and the flesh should not be mortified, as the church had suggested in the past. No wonder the movement was so popularly followed. However, freedom of the flesh was only likely to be used responsibly if the mind had been educated to manage it wisely. Uncircumscribed strength was not what muscular Christians espoused. Self-control and self-discipline to realise the full potential of the individual was the ideal to which Victorian young men should aspire.

Hughes himself explained that 'the least of the muscular Christians has hold of the old chivalrous and Christian belief, that a man's body is given him to be trained and brought into subjection and then used for the protection of the weak, the advancement of all righteous causes, and the subduing of the earth which God has given to the children of men. He does not hold that mere strength or activity are in themselves worthy of any respect or worship, or that one man is a bit better than another because he can knock him down, or carry a bigger sack of potatoes than he'.

This vision of manhood was extraordinarily powerful, and affected young men for at least a century afterwards. It was open to abuse, particularly in the expansion of the Empire in the later 19th century. As expressed by Brookes, though, it takes rather the form, as the century goes on and the threat from Prussia in particular grows, of protecting the old country from going soft as a result of industrialisation, commerce and the over-emphasis in education on the intellect at the expense of the body.

More important to Brookes than all of this, though, was the remarkable development announced in August 1858, that thanks to the generosity of wealthy ex-patriot Greek Evangelos Zappas, a royal decree had been signed to revive the Olympic Games at Athens in 1859. It was probably Brookes who fired off the news to *Eddowes's Shrewsbury Journal*. It reported on Wednesday 6 October 1858 that the games would be held in an ancient stadium that was 'still in a very perfect state of preservation'. The proposed events included horseracing, wrestling, throwing quoits, and other athletic sports, singing, music and dancing, 'besides which there is to be an exhibition of flowers, fruits, cattle and other articles of Greek produce or manufactures'.

This was partly a result of Ernst Curtius's request in 1852 for permission to excavate Olympia, and his proposal at the same time that the ancient games be revived. Before Curtius, Greek poet Panagiotis Soutsos (educated like Brookes, though seven to nine years earlier, in Paris and Padua) had been calling for the restoration of the Olympic Games to help re-establish his new nation's culture and identity in the modern world. Unsuccessful, but undeterred, Soutsos had repeated his demand in 1842, 1845 and 1851. Now, it seemed, Zappas would make Soutsos's Olympian dream come true.

Since at least 1856, Zappas had been agitating through diplomatic channels to reinstate the games but was fobbed off with military honours by the unenthusiastic foreign minister, Alexandros Rangavis. Rangavis observed that 'Today, nations do not become distinguished, as then, by having the best athletes and runners, but the champions in industry, handiwork, and agriculture.' Zappas and Soutsos combined, and Rangavis was sent 2000 Austrian florins to cover the costs of the first of the 'Olympiads of Zappas'. In particular, he wanted his money spent on the restoration of the ancient stadium in Athens (which, contrary to the confidence of *Eddowes's Journal,* was dilapidated, but which would be used for the first IOC games in 1896).

Despite this extraordinary generosity, Zappas's wishes were ignored. Instead, a month of Sundays in October 1859 was dedicated to a celebration of Greek industry, modelled more on Britain's Great Exhibition of 1851 than the ancient Olympic Games. Some sports were staged in today's Koumoundourou Square in Athens, to which competitors were drawn from all over the Greek-speaking world. However, the weather was not kind and, standing several deep around the square, few of the spectators could see.

The main effect of the Zappas Games for Wenlock was that Brookes was motivated to contact the Greeks directly, and so to begin to see athletics as an international endeavour. Just before Christmas 1858, Brookes took it upon himself to advise the organisers, through the British ambassador in Athens, Sir Thomas Wyse to include Wenlock-style high and long jump, hurdles, foot races, putting the stone, and tilting at the ring. Despite Wyse considering this far too ambitious, Brookes forwarded £10 from the Wenlock committee as the prize for the Athens tilting competition. Wyse confirmed on 14 July 1859 that he had forwarded it to the organising committee.

In fact the Zappas Games of 1859 included footraces, three jumping events, two discus, two javelin throws and a pole climb. In the predictable absence of tilting at the ring, the Wenlock prize was awarded for the winner of the 'dolichos', a footrace of seven laps of the square, or just under a mile. When the race leader collapsed, Petros Velissarios from Smyrna (Izmir) swept past to take the Wenlock prize and honorary membership of the Olympian Class of WARS. It might not have been spectacular, but the Wenlock/Athens connection had been made.

At the end of their first decade, therefore, the 1859 Games at Much Wenlock (held just before the Zappas Games) saw 12 adult athletics events, of which the 200yd footrace, the football, high jump, javelin, archery, hurdles and half-mile footrace are still (in their metric equivalents) events in the Olympic Games today. Quoits was related to the discus, and arguably Wenlock's tilting represented an early form of competitive equestrianism that was distinct from flat racing or steeplechasing.

Add to this a dedicated games field with a grandstand, natural raked seating, a running track, processions, flags, pageantry, speech-making and a degree of junketing, and it can be seen that the claim of Wenlock's Games to represent the proto-Olympic Games is not so far-fetched. Furthermore, Brookes had made a direct connection with the revival of Olympic Games in Greece by this time – four years before Pierre de Coubertin had been born, and 35 years before the revival of the modern Olympic Games was agreed.

It is not just in the context of the Olympic Games that Brookes's achievement is noteworthy, but also in that of sport in Britain by 1860. Wenlock's Games pre-dated athletics at Cambridge University by seven years, and at Oxford University by 10, the latter's Athletics Club being formed after a meeting in the Merton College rooms of Edwyn Arkwright of Herefordshire, in 1860. Dr Hawtrey, the head at Eton, in 1856, had banned the College XI from participating in the annual cricket matches against Harrow in London 'on the ground that they lead to licentiousness and profuse expenditure'. There was as yet no Football Association, no Ashes cricket, and no swimming association. Bicycles with pedals, and tennis had yet to be invented.

Competitive walking and running – pedestrianism – had been practised in Britain for over a century. Rarely, though, were so many disciplines competed for on the same day, and Wenlock's games were remarkable for doing so, so early. One exception was in Scotland, where Highland Games had been held since at least the 11th century. R.A. Slaney went to Blair Atholl in 1841 where he saw 'running, throwing weights, Broad Sword, Dance &c', and noted that 'Such meeting might be *well worthy our imitation.*' The popularity of Highland Games grew after Queen Victoria, in 1848, took her family to the Braemar Gathering (first held in 1832). Also on the celtic extremity of Britain, southern Ireland was quick to take up athletics once they began to gain ground. Their heritage in athletics outstripped even that of the ancient Greeks. The Tailteann Games, an annual clan gathering on the banks of the Blackwater River in County Meath, Ireland, in honour of Queen Tailte were tests of speed and strength. They are believed to date from 1829BC and to have survived until the Norman invasion there, in AD1168.

It can, therefore, be seen that, founded in 1850, the Wenlock Olympian Games were ahead of their time, particularly for an athletic meeting independent of a public school or university. Here was a little community not paying lip-service to the needs of its population, but taking action. At the Society's annual dinner after the bazaar on 5 December 1856, it was local landowner and MP, James Milnes Gaskell, who defined the achievement of the organisers of the Wenlock Olympian Class. 'While some among your neighbours have talked only, you have acted, and you have applied yourselves with zeal and energy to the object on which you had set your hearts'.

The mood at the 10-year milestone for Wenlock was captured by a letter to the *Shrewsbury Chronicle* of 26 August 1859 from 'Bona Fide'. 'Honour is due, particularly to WP Brookes, Esq., to whom the public at large, especially of Wenlock and its neighbourhood, owe a lasting debt of gratitude…While thousands throughout the country expend their sympathies in idle talk about such matters, Mr Brookes promptly put his professions in practice, and established…the Olympic Games…These athletic games, I rejoice to know, are widely spreading their blessings through the length and breadth of our land…Few men have done more real good in their day with less of ostentation.'

Chapter 2

'"How far and in what way shall we promote and support the wholesome recreation of the people?"…The matter is not of trifling importance…I would call attention to the Olympian Games at Wenlock, in Shropshire, tested by the experience of ten years, for the encouragement of athletic exercises. Sure I am that this manifestation of interest begets a sympathy between all classes. A man will oftentimes be more gratified by your attention to his amusements than by your regard for his necessities.'

The Earl of Shaftesbury at a meeting of the National Association for the Promotion of Social Science, Bradford, October 1859

'Ten years ago,' reported the *Liverpool Courier* of 1860, 'a few gentlemen residing at Much Wenlock, in Shropshire originated a class which was laughed at and discountenanced by their neighbours; but the originators had the moral courage to return smiles for laughter, and to carry on their work until they succeeded in winning over those who scoffed at them, and made their class an acknowledged local institution and a substantial good.' It continued, 'Why should not these societies be literary in the winter months, and in the summer months resolve themselves into out door amusement clubs? Let the mind be trained; but do not forget the body.'

Wenlock's Olympian Games were indeed, after 10 years, an institution, and a popular one. The 1860 Wenlock Games were stepped up in several ways, not just because of the 1859 Zappas Games in Athens, but also in anticipation of the advent of the railway the following year. The Games needed to bring in the crowds in 1861 and so benefit both the Society and the Wenlock and Severn Junction Railway Company. Unfortunately, the weather in August 1860 was 'vile' – wet and blowy – and most of the competitions had to be postponed for a week.

The invited celebrity, Lt Col Herbert Edwardes, a Salopian and distinguished military man, attended on the original date, 22 August, dined and stayed with Brookes at Wilmore Street. Edwardes made a generous speech at the Raven after a luncheon of hams, veals, and tongues, grapes and pineapples from the Forester and Gaskell hot-houses, washed down with champagne. 'There's a great deal too much work in the world,' he began. 'Men are too much slaves to their occupations now-a-days. There is a perfect idolatry of labour, which leaves no margin for home, or holiday, or the inner life (hear, hear)…This Olympian Class is a great idea, and it does honour to your public-spirited townsman, Mr Brookes…the Wenlock Agricultural Reading Society…has a lending library, and a drawing class, a music class, a class for chemistry and botany, collects photographs and autographs of distinguished men, and fossils; and has a Working Men's branch besides…

'Here is a Society really doing good! Here in the heart of a midland county, out of the reach of the great centres of learning, arts, politics, and fashion, in a quiet corner of Old England'. Praise indeed, but if Brookes's delight was unbounded up to this point, it soon turned to horror as Edwardes went on to suggest that the games be called 'The Shropshire Class of British Work and Play, or anything else you will; but let it tell of English men and women, English boys and girls.' Edwardes was no philhellene.

Next, the winners of a prize ode competition about the Games were announced. Entries were submitted under a pseudonym, and the real identity of the poet sealed in a separate envelope. The winner of the first prize of £4 turned out to be Jonathan Douglas, editor of *Eddowes's Shrewsbury Journal*. The second prize envelope was then opened. The name 'William Brookes' was called. Brookes, evidently suspecting a trick, denied that he was the author. Quietly, though, his son William stood up, provoking 'a loud and spontaneous cheer' from the assembly, and no doubt uproarious laughter from his proud father.

William, called 'Willie' (variously spelt), was now 15 and an especially precious son. His elder brother, John, had died aged 11 on 11 April 1854. Also that year, Anne Wilkinson had sent her daughter Mary Anne from London to Much Wenlock, in hopes that Mary Anne's weak lungs might benefit from fresher air and proximity to two surgeon-uncles. However, despite everyone's best efforts, Mary Anne, too, died of consumption in 1854. Anne was devastated and fretted that she had not heard from William and Jane, but her mother explained that 'Jane is too much engrossed with her own sorrow to write to any one at present'.

Willie's health was indifferent. On 12 March 1856, Jane wrote to Anne in London, 'I am feeling anxious about Willie, he is looking rather pale the last few days. William was talking to me yesterday and said I must take great care of him or he would become consumptive. He coughs very little, but is constantly taking fresh colds. I have now fire in his bed room and regret I left it off so soon.' Despite Willie's delicacy, Brookes sent him to boarding school in Wem, with instructions to Mr Boulton for his son's care. It worked, for in 1858 Willie 'came home on Saturday last…in a Fly to Shrewsbury', where Jane went to meet him. His grandmother reported him 'looking quite ruddy' and 'stouter and stronger can walk 10 or 12 miles and at a good pace too…he has shown his sisters & me his themes and they are well expressed, (he has read his Hebrew by himself and practised his violin…) all of which pleases his papa who…in his letter of thanks to Mr Boulton…told him that he would rather see him good than great'.

As his poetry prize demonstrates, by 1860, Willie was showing great promise. The abandoned sports were resumed the following week, on Wednesday 29 August. Of these postponed games, we have the only surviving mention of any games by a member of the Brookes family. William's sister Maria wrote to Anne on 30 August 'Yesterday was a lovely day & the games went off very nicely – Lord & Lady Forester were there the Gaskills & many other carriages with ladies & gentlemen but I did not leave Mother so did not witness it – William thinks about 4000 must have been there – The Procession was very nice indeed, but the Friday paper will give you a better description than I am able to do –'

The procession set off from the Reading-Room at 2pm. 'The herald's dress excited universal admiration.' Brookes had written to the costume department of Covent Garden, London for advice on the correct tournament costume of the period of Henry VIII. It consisted of 'a green silk velvet tunic, richly embroidered with gold, over which was thrown a crimson mantle. He wore also white buckskin trousers, with buff leather boots, piped with red; also, a blue silk velvet cap, turned up with crimson, and carried the silver decoration of the class, encircled with a silver garter with the motto of the class, an elegant white plume rising out of a silver encasement.' (plate 4) His pony had a rich single plume on its head.

The herald was followed by eight olive-crown bearers, about five years old, then two mounted pages, elegantly dressed, bearing the rifle and tilting cups. 'Besides, there were models of those implements most conspicuous in the games. A neatly-made hurdle was borne aloft on a wand, and adorned with flowers, &c. A foot-ball and other things were represented in the same way.' The procession turned right up Barrow Street to the new gasworks, made an about-turn and returned up Barrow Street past the Raven, and on down Wilmore Street, and Sheinton Street, before reaching Windmill Field. This was the first time that the procession had been undertaken mostly for the purpose of spectacle.

Brookes made his opening address. Another first was his clear statement that 'We are endeavouring humbly to follow the example of the ancient Greeks, who, as Mr Gladstone [then Chancellor of the Exchequer] lately remarked at Glasgow, "had the largest ideas upon the training of man, and produced specimens of our kind with gifts that have never been surpassed."' The *Shrewsbury Chronicle* similarly referred to Greece and the ancient games, before observing that 'It might have been supposed that the revival of so ancient an institution would have been undertaken by a great town or city. But we find, what contrasts in one sense very oddly, a few gallant spirits in a thriving little Salopian borough leading the van in the resuscitation of games originally rudely practised by the sons of one of the most renowned nations on the face of the earth.'

Brookes quoted from the thank you letter of Sir Herbert Edwardes. He had been 'very glad to see that the professionals were beaten in a foot-hurdle race by a Wenlock man,' William Roberts. Roberts was to be the most successful athlete at the games throughout the 1860s (plate 11). He was also to be a consistent servant of the Society; his first win was in the under-14 boys' race in the third-ever games in 1852, he became the starter for the races in 1881, and he helped to decide on an appropriate memorial to Brookes after his death at the end of the century – an almost unparalleled involvement in the Games (plate 26).

At this time, Roberts reigned supreme in the one-mile hurdles (14 flights), which he won from 1858 until 1861 (inclusive) and again in 1868 (when he was also third in the steeplechase), switching to victory in the 150-yard hurdles (10 flights) in 1869. In addition, he won both the high jump and long jump from 1861 (when he jumped 18ft 4in in long jump) until 1864 (inclusive). In the high jump he cleared 5ft 2in in 1862 and 5ft 6in in 1863, landing on his feet. Roberts was, for the rest of the year, a painter by trade, and the publican of the Plough Inn, and later the Royal Oak, both in Barrow Street. His physical prowess won him, by 1867, a Much Wenlock bride, Sarah, five years younger than him, with whom he would have 11 children.

Other significant winners in the 1860s include Archibald Cooper, who won the half-mile hurdles in 1861, and in 1863 the one-mile foot race 'with great ease'. He won the one-mile hurdles in October 1864, but lost the running high leap that year to Roberts. By 1878, he appears to have moved to Wrexham. Samuel Hoare or Oare of Bourton came second in the one-mile hurdles to Cooper in October 1864, and at the same games won the half-mile flat foot race 'open to farm labourers residing in the county of Salop'. He was the favourite, too, so obviously fancied by the spectators. The following year, Hoare was victorious in the one-mile foot race, beating J.C. Bowdler, and in 1866 won the one-mile hurdles. In 1867 and 1868, Hoare's main threat in the mile footrace was George Palmer, whom he beat in 1867, but to whom he was second in 1868.

William Grainger, a farmer's son from Stanway, south of Much Wenlock, was another of the 1860s' local greats, being victorious in the 1863 one-mile hurdles, beating Samuel Hoare. He also had a go at the tilting in 1866, and won the long jump in 1868, an eclectic selection of events. J. Gollings of Broseley also had brief glory in 1869, winning both the 200 yards footrace and the 150 yards hurdles, in which he defeated William Roberts, after a 'hard and exciting race'. Finally, Thomas Barnett came to prominence in 1868 and 1869, and like Roberts was faithful to the Society, outlasting Brookes, and serving as a judge towards the end of the century. His wife was also an asset to the Society. When the town's decorations were much admired by the newspaper in 1864, she was bracketed with Secretary, Edwin Yardley's wife, Esther – 'two ladies to whom Wenlock always looks when it wants any decoration for its festive occasion, and never looks in vain.' In 1865, for the only time, a competition was held for the occupiers of houses in Much Wenlock, rented for under £6, 'the fronts of which shall be most tastefully planted with Shrubs and Flowers, and with Creepers trained against the house walls'. First prize was 10 shillings, second five. Sadly, the winners of this proto-'Britain in Bloom' were not recorded.

In August 1860, the odes of Jonathan Douglas and Willie Brookes were printed in Edinburgh, and Willie's set to music by Arthur O'Leary and published by Ewer and Co. in London. It was performed by students of the Royal Academy of Music at Hanover Square, London, so coming to the attention of Spyridon Trikoupis, Greece's Envoy Extraordinary & Minister Penipotentiary, who asked for further information. Brookes wrote to Greece's Queen Amalia in October 1860 making reference to Gladstone's remarks about physical exercise, and relating the Society's activities since 1850. He sent her a medal and a belt clasp worn by the female relatives of the members of the Class. (None of these clasps has yet been found.) Also that October, he forwarded the Society's silver medal to Petros Velissarios of Smyrna who had won the Wenlock race at the Zappas Games, via N.G. Theocharis, President of the organising committee of the Zappas Games. Brookes also wrote to the Prince Consort, Prince Albert, to inform him of Wenlock's endeavour.

Within a week of Brookes's letter to Trikoupis, came a significant watershed. On Friday 16 November 1860, a stormy meeting of WARS was held in the Reading Room of the Corn Market. This was the 19th annual meeting, and difficulties for the institute were becoming apparent. Irregularities in the accounts had been left unexplained by the former Treasurer. Brookes wanted to raise the subscriptions to WARS Library and Reading-Room to 8s each, instead of 6s to the Library and 10s to the Reading Room as before. 'A discussion' ensued. It became apparent that 'the proposed change was not desirable'. No doubt piqued at this uncharacteristic rejection, Brookes next delivered the report of WARS for the year. Despite 'the strictest economy', the library had been unable to afford any new books for three years. This had led to a decline in library membership which had further reduced income, compounding the problem.

Brookes's report covered the number of volumes now in the library (1,828, and 262 for the working men), the number of subscribers (too few to break even), recent donations (including that by J.M. Gaskell of the garden at the back of the Corn Market, saving them the rent of two guineas a year) and the outcome of the Government's Inspection of the Drawing Class (a drawing by Miss Morris of Cressage was to be forwarded to London for national competition). He reported that the Working Men's new night school for reading, writing and arithmetic, established by the popular curate Nathaniel Heywood, had been 'well-attended'. They hoped to establish 'a penny savings bank'. Finally, Brookes turned to the activities of the Olympian Class.

At this point, Revd William Wayne, the vicar of Much Wenlock interrupted. He wondered 'how it was that the Olympian Class should be connected with the Wenlock Agricultural Reading Society?' Brookes, already prickly, could barely comprehend the question, but checked his notes and had to admit that he 'could not find any entry' to say that the Olympian Class was associated with the Reading Society. But the rules of WARS 'did not object to its being connected with any useful object'. Revd Wayne went further, saying that 'he did not think that the Olympian class was thoroughly in unison with the character of the reading society'. Brookes replied that he 'attached importance to physical improvement as well as mental culture'.

Ralph A. Benson, shifting in his seat and trying to move matters on, suggested that Revd Wayne give notice of a motion to the effect of what he was saying. Wayne said he 'quite agreed with the importance of physical training, 'but what he did not like was the mixing up of the physical with the mental. The two should be separated'. He moved that 'the reference made to the Olympic class should be left out' of the report. Brookes 'expressed his surprise at the course which Mr Wayne had thought fit to take'. He referred to instructions from the Society of Arts in London that it was desirable in institutions 'of an educational character that physical recreation should not be forgotten' if they were to be beneficial to members. Brookes mischievously recommended to Mr Wayne 'the book entitled *Recreations of a Country Parson*' which produced laughter in the room.

Wayne retorted that yes, he agreed 'so far as it is beneficial to the health of the members'. Brookes correctly surmised the basis of Wayne's objection, and added 'without promoting intemperance?' Wayne confirmed 'that is the part of the subject to which my remarks had reference. I have heard that the Olympic games are productive of an amount of intemperance; that amongst the people there is a loss of money and time, and that drinking is produced. All that I wish is that such practices as far as possible should not be sanctioned. I therefore move that the paragraph in the report to that effect should be left out.'

Brookes told the meeting that Mr Blakeway had signed a statement saying that in his capacity as town clerk he had twice attended the games, and had seen 'thousands of people assembled and only witnessed two cases of intoxication.' Brookes added that in 11 years as a magistrate, only one person had been brought before him for being intoxicated at the games. 'You must have healthful recreation to the people; if not, you give encouragement to the beerhouses. I know that at the time the Olympic games are being practised the beerhouses are empty; and it is well known that in Shrewsbury it is on that account principally that there is a feeling against them. I do hold, therefore, that the observations made by Mr Wayne are really unfounded and uncalled-for.'

Benson, increasingly uncomfortable, asserted himself as chairman. 'Move a formal amendment, Mr Wayne.'

'I cannot do that,' said Wayne, 'unless I know that, according to the record of our proceedings, the Olympic games are united with this society. It appears there is no statement to that effect. If that be so, then legally they are not united.' Brookes went head to head. 'I move that the report be adopted in its entirety.'

Poor Benson admitted himself to be in 'an awkward position, having proposed myself that the report should be adopted.' He conceded to Wayne that 'there is no real connection between the two, yet the Olympian Class has been looked upon as a branch. The question should be mooted at a public meeting.' The Revd R.H.G. More came to Benson's aid, suggesting that 'Since the Olympic Class receives no benefit from being connected with the reading society, what objection can there be to its separation?'

Brookes retorted, 'Charges have been made against it'.

'I have not made any charge', responded Wayne.

'No, no, no; but you have made what are, in one sense, charges enough against the games – of being productive of drunkenness.'

'Well, I have been informed that men have left their families during that week, have not worked as they ought, and not brought home, consequently, so much money; and that there has been drinking.'

Benson tried Wayne once again, 'You had better make a proposition.' Wayne replied, 'I move then "That the report be adopted, with the omission of such words as connect the Olympic Class with this institution as an integral part of it."' He was seconded by Revd More. A pin could surely have been heard to fall on the floor of the Reading Room as Benson asked for a show of hands. How the eight men must have wished for a secret ballot as their votes were scrutinised by Brookes and Wayne, the two Titans of the borough. 'For the amendment, three; for the original motion as Brookes had proposed it, five.' George Harnage abstained.

Wayne had been defeated, but 'gave notice of his intention to bring forward his resolution at a future meeting.' The issue had only been postponed. Moving on, Benson was re-elected as President. At the conclusion of the meeting, Brookes must have burst through his front door like a whirlwind, intent on finding evidence that the Class was indeed allied to WARS. While he turned over his records, Brookes might have reflected that the ancient Olympic Games had ceased around AD 390 because of edicts from Theodosius I outlawing pagan rituals in the newly Christian Byzantine Empire. Almost 1,500 years later, Brookes was not going to let the Church bring down his own Olympian Games. He immediately drew up a circular 'to consider whether the general interest of the (Olympian) Class would not be best promoted by a separation from the Wenlock Agricultural Reading Society.' Stalwart allies put it about while Brookes attended the mercifully uneventful annual WARS dinner at the Raven on Barrow Street.

The next day, Saturday, Brookes found 100 of the tradespeople and working men gathered in the downstairs Reading Room. The town's draper, Henry Pinckstone was in the chair, to keep order over those who had 'rallied round the standard…and testified by their zest how much they valued a properly conducted species of recreation, and how loath they were to allow it to suffer deterioration in the eyes of the multitude.' Brookes confirmed that he had proof that the Olympian Class was indeed 'a part and parcel' of the Reading Society. A reading of the minutes confirmed that Wayne had been a party to the formation of the Class and its rules. Brookes made a point of reading 'that any person guilty of drunkenness, or using profane or improper language…should be liable to be fined from one to five shillings by the committee, or to be expelled the class.'

'Considering, therefore, that the accusation made against this class, "that it promotes drunkenness," is unfounded', Brookes proposed separation of the Olympian Class from WARS, and that it be 'continued, henceforth, under the title of 'the Wenlock Olympian Society.' (Loud Cheers.)' Thomas Jukes of the Coates proposed that Brookes 'be the President of the Olympian Class'. He was seconded by baker Thomas Owen, 'a forest of hands was held up in its favour, and a burst of cheering signified that it was heartily carried.' Thus the Olympian Class was renamed the Wenlock Olympian Society, 10 years after the Games had begun. Brookes responded by confirming 'I shall resign my office as secretary to the Reading Society' so that he might 'have more time to devote to your institution'.

The struggling WARS had just lost its greatest asset. Brookes could now devote his prodigious energy to the Olympian Society. He told them, 'You must not be discouraged if you meet with opposition when engaged in good work…You cannot expect to accomplish at once all you desire; as the tree increases in growth, as it puts forth more branches, it will produce more fruit. You must not be discouraged if the objects of your society are misunderstood, or its results misrepresented.' He urged them to take courage from the fact that 'the noble of the land, who can appreciate the value of physical training, sympathise with you in your aspiration, are generous in their construction of your motives, and liberal in their support of your efforts'.

Brookes accepted the presidency of the society. 'I do so, trusting that every member will show by his conduct that he is anxious to preserve its character untarnished, relying, too, upon his cordial and active support in carrying out all its objects, the moral, and intellectual, no less than the physical improvement of the people. We want to provide out-door recreation as a substitute for sensual and degrading pursuits. We want to get rid of drunkenness, as a moral stain upon human nature, as an offence against society, and, what is of far greater moment, as an offence against Heaven.' This was a man on a crusade, poaching moreover, the language of Wayne's pulpit. 'Our greater antagonist will be the demon drunkenness. Drunkenness, as you all know, destroys alike body, mind, and soul.'

The working men of Wenlock recognised the opportunity that had befallen them, thanks to the intransigence of the vicar. At a time when many working-class families were symbolically turning their back on the Church of England with its traditional links with the big estate (younger sons often being vicars), in favour of non-conformist chapels in their various forms (Much Wenlock's Primitive Methodists erected their chapel on King Street in 1862), this was a movement in step with its times, another way in which the working man could exert his independence from the old controlling interests. Three cheers were raised for 'our worthy president; we shall never have a better opportunity…Stentorian voices soon made the walls of the building ring with hearty shouts of gladness. To make the ovation complete, three other cheers were raised for 'Mrs. Brookes and family,' and they were given with additional vigour.'

The break from WARS gave Brookes greater clarity of purpose. In some ways, it was an outcome that he might have desired. In his speech after the 1858 Games, Brookes had confessed that 'If there be one branch of your institution, for the permanence and prosperity of which I feel more solicitous than another, it is your olympian class'. A small revolution had occurred. Far below the noise of the world, tucked away, sunk deep in its pillow of surrounding hills, the Wenlock Olympian Society had been born, with a knight errant out to vanquish the snobbery of the middle class and its prejudice. He would risk all for the working class, as he had done on that day a decade before, when he had run the gauntlet of ridicule by leading their little procession through the town. He had not been disappointed. He could be confident, now, that they would not let him down. The men of Wenlock were in the vanguard of honest recreation in which all grades could take part.

The split from WARS coincided with the arrival of the railway in Wenlock. At the 1859 (10th anniversary) Games, parking had been an issue after the field 'was approached by parties from all directions. Even the break-neck Wenlock-edge offered no obstacle to passengers by carriage or on foot; for they one and all seemed to make for the scene of display,' and 'traps phaetons, carriages, &c., rolled rapidly up and took "stands".' The following year, the Games programme announced that 'In order to prevent confusion, and to afford facilities to all witnessing the games, persons will be appointed to station carriages as they arrive on the ground.' The newspapers reported that 'on the opposite side of the track [from the grandstand] marked out were lines of carriages, phaetons, traps, flys, and innumerable waggons, with parties select and mixed.'

Construction of the railway was already underway, in hopes that it might facilitate the transport of the 36,600 tonnes of limestone annually quarried west of Much Wenlock to Coalbrookdale, instead of its being lugged by heavily-laden packhorses, or in wagons, down precipitous tracks through Farley Dingle. It would be a very steep line, but engineer Thomas Brassey was undaunted and linked it to the Severn Valley Railway at a junction just beyond the river Severn at Buildwas. Andrew Brookes was chairman of the company formed in 1859, Roger Blakeway the secretary, and William Penny Brookes one of the directors.

It took five and a quarter years to square local interests and confirm the precise route of the line. For Andrew Brookes, it meant leaving his family home in Cressage, four miles from Much Wenlock, where he had lived and practised for about 16 years by 1860. The 'pretty mound of trees' in his garden was directly on the route of the Severn Valley line. The Brookes were a close family, and sadness had bound them closer still. After the deaths in 1854 of Mary Anne and John, in 1861, Andrew Brookes and Eliza were to lose their son, Alfred. That Christmas, it had been hoped that Andrew and Eliza would join the family at Wilmore Street, but typhoid fever was raging (Prince Albert died of it on 14 December) and they were afraid to bring their daughter Edith. 'Of course they could not be separated – Lizzie's grief…is overwhelming at times'.

A special leaving dinner was held for Andrew at the Eagles Inn, Cressage on 29 June 1860, chaired by Sir George Harnage of Belswardyne for whose wife Andrew had cared until her death. He therefore spoke with feeling of 'our worthy friend…for 10 long years or nearly so…a constant visitor at my house at least three or four times a week; and the satisfaction he always gave, indeed the great relief he invariably afforded, were always strikingly apparent when he left my house. He was not only well skilled in his profession, but his kindness of manner at all times did more good almost than was effected by his medical skill…his kindness was unbounded. (Hear, hear.)'

Andrew took a trip to Ireland and returned to Shrewsbury to join the practice of the great William J. Clement, not only a mentor in medicine, but one of the foremost men in the Liberal party in the county, MP for Shrewsbury from 1865 until his death in 1870, and mayor of the county town from 1863 until 1865. Clement suffered for his political views, allegedly being squeezed out of his role at Salop Royal Infirmary by the overwhelmingly Tory hierarchy. Andrew Brookes lived near St Chad's, and after Clement's death moved to his former residence, the Council House (the meeting place of the Council in the Marches of Wales several centuries before) behind a half-timbered gatehouse near the castle. Andrew's successor in the Cressage practice, Dr Willings, was appointed.

On 26 March 1860, Brookes's daughter Maria (now about 23 years old) was brought to the field between the priory and the future station, close to Windmill Field and there cut the first sod of the line, put it into a special wheelbarrow and ran it along a plank. Herculean navvies began work, about 50 of them lodging in Much Wenlock. Their reputation for hell-raising went before them. Brookes, with his egalitarian credentials no doubt welcomed them, besides dealing with their injuries, but unlike his local labourers, the navvies were more difficult to govern. In October 1860 the *Wellington Journal* reported that four Irish navvies were arrested for causing affray in Much Wenlock, observing that 'incidences of this kind seem to have been all too frequent of late by labourers involved in building the railway from Much Wenlock to Buildwas'. Unfortunately, there is no evidence that these men took part in the games of 1860, for they could surely have thrown a hammer or stone as far as any man there, albeit not necessarily with the chivalric niceties that Brookes sought to encourage.

Whatever the benefits to trade, there is no doubt that the new railway line benefited the Wenlock Olympian Games. Much Wenlock station, originally planned to be near the Wynnstay Arms (now the Gaskell Arms) would from 1864 be built close to the gates into the Games field. Until it was built, the Goods Station was used (whose building is today the bowls club's pavilion on the Field). The line was expected to be open for the 1861 inaugural Wenlock Olympian Society Games, but there was a hitch. The new line had not yet been passed by the Board of Trade Inspector for public use. Brookes, undaunted as ever, negotiated permission to run a special train 'taking up by the way such ladies and gentlemen as had confidence in the security of the line'.

The Olympian Games train, complete with the Shropshire Artillery Band, pulled out of Coleham Station south of the river in central Shrewsbury at 10am on 23 October 1861. As it neared Much Wenlock, 'crowds had assembled at various spots commanding a view of the line; and amid waving of handkerchiefs, and loud cheers the train steamed past the Windmill Field, slowed over the bridge above Sheinton Street, and pulled up to the platform.' There the train was met by the indispensable juvenile fife and drum band and the whole Olympian procession, including the tilters, whose horses must have needed some control as the train hissed and belched to a halt.

In the absence of both of the Brookes brothers in mourning for Andrew's son, Ralph Benson made a speech that alluded to the immensity of the development. 'They had seen the steam engine scale those heights which had been looked upon as barriers not to be passed, as the broad Atlantic was before the days of Columbus…Now London was infinitely more reachable than Ludlow was not many years ago.' Revd Wayne had made a similar point, at the cutting of the first sod of the railway. Steam-boats had started the New York to Albany route in 1807, and 'in this month of March 1860, a steam-ship has crossed the mighty Atlantic Ocean, from Newfoundland to Ireland, in six days and eight hours!' In 1901 a German liner would have got the journey time down to under five days. In 1866, the laying of the first transatlantic cable would enable the relay of telegraphic communications across the ocean, sending instant messages between the continents.

The world was shrinking. The possibility of challenging men in athletic competition from elsewhere in the county, then the country and ultimately the world began to seem not just possible, but entirely practicable as the century rolled on. In 1861, the first ever English team went to Australia on the SS *Great Britain* (whose iron plates were made at Horsehay near Much Wenlock) to play cricket. Nationalisation of standards in other spheres was already under way. In 1860, WARS had become affiliated to the Society of Arts in London, so that paintings and drawings could be entered into competition with works from all over the country. In 1862, Brookes's middle daughter Adeline would, for a second time, win a national medallion for her work. Of more practical use, examinations taken in Much Wenlock could result in certificates valid for employment all over the country.

In October 1858 the *Shrewsbury Chronicle* had suggested, in considering the Wenlock Games that 'If several classes were formed then there could be a county competition at which 'the members from all the local classes should be invited to compete'. Brookes now had spare capacity to pursue exactly that. At the start of this process of expansion, in 1860, Brookes sent out the programme of the Wenlock Society's Games to every Mayor in the land, hoping that some of his wind-borne seeds might fall on fertile ground. He had also set in train an expansion of his project. Their meeting in May 1860 resolved that 'it is desirable that annual Meetings for Olympian Games for the whole county, to be called 'The Shropshire Olympian Games', should be held in rotation in the following Boroughs and other large towns. Shrewsbury, Ludlow, Oswestry, Bridgnorth, Wenlock, Wellington etc.' Brookes had written to the mayors of these towns to ask them to act on a committee for carrying out the plan.

By July 1860, Brookes had matters well in hand. *Eddowes's Shrewsbury Journal* looked forward to that year's games in Wenlock while observing that the movement for physical recreation 'may now be fairly considered a national one, and such steps are being taken with regard to the establishment of Olympian Games and sports of a kindred character in Shropshire especially, as can hardly fail to be conducive to public health and morals'. Further afield, *The Court News* was reporting Wenlock's revival of the Olympic Games, heartily desiring that 'the neighbouring counties have caught the flame that has been so auspiciously lighted at Wenlock. Would that the Wrekin would light up, and send the fire far and wide through Warwickshire and Staffordshire, and they hand it on to Worcestershire, Oxfordshire, Gloucestershire, and Bucks, and that next year we may have the good fortune to record the revival of the Isthmian games in Yorkshire, the Nemean in Devon, and the Pythian in Northamptonshire.'

In the event, the Shropshire Olympian Games were held four times. In 1861 at Wellington (Shropshire), in 1862 and 1863 at Much Wenlock, and in 1864 at Shrewsbury. This may seem a small achievement, but Brookes's rapid push towards the nationalisation of sports would quickly supersede competition at county level. Nevertheless, this series of Games is important for several reasons. Firstly, they were held in different locations annually, hoping thereby to spread the passion for recreational sport. This peripatetic feature was eventually to become part of the modern Olympic Games. Secondly, the larger-scale games attracted competitors from further afield. Shrewsbury was on several railways, indeed was 'the embryo "Crewe" of Salop' making it more accessible. Brookes's Shropshire Olympian Games are therefore among the first championships of a national character in Britain. Thirdly, they brought additional coverage to Brookes's endeavours, bringing him into contact with others who would help the national movement come alive.

The build up to the Shropshire Olympian Games at Wellington in May 1861 began in earnest in April. The *Shropshire News* believed it 'a step in the right direction' as some 'honest recreation in which all grades can take part' was needed to replace those that had been lost or which, 'unfit to bear the light of day, still skulk amid the backslums of towns and serve but to brutalize and enervate, without one redeeming quality in return'. Men had been allowed to become 'something like machines,' employing the same muscles all day every day until they became 'more or less deformed'. The writer claimed that 'you can tell the trade they follow by walking behind them in the street. One man lies doubled up in a coalpit till his legs form the segment of a circle'.

The choice of Wellington was influenced by Brookes's confidence in influential local patronage from Robert Slaney, and his long friendship with Thomas W. Jones the local auctioneer and valuer of Church Street, Wellington, who was also a walker and high-jumper. In handing out the prizes, Slaney would describe a 'spirit of thankfulness for the good conduct which has characterised the proceedings'. He noted that when discussing the Games, 'we were cautioned that the experiment of bringing together large masses of work people from the mines and forges and such like establishments was a somewhat perilous one, and that in all probability confusion, clamour, and perhaps something worse, would be the result. How that prediction has been falsified.'

The first Shropshire Olympian Games, held on Monday and Tuesday 20 and 21 May 1861, had 34 classes in total, 24 of them broadly athletic, three of them for shooting and open only to the Wellington Rifle Volunteers, and the rest for poetry, painting, arithmetic, writing, history, sewing and other intellectual pursuits. In reporting the events in May, the *Shropshire Chronicle*, (demonstrating the novelty of what Brookes was doing by struggling for the correct adjective) made great play of the benefits of 'gymnical exercises' to the Greeks. The Games drew visitors from Chester, Wrexham, Oswestry, Birmingham, Manchester and Stafford. The site was three fields belonging to Mr Nichols of the Crown, near the Haygate on the Shrewsbury-road side, so giving the event the stunning Wrekin hill as its backdrop. It was estimated that 6,000–7,000 people attended on the Monday and more than 10,000 on Tuesday. On the Windmill Field model, the site had a grandstand, refreshment booths, and stalls selling nuts, oranges, ginger-beer, cakes and sandwiches. The sun shone and the bands of the Shropshire Artillery Corps and the Wellington Rifle Corps played.

One of the main attractions was the water jump for some of the foot races, cut two to three feet deep. It was used in both the under-15s' 300-yard race in which 21 competed, the water leap being 'productive of much fun', and the under-18s' 300-yard race for those 'employed in the mines', followed by the same for those employed in the forge – 'a beautiful race' with a close finish right to the judge (T. W. Jones's) chair 'amidst the cheering of the spectators and the encouraging cries of the supporters of the respective competitors'. The winner was John Proudley of Wellington, with an exciting dead heat for third. Also noted was the wheel race – each competitor was 'to bring his own wheel' – won by William Dolphin of Wellington. Leaving the ground, an unsuccessful competitor was heard whistling 'I canna mind my wheel, mither'.

A Wenlock party made the journey to Wellington on both days. Thomas Jukes of the Coates Farm won the pony tilting on the Monday as well as the tilting on Tuesday (the only competitor to take a ring three times), while a purely athletic group attended on the Tuesday. William Roberts triumphed in the high jump (5ft 2in) and 'easily' beat Job Smith of Manchester in the one-mile hurdles (14 flights) 'open to All England'. William Shingler, a 25-year-old labourer from Mardol Lane in Wenlock, won the long jump (15ft 3in), while the juvenile fife and drum band under George Yates beat Wellington and Shrewsbury. The games won too, as notably only one person was taken into custody during the two days, and 'not one case of pocket-picking took place'.

The second and third Shropshire Olympian Games were held in Much Wenlock in 1862 and 1863 (in addition to their own games). The 1862 games were the more notable of the two, because of the attendance of the famous runner Jack White, the 'Gateshead Clipper', from Newcastle-upon-Tyne. He had first raced professionally in Newcastle in 1857, and by 1860 he had been taken up by George Martin from Manchester, a famous trainer and promoter of the period, known as 'the wizard of pedestrianism'.

In 1860 the versatile White had held the national four, six and 10-mile running belts and his career that year was said to have 'surpassed that of any pedestrian ever known in England.' The following year, 5,000 people watched him race close rival James Rowan over half a mile for £50, though Rowan won. In 1863, when White had run 10 miles in 52 minutes and 14 seconds he was called 'the best ped the world has ever seen'. He raised the profile of running in the North East, especially after music hall songs like *Wor Tyneside Champions* celebrated 'Little White' (5ft 3in and just under 8st) and Rowan.

In the run-up to the 1862 Shropshire Olympian Games, 'Little White' was said to have been 'matched in pace with 'Deerfoot'', the running name of native American Seneca Indian, Lewis Bennett, born in 1830. Deerfoot was brought to England by White's manager Martin on several occasions from 1861. He caused a sensation, running bare-chested (which broadened the Victorian female audience for athletics) and in moccasins, with a band and feather round his head. He was Longfellow's *Hiawatha* (1855) 'swift of foot', made flesh. The Prince of Wales watched, and dined with Deerfoot at Cambridge, adding to athletics' cachet.

Adding spice to the appearance of White at the Shropshire Olympian Games at Much Wenlock in 1862 was the fact that he would be in direct competition with William Roberts. Many spectators fancied their man's chance. Although many acknowledged that White was a great runner 'many doubted that he was a jumper, consequently the friends of Roberts felt the greatest confidence in their man'. Windmill Field was prickling with anticipation as the runners came on to the grass. They were almost ready when White's backers objected to the height of the hurdles. They had been set up as usual, but a concession was made. While the crowd grew restless, each hurdle was driven in several inches lower. Brookes, accompanied by the supporters of each man, then wisely walked the course to secure their approval.

Finally, the four competitors stood at the starting line, bent slightly forward, and were off. Both Roberts and White got away together well. White, however, soon shot ahead. At the first hurdle, though, he put his hand on the top bar and '*vaulted over*'. Consternation erupted from the grandstand and spread across Windmill Hill. 'Loud cries of disapprobation were heard from all quarters'. White was undeterred and pressed on, vaulting each hurdle and passing the winning post about 25 yards ahead of Roberts, followed by Samuel Hoare and Archibald Cooper, 'who all topped the hurdles in very good style'. Brookes's old friend T.W. Jones, no doubt rose uneasily from his judge's chair, as furious appeals were raised all around him.

After due consideration (and thankful, no doubt, that the rules had stated from the very first games that the judge's decision was final), Jones delivered his verdict. 'The order of running has been to leap fairly over the hurdles, and if a party deviates from that rule, I do not think he is competent to be the winner of the prize…I do not think it is fair for a man to go over the hurdle by putting his hands upon it…I now give my decision in favour of Roberts.' Brookes was sure 'no man would give a more impartial judgment than Mr Jones'. It was a mercy that rain stopped play.

This incident reinforced the reputation of professionals for dubious practice and was a clear indication of the rising need for national rules for athletics. In 1863 the Wenlock Olympian Games programme explicitly stated for the first time that hurdles were 'to be clearly leaped without touching'. Not unlike Brookes's profession, for which 18 different British institutions had been able to grant medical qualifications in the early 1800s, athletics needed uniformity for practise nationwide, now that clubs and competitive games were springing up everywhere. In 1861, the Liverpool Athletic Club was founded. On 30 November 1861, a few gentlemen of the West London Rowing Club hired the West London Cricket Ground at Brompton and ran a few races. The event was an instant hit and was regularly repeated.

In 1863 (the year that the Football Association was formed to standardise rules for that game nationally) the Pear Tree Ground opened in Bristol. A varsity meeting of Oxford and

Cambridge's athletics clubs was held for the first time at Christ Church cricket ground on 3 March 1864 (quite possibly attended by Willie Brookes, who had matriculated from the college the previous year). Just outside Manchester, George Martin, White's manager, opened the Royal Oak Grounds in 1864. Martin staged the first annual grand Olympic Festival for the Encouragement of Physical Education in 1864. In 1865, in the North East, Huddersfield Cricket and Athletic Club came into existence, the first of many in the region.

The discomforts of 1862 were surpassed at the Games the following year, but not for reasons of athletic misdemeanour. This time, Brookes had the unwelcome experience of providing the spectacle for the wrong reasons. All of Wenlock had been aghast when Brookes was assaulted in the High Street in Much Wenlock on 6 April 1863. Brookes felt obliged to seek redress in the courts against his attacker, James Beddoes. Beddoes claimed that Brookes had been having an affair with the wife of Beddoes's half-brother, Charles Weale.

The case was brought before the Petty Sessions of the borough magistrates on Thursday 9 April 1863. Brookes suffered the humiliation of standing in the Guildhall that he had spent so much of his own money to renovate, before his fellow magistrates to give an account of himself and then to be cross-questioned by them. Brookes's solicitor Roger Blakeway had drafted in a Lincoln's Inn barrister, 22-year-old Mr Steward, to make his case.

Steward, after opening with an assertion of Brookes's unimpeachable character then outlined how Brookes had gone to the house of one of his tenants, Mrs Hughes, where he met Lucy Weale, who spoke to Brookes briefly before leaving. Brookes was speaking with Mrs Hughes, whose mother and lodgers were among his patients, when they were warned of Beddoes's approach. At Mrs Hughes's suggestion, Brookes hid under the bed in the room. The window was then smashed and two men entered, Beddoes through the back door and his 'illegitimate brother', Mrs Weale's husband Charley, through the kitchen door. After Beddoes and Weale ran through the room in search of him, Brookes slid out from under the bed and tried to escape through the smashed window, only to find it barred. Beddoes and Weale returned, caught hold of Brookes, flung him over an oak chest and hit him several times on the back of the head with the butt end of a whip, reinforced with iron (he had his hat on). The redoubtable Mrs Hughes caught hold of the whip, enabling Brookes to escape, but he was further beaten in the street until he took refuge in a cottage.

'It is no secret what the line of defence will be in this case', said Steward, 'that there was an improper intimacy between Mr Brookes and Mrs. Weale'. In return, Steward claimed that Beddoes' motivation for the attack was that Beddoes had tried 'to violate [Mrs Weale's] person, accompanied with violence' the previous year. Brookes, being confided in by Mrs Weale, had felt sympathy for her, a sympathy resented by both Beddoes and Weale.

Brookes, when questioned, admitted previously receiving 'a caution' from Beddoes. He had therefore made 'an assignation with Mrs Weale at Mrs Hughes's to offer her support. I had met with Mrs. Weale, and walked with her'. Brookes was also obliged to divulge that 'I have given Mrs. Weale presents', a gold brooch, with an emerald engraved 'For ever' (after a song Mrs Weale used to sing), a locket with the same inscription, a ring, and a shawl brooch. The latter was engraved in French, 'J'espre,' [sic] 'which meant to convey that under any difficulty she was to rely on me as a friend. They were not given with her husband's consent.' He had given her his photograph and had paid for Mrs Weale's for himself. Mrs Weale had written to him, occasionally on foreign paper, coloured and lined. 'Mrs. Weale gave lessons to my daughters in music, and me. I played on my own instrument.'

Mrs Hughes testified to the events as described, and Lucy Weale was called. Beddoes, she claimed, 'has an animosity to me because I would not submit to him, and be his wife as well as his brother's.' She said that she had sought Brookes's opinion after her husband had refused to advise her. She also claimed that Beddoes 'struck me several blows, while I was at Mrs. Hughes'.' On seeing this, her husband Charley Weale, somewhat short of the chivalrous ideal, had cried out, 'James, leave off; she is my wife, I will beat her.'

After this account of alleged extra-marital sex, attempted rape, incest and wife-beating, the magistrates had heard enough. They sent the case for trial at the next borough sessions in early July, when the Recorder acknowledged, with masterful understatement, that the case 'possibly has caused a great deal of sensation in this neighbourhood'. For the gossips, this hearing turned out to be a damp squib, for the defence counsel, Mr Neale, persuaded Beddoes to plead guilty to a lesser charge of common assault provided that in return, he drop all the claims of Brookes's affair with Lucy Weale, claims that had 'imported agony with his family'. With much allusion to Brookes's pained wife Jane, to happy homes and children in peace, Lyde Benson (acting for Brookes) attempted to smooth everything over. Beddoes was ordered to pay £10 and keep the peace towards Brookes for a year.

The timing of the scandal was also unfortunate because Brookes's youngest daughter Isabella was to marry on 6 October 1863 the Revd Charles Great Rex, Much Wenlock's curate. Wenlock seems to have regained its usual equilibrium by the time the wedding came round. The road to the church was carpeted in red, two dozen girls strewed flowers before Isabella as she went to church in a 'handsome and richly embroidered white dress, with wreath of jessamine mingled with orange blossom, and tulle fall'. Five bridesmaids followed, over five hundred people gathered to watch, the streets were overarched with flowers, seven sheep were roasted in the town for the poor, bells rang, cannon boomed, and a brass band paraded the streets from eight in the morning. The wedding party was held at the Talbot with a public ball for 150 afterwards, at which dancing was kept up 'till a late hour'. Brookes became a grandfather the following year with the birth of Arthur Charles Great Rex.

The final Shropshire Olympian Games were held over two days in Shrewsbury in 1864. On Wednesday 7 September, in rather autumnal weather, the programme of 17 events included sword exercises (by the North and South Shropshire Yeomanry), a half-mile walking match, shot putting, tilting at the ring and single stick, besides flat races of a quarter and half mile, hurdles of half a mile and one mile, wrestling, high standing leap and high running leap, wide standing leap and wide running leap. The programme for Thursday 8 September under sunnier conditions included rifle shooting (open to the militia, artillery and rifle volunteers using Government long Enfield Rifles) and Carbine shooting, to be held north of Shrewsbury at Berwick, the home of Mr Gough.

This was followed by swimming, an innovation for games in which Brookes had been involved. The swimming was to take place in the River Severn which flowed through the picturesque Quarry site in the heart of Shrewsbury. The river also facilitated a Regatta, with events for four to six-oared outrigged boats and sculls, a half-mile race for whiffs and wherries, a three-quarter-mile gig race, a coracle race over a quarter of a mile and a 1.2 mile single-handed punt race. Intellectual competitions included a poem on 'The Paradise of Cymru' (Wales), and prizes for the best watercolour drawing, for the best shaded drawing from the round, and for the best outline.

The number of entrants for the Shropshire Olympian Games at Shrewsbury in 1864 was perhaps disappointing, but the races were exciting, particularly the half-mile hurdles which was hotly contested by A. Smith of Chester, George Griffiths of Wellington and H. Simpson of Seaforth, Liverpool. 'At the start Griffiths went away with the lead, but soon gave way to Smith, who, when halfway over the last lap was passed by Simpson; at this time Griffiths was last, and his chance of winning seemed hopeless, but when approaching within a very short distance of the post, he put on a gallant spurt, and passed to the front, amidst the cheers of the spectators.' Simpson went on to win the one-mile hurdles, and the high jump, when he cleared 5ft 3in 'in beautiful style'.

The regatta was a glorious spectacle, presenting 'a sight rarely witnessed'. As a competition it was a little frustrating because many of the crews in second place as they passed the boat house, pulled in and gave up, leaving the leader to go on and win alone (frequent practice in foot races of the period, the runners often wanting to save themselves for another race the same day). The first race provided drama though, when the victors stood up to salute, wobbled and tipped the boat over. All could swim except the unfortunate cox, a 'little boy' who had to be rescued by Dr Fenton. The coracle race was especially competitive. H. Barrett and G. Allen, both of Overton, in their little boats like walnut shells, passed the flag in a dead heat and divided their winnings.

By the time of these Games, Brookes must have been delighted to see similar athletics meetings held annually in Liverpool. Answering the call of the *Liverpool Courier* of 1860, Liverpool Athletic Club was founded around January 1861 by John Hulley (1832–75) and Charles Melly (1829–88), educated at Rugby School under Arnold from 1844, of the philanthropic liberal Liverpool family that was later to produce the jazz musician George Melly. Mount Vernon parade ground welcomed 10,000 spectators for the first Grand Olympic Festival organised by Liverpool Athletic Club on 14 June 1862 and again in 1863. These Festivals continued until 1867.

The *Liverpool Courier* of 18 October 1862, recording the developments, praised Brookes's perseverance at Wenlock. It noted that 13 years' work had resulted in his example being 'followed in other parts of the county – may we not add, also, in Liverpool?' It was suggested that William Dargan, the great railway developer in Ireland had also been influenced by Brookes. He 'set apart a piece of ground at Bray [Co. Wicklow] for the purpose of encouraging athletic sports'. Dargan's athletic ground (today home to Bray Wanderers AFC) opened in 1862, complete with Turkish baths.

John Hulley (whose father and two uncles were surgeons) was a keen proponent of gymnastic exercise. He was based at the gymnasium (also the headquarters of Liverpool AC) at the Rotunda, Bold Street. Hulley, a flamboyant character, 'with the body of a Hercules and the head of an Apollo', was unashamedly eccentric, and adopted the somewhat Old Testament title of 'Gymnasiarch'. Hulley's physical prowess was in no doubt. He was known as 'the greatest athlete of his time. He it was who offered to fight Tom Sayers, England's champion pugilist, he who walked from Liverpool to London, swam across the Mersey several times, raised himself from the ground with one arm, lifted prodigious weights, and performed various other remarkable feats which attracted hosts of admirers, and gave him a unique reputation.'

Hulley, by 1860, was 'stirring all Liverpool with his new theories of muscular Christianity'. He was helped by his magnetic personality that attracted numerous disciples in the booming port city. At Brookes's invitation Hulley attended the Wenlock Games in October 1862, bearing the bronze medal of the Liverpool AC, which Brookes presented to winning tilter Bromley Jones. Brookes, on proposing the health of Hulley suggested 'that he be elected an honorary member of the Shropshire and Wenlock Olympian Societies.' He also quoted from an essay delivered by Hulley at Liverpool's Theatre Royal in 1861, which demonstrates how similarly the two men thought:

'Do we think that any one of us, whatever be his mental merits, can allow his physical strength to decline, can leave his bodily powers uncultivated, without becoming degraded and imperfect, and without paying the sure penalty?...[Nature] demands that an equal and impartial attention be paid to all the faculties, and that an equal interest be taken in physical as in mental culture.'

Brookes also linked up now (perhaps through Hulley) with Ernst Ravenstein (1834–1913), director of the German Gymnastic Society (GGS) that in 1864–65 would build the German Gymnasium or 'Turnhalle' at 26 St Pancras Street, London (where it stands still, opposite the domestic entrance to the international rail terminal – plate 9). Ravenstein's father had studied under Friedrich Ludwig Jahn, 'the father of German gymnastics'. GGS membership, (1,100 in 1866, of which 650 were Britons, mostly tradesmen) included more than 30 nationalities. Besides gymnastics, fencing and boxing, GGS activities included an amateur band, a singing club, a literary club (their library had 2,500 books) and an English dramatic club. Ravenstein was also president of the London swimming club. A fellow of the Royal Geographical Society in London, Ravenstein was a leading cartographer, but is remembered chiefly for his laws of migration. He was awarded the first Victoria gold medal of the RGS in 1902.

By the time of the 1864 Shropshire Games in Shrewsbury, the first stone had been laid of Hulley's new gymnasium in Liverpool – the largest in Europe at 105ft long x 75ft wide x 60ft high – opposite the Philharmonic Hall on Myrtle Street. Melly and J.R. Jeffery helped Hulley raise the £15,000 required. Prior to its opening, Hulley would assemble a first-rate group of teachers including James 'Jem' Mace, champion boxer, André Durbec from Paris for fencing, and Cumberland wrestlers R. Irving and J. Becton. Hulley invited the Shropshire Olympian Games Committee to the grand opening on 6 November 1865.

Brookes went to Liverpool with Thomas Phillips, the chemist of the Mardol, Shrewsbury. On Myrtle Street, Brookes and Phillips found an imposing classical building across whose pedimented stone front were emblazoned the Gymnasium's (and the Victorian age's) motto by Juvenal, 'Mens sana in corpore sano' – a healthy mind in a healthy body. This vast cathedral to health was lit by windows high in the walls and a skylight. Hulley had toured the continent to research the latest equipment, including enough ropes to rig out a man-o-war, and a climbing wall with imitation castle stonework. Along two sides were balconies for male and female visitors (plate 8). There was a separate school of arms for fencing, boxing and broadsword practice under Durbec, and rooms at the side of the main entrance hall for Hulley's offices as Managing Director.

Lord Stanley, the former and future Prime Minister, in his speech, alluded to the great change in Britain, that for the first time in history, more than half the population lived in urban areas. He acknowledged that the gym was unlikely to be used by the labouring classes, but suggested that it would be a great boon for the armies of clerks, shop workers 'and all whose days are passed sitting in offices,' often close and overcrowded, resulting in feeble frames 'not physically speaking, the stuff out of which one wishes the middle classes of England to be made'. The object of the gym was not, Stanley insisted, to make champions of England, 'but to give them strong constitutions'. Interestingly for Brookes, local influential clergyman Revd Nevison Loraine spoke, asking rhetorically, what the clergy had to do with physical education. He felt it his responsibility 'to use all the influence that he possessed to promote not only the moral and spiritual, but also the intellectual, physical, and social well-being of the people. (Applause.)'

Liverpool Gymnasium became 'one of the acknowledged centres of sporting life in England', attended by men from the leading families of Liverpool including the Inmans, McIvers, Ismays, and Holts, besides visitors from elsewhere in England, and Americans en route to the port. These included not surprisingly, Charles Kingsley and Thomas Hughes, Prince Alfred the Duke of Edinburgh, Charles Dickens, and P.T. Barnum the great American showman, who tried unsuccessfully to whisk away Hulley's apprentice Alexander Alexander to perform in the United States.

More significant for Brookes's endeavours was a meeting held in the gym earlier on 6 November 1865, chaired by Hulley. Here, Brookes, Ravenstein and Hulley, along with Phillips, athlete William Mitchell, John T. Murray of London, Ambrose Lee of the Mechanics' Institution Gymnastic Society of Manchester, D.C. Keeling Secretary of Liverpool Athletic Club, J.B. Lee a member of Liverpool Athletic Club, and the fencing master André Durbec met, with the object, set out by Brookes, of considering 'how they could further the cause of physical education throughout the country.'

Brookes proposed formally 'That a National Olympian Association be established for the encouragement and reward of skill and strength in manly exercises by awarding medals or other prizes, money excepted, at general meetings of the association, to be held annually, and in rotation, in or near one of the principal cities or towns of Great Britain.' He further suggested that the society should 'show the advantages of combining mental with physical culture', and

'That professional athletes shall be excluded from competition.' His proposal was passed unanimously.

Significantly, Brookes also proposed that 'this association shall form a centre of union for different olympian, athletic, gymnastic, boating, swimming, cricket, and other similar societies, enabling them, through the medium of a year-book, to assist one another by mutual suggestions, and to collect and diffuse information on subjects of physical education…that the competitions of the association shall be international and open to all comers.' The NOA's motto was to be 'Civium virtus civitates tutamen' – in the strength of the individual is the strength of the nation.

At this meeting, 'suggestions were made for sending a formal challenge to the athletes of France and other countries'. The NOA had ambitions for its inaugural Games in London in July 1866 to be an international championship – the first of its kind. A committee was established, of which Brookes, the NOA's 'cheval de bataille', was the Secretary. Responsibility for spreading the word and for drumming up support through subscriptions was split between Ravenstein for London and the southern counties, Brookes for the midland counties, and Mitchell for the northern counties.

Brookes had had most of this in place before the meeting in Liverpool on 6 November. *Eddowes's Shrewsbury Journal* had received a prospectus of the NOA by 25 October 1865, and the objectives and details had been set out in an article in the *Shrewsbury Chronicle* of Friday 3 November. For funds, Brookes set to with yet another round of letter-writing. The *Shrewsbury Chronicle* noted that 'Shropshire has already responded heartily to the scheme, with Liverpool, Worcester, Birmingham and other towns also contributing liberally to the fund.'

Brookes embarked on an NOA fund-raising tour of the Midlands. The *Worcester Journal* was stirred by his visit in late November 1865, after which it reported that principal subscribers included Thomas Southall, the Mayor, and John Perrins (a gun-maker, not the brewer of Worcestershire Sauce). Birmingham's leading citizens met to consider a gymnasium for the city on 18 December 1865. George Dawson, the leading philanthropist and charismatic non-conformist Unitarian minister 'cordially supported the proposition'. Birmingham Athletic Club was founded in 1866 and owed its survival to Joseph M. Hubbard, who 'had no equal'. BAC acquired athletic grounds at Portland Road, and built a pavilion, but for a gymnasium had to make do with the 'poultry bay' of Bingley Hall exhibition centre. Not until 1891 when Birmingham Athletic Institute opened on John Bright Street, did the BAC have a purpose-built gymnasium. In London, Ravenstein's efforts received support from Major Hammersley, the Inspector of Military Gymnasia, and from Thomas Hughes MP (author of *Tom Brown*).

Mitchell was also agitating, for the *Bacup and Rossendale News* in February 1866 stated that the NOA was meeting 'the obvious necessity of providing a central association, as a medium of communication among the various athletic clubs now in existence throughout the country.' It believed that grand national competitions [the Aintree horse race had begun in the late 1830s] were required for athletes too, 'where Englishmen may contend in generous rivalry against the flower of the youth of France, Russia, Germany, and the world at large.' It acknowledged the rapid spread of gymnasia throughout England and supported their consolidation into 'one grand centre of union' with 'the institution of annual contests to fan the flame of youthful ardour and enthusiasm'. The National Olympian Association, it concluded was of 'vital importance'.

The first half of the 1860s had seen Brookes undertake an exhausting expansion of his Wenlock athletic enterprise. The Olympian Class had broken away from WARS and had continued to stage its annual Games on the Windmill Field, Much Wenlock before growing crowds. The movement had spread to county level, Shropshire Olympian Games being staged annually from 1860-64 (inclusive). In November 1865, Brookes had drawn up, circulated and had approved proposals for the formation of a National Olympian Association, to promote physical recreation nationwide. It would stage national and perhaps international championships. It would also centralise the various new sporting clubs and societies all over the country. Although this represented a breath-taking rate of expansion for Brookes, it was necessary to keep up with the speed of expansion of sport in Britain at the start of the 1860s.

As the July 1866 date for the National Olympian Games in London approached, the marketing effort had proved successful, for the aims of the NOA were clearly understood. The *Birmingham Daily Gazette* in July 1866 said 'It is intended to constitute a centre of union for all the local cricket, boating, swimming, and other clubs of a like nature that may choose to put themselves in correspondence with it.' However, the successful dissemination of the NOA's aims produced some less-welcome results.

CHAPTER 3

'It was this frank and rough fellowship in their field sports...their bold rivalry in their hurling and their football, their wrestling and their single stick, their archery, their land and water quintain, which knitted the squire and the yeoman and the ploughman – the merchant, the artificer, and the sturdy apprentice, in a companionship which made them strong enough to defy the world in Elizabeth's heroic time.'
Knight's *Popular History of England (1856)*, quoted on the programme for the Shropshire Olympian Games, 1861

'**C**ricketing, boating, boxing, &c.,' said The *Birmingham Daily Gazette* of July 1866, 'are now become "commercial transactions", and occasionally not very creditable commercial transactions... the committee of the new [National Olympian] Association have therefore, on the whole, we think, judiciously determined not to offer prizes in money. They will thus escape the swarm of "professional gentlemen" who would otherwise attend their meetings for the sake of what they could pick up in cash, and attract those for whom the Association was more especially established.'

There is a whiff of exclusivity in the *Gazette's* piece, an eloquent reflection of a new division entering the development of sport in Victorian Britain. The *Gazette* was inaccurate to imply that the NOA was established for any particular class of society. Brookes's egalitarian principles are abundantly clear. However, the moral code of muscular Christianity had become associated with the making of a gentleman and so by extension, the amateur had become associated with the upper classes only. In fact, the professional/amateur distinction had originated in rowing, not out of snobbery, but out of the legitimate claim that men who spent all day rowing as a profession, like the lightermen who unloaded boats midstream on the River Thames for delivery to Wilkinson's Botolph Wharf, would inevitably be stronger than the university students who rowed as a pastime, so the two should not compete together.

Over time, however, the conflation of the professional and amateur distinction with social class, particularly in the Oxbridge and metropolitan south-east of the country clouded the issue for other sports. There followed an uncomfortable period of resistance to all classes competing together on equal terms. That the ostler of a Wenlock inn should share a Windmill Field dressing tent with an Eton and Christ Church-educated scion of the broad-acred aristocracy would require a change of attitude that would take a long while to achieve. As a result, the professional/amateur debate was to dog many sports (and the Olympic Games) for years to come. The game founded at Arnold's Rugby was among the first victims. The row over payments to players for loss of earnings (while they participated in matches) resulted in the split between rugby league and rugby union in 1895.

The *Gazette* was, though, absolutely correct that athletics needed closer monitoring, especially pedestrianism, where monetary gain motivated malpractice among professional competitors and their backers. This was relatively easy (in theory) to define, prove and prune out, and this is what the NOA was hoping to achieve by taking money (professionals) out of athletics. Runners had been competing for money for over a century. Pedestrianism's foundations – the aristocracy betting on its footmen in private races – rested on such 'transactions'. Next, young men with a particular talent began touring the country, challenging all-comers, or, like circus acts, undertaking superhuman feats. Their reward was a share in the takings, or a cut of the wagers. The most famous 'ped' was Scotsman Captain Robert Barclay Allardice who, at 15, won a hundred guineas for walking six miles in an hour on the Croydon road. This rose to 5,000 guineas soon afterwards when he walked 90 miles in under 21 and a half hours. Barclay also made money running, but his most famous achievement was walking 1,000 miles in 1,000 hours (42 days non-stop) in 1809. This allegedly won him £16,000 (more than half a million pounds today).

Not surprisingly, young men of all classes were attracted to pedestrianism. As its popularity rose, magistrates around the country had to start fining men for running on the highway, prompting the opening of the earliest tracks. By 1850, several cricket grounds had installed sprint tracks, usually made from gravel, including Sheffield Hyde Park by 1836, Leicester Cricket Ground (1845), and Lord's in London which had a two-man-wide path by 1837 (running round the pitch and behind the Pavilion) that was relaid in 1842, 1850 and 1857.

About a dozen other purpose-built tracks had been laid by 1850, often near taverns, including at Mrs Betty Berry's Snipe Inn, Audenshaw near Manchester (by 1840, extended 1857), the Higginshaw Ground in Oldham (relaid 1854), and the Bull's Head at Birchfield in Birmingham (1847). In London, tracks were laid at the Bee Hive, Walworth (1843), the Old Hat in Ealing (1845), Copenhagen House in Islington (from the late 1840s) which held the first national running championships in 1851 (the year after the first Wenlock Games), the New Surrey Ped Ground in Garrett Lane, Wandsworth (a 440-yard track from 1859) and at the Cheese Brothers' Flora Grounds in Bayswater, which opened in 1849 but by 1850 were the best in the country, attracting 15,000 spectators.

This is when the 'transactions' began to become more questionable. Running for the cash incentive attracted the less scrupulous and led to dubious practices. These included 'roping' (deliberately running slowly to lose a race) or 'running to the book' (in which true form was disguised to avoid handicapping, which was to become common in the 1870s), and 'ringing it' (in which promoters conspired to fix handicapping unfairly). From 1850 until 1863, Wenlock's prizes had always been in cash (the hurdles the most prestigious, worth £10 in 1863) except for some like the 1851 ladies' race for a pound of tea. Indeed, Lord John Manners's gift, in the first games, of £1 for a running race supported this approach. The 1862 Shropshire Games, with the controversy over White's hurdle vaulting demonstrated the danger of the cash incentive. Coming in first, by any means, was all that mattered.

The Shropshire Olympian Games at the Quarry in Shrewsbury in 1864, however, offered only medals for prizes, with the exception of the coracle and punt races. That October, Brookes referred at his Wenlock Olympian Games to the current 'dispute' over whether money or medals should be offered. He believed there was no point in giving medals to the working classes, when money was what they needed. However, he acknowledged that they also wanted the 'better classes' to compete and they would only do so for medals. 'There should always be, therefore, two kinds of competition;' he concluded, 'one for money, and the other for medals.'

Ironically, at the 1864 Wenlock games, the one-mile footrace produced just the kind of fiasco that brought Brookes's equivocal view into question. The competitors that year were supposed to prove that they were not professionals – proving a negative never being easy. The races were for the first time, 'strictly confined to amateurs', with the exception of the mile race, for which a £10 prize was offered. The professional race was, the *Shrewsbury Chronicle* reported, a 'disgrace...a regular sell'. The four competitors had travelled together from Birmingham, 'and *en route* very amicably settled the issue of the race. They had not run 200 yards...before one fell lame and gave up the race; a little further on a second one gave up, and for the rest of the course the race was an easy trot by the other two, one leading at a distance of about 50 yards.' The winner was called Sanderson, his runner-up James Nuttall, and the pair 'came home in solemn silence'. They were much mistaken if they had thought that in their urban sophistication they could hoodwink the rural Wenlock crowd, or indeed the stewards.

This was not the only problem that the professionals caused at Wenlock in 1864. 'Their presence had brought together a number of lesser stars in the racing firmament, who caused a deal of extra trouble to the judges by attempting to enter themselves for races strictly confined to amateurs. One of these gentry, who, judging from his appearance, would have been at a loss to describe the difference between a plough and a harrow, solemnly declared that he was a farm labourer, and demanded to be allowed to run as such.'

Brookes tried to square this circle in 1865 at Wenlock, the year that the Olympian Games settled definitively on Whit Tuesday (always in May or June) with a complicated compromise. Some competitions (the half- and one-mile hurdles, and the one-mile flat race) were run for medals and restricted to members of the Liverpool and Manchester Athletic Clubs, the Shropshire and Wenlock Olympian Societies and the Bridgnorth Gymnasium 'who have never competed for money'. The other races, all for cash prizes, were open only to Shropshire residents.

In 1866, the Wenlock Olympian prizes were once again all cash prizes, in many cases given by local sponsors, including the Lilleshall Company and the Cannock Chase Company, and individuals including Lord Forester, Jasper More, and J.M. Gaskell. The top cash prize of £3 was for the half-mile hurdles. Professional runners were excluded. The same occurred in the summer Games of 1867, with a top prize of £5 for the one-mile hurdles (donated by Lord Forester), but this was the last time that money prizes were paid at Wenlock. A dramatic change had occurred by the local men's autumn games the same year. All of the prizes were 'to the value of' and took the form of a writing case, books, and portrait photographs of Brookes and of the previous Festival. The programme for the 1868 summer Wenlock Olympian Games expressly stated that 'Professional Athletes are excluded from all amateur contests'. This first year of the General Competition (Pentathlon) saw local winner, Thomas Barnett, rewarded with a gold scarf pin donated by Hunt & Roskell, the Queen's silversmith, of London.

Since this was the way that things were now to go, Brookes commissioned from Hunt & Roskell a new medal for Wenlock. It needed to be exceptional to continue to draw top flight competitors to the Games. It featured Nike, the Greek goddess of Victory (another example of a fine idea by Brookes), the die for which was by the celebrated sculptor Edward William Wyon (1811–85). Wyon had been a regular exhibitor at the Royal Academy from 1831, and had been commissioned by Wedgwood to produce a series of busts of famous people for reproduction on their products.

Nike is depicted as she was in images of the lost wonder of the world, the statue of Zeus at Olympia – a beautiful winged figure, standing on an orb holding a tiny crown of olives – set in an oval of olive leaves in the centre of a Maltese cross (plate 13). Above her were words from Pindar's Olympic Ode, 'there are rewards for glorious deeds'. The cross was suspended from a bar decorated with four emblems: a scroll and lyre for literature and music; a bust and palette for sculpture and painting; a tilting ring and lance, a quoit and cricket bat for sport; and a rifle and sword for military exercises. These were interlaced by a sash with clasps bearing the motto 'Arte et Viribus' (skill and strength), the whole surmounted by a raised hand holding a crown of laurels – the emblem of the Wenlock Olympian Games.

In 1868, the Nike Medal was awarded to Warren FitzWarren, winner of the General Competition for amateurs, and also to Miss Harris of Malins Lee near Much Wenlock for her watercolour of a Shropshire church. From 1871 the Nike medal in silver became the first prize for the General Competition, and the medal featured on the cover of the Games programme from that year until 1877. The die was an extraordinarily expensive investment by the Society at £84 4s. Furthermore, each of the first-class silver medals cost £14 to produce. (A cheaper metallic mix of the same medal was given for second place in the General Competition, and called, confusingly, the Society's third-class medal).

Far more difficult to define than malpractice was amateurism, the question exercising the South East, where the influence of the public schools and the universities was most strongly felt. Sport, on the muscular Christian model, was now intensely popular. The Eton versus Harrow cricket match in London was an important fixture on the summer calendar of British society. The boat race had been there since 1856. Athletics would not be far behind. The publicly-schooled, Oxbridge-educated men of London, the political secretaries, Treasury or Foreign Office staff, or army officers – the younger sons of the leisured classes – who wished to continue their sports had formed themselves into a loose band. By 1865 besides the Brompton meetings, they had taken to competing at Hackney Wick and Bow. As the 'gentlemen amateurs' they would never be caught training or even showing much desire to win – languorous insouciance was their style.

Socially beneath them was the army of office workers, shop servants, and banking or solicitors' clerks of the new middle class who took their athletics seriously. Though they considered themselves amateurs as they did not earn their income from sport, they were not embarrassed to compete for monetary prizes, like the men at Wenlock. They formed themselves into the Mincing Lane Athletic Club in 1863, holding their first athletic meeting the following year, at Beaufort House grounds, Brompton on 9 April, and meeting again on 21 May. They worked at their sport, holding several meetings a year at Brompton until 1869, and making use, too, of the Old Deer Park, Richmond. (This club's administration and organisation supplied the model for the New York Athletic Club founded in 1868.) The Civil Service formed its own club in 1864, also meeting at Brompton, and Brookes would have welcomed the formation in 1867 of the United Hospitals Athletic Club.

Into this settling south-eastern stewpond of class-conscious sporting strata landed, in November 1865, the hammer throw flung by the NOA from the provincial north-western Liverpool Gymnasium. A Gymnasiarch, a German and a General Practitioner were threatening to take over the centralisation of all clubs, the regulation of athletic and gymnastic sports, and the organisation of a national (and international) championship in seven months' time, *and* in London. The gentlemen amateurs' insouciance was shed in world-record time. Polished heels were lifted off leather-topped tables, cigars stubbed out and newspapers folded. Something must be done. Instead of bringing the enemy within and overpowering it, by joining forces with the NOA and adding 'Gentlemen' to the three Gs, they assembled to plan a little handicapping of their own. They would form a club and get a head-start on the provincial interlopers.

The man that made this possible was John G. Chambers (1843–1883), the Eton and Trinity, Cambridge-educated son of a Welsh landowner fallen on difficult times. Chambers was a truly outstanding sports administrator – President of his University Boat Club and self-appointed manager of the University's Athletics Club, which he reorganised into a serious sport. He was mainly responsible for the programme of the first varsity athletics match in March 1864. Down from Cambridge and finding himself unexpectedly required to work, he became a journalist at the weekly journal *Land and Water*.

Chambers was the driving force of the antagonistic society that formed in December 1865, the Amateur Athletics Club (AAC). Its definition of an amateur was 'any person who has never competed in an open competition, or for public money, or for admission money, and who has never at any period of his life taught or assisted in the pursuit of athletic exercises as a means of livelihood.' There was nothing in there that ought to exclude the Wenlock men from membership or competition. With the NOA's championship planned for late July 1866, *The Sporting Gazette* of 23 December 1865 announced that the AAC would hold its championship four months before the NOA, in March 1866, on a London ground.

Land and Water followed up with a supportive piece in February 1866. 'There can be but one locality for the formation of such a club', it asserted, 'and that is London...London as a centre is as essential to its success as Newmarket to a Jockey Club.' The comparison was significant, as this was how Chambers saw the role of the AAC, as a club 'to supply...some established ground on which the numerous competitions in athletic sports and foot races may take place', and a gentleman's club at that. The NOA, not being of London, and its promoters not altogether gentlemen, was not quite the ticket, born on the wrong side of the blanket, born out of wedlock, or as it were, out of Wenlock. However, the Jockey Club had been formed in the agrarian 1750s by a circle of aristocratic gourmands and gamblers in the Star and Garter pub in Pall Mall, to govern the sport of kings. Athletics needed organisation, administration and regulation (besides a location for an annual championship) in the urban age of Reform.

Undeniably, the AAC successfully gazumped the NOA in 1866. As Peter Lovesey observed, in his centenary history of the Amateur Athletic Association, 'the AAC prospectus, published in February, 1866, bears signs of having been cobbled together over Christmas with no more purpose than to thwart the National Olympian Association.' Being held the day after the Boat Race, a huge social draw, they would be assured of large crowds. More significant for athletics than the gazumping of the NOA was the recognition by the Mincing Lane Athletic Club that in the AAC it had a rival. It started a long-term campaign of animosity till all heads were banged together, finally, in 1880, and the AAA (Amateur Athletics Association) emerged. For now, the Mincing Lane members met on 16 January 1866 and changed the club's name to the London Athletic Club. Between 6 November 1865 and 16 January 1866, therefore, three major new Athletics bodies had been formed: the NOA, the AAC and the LAC.

The egalitarian NOA's venue for Britain's first National Olympian Games was, appropriately, Joseph Paxton's glittering Crystal Palace – 'the People's Palace'. The former home of the 1851 Great Exhibition in Hyde Park had been relocated to Sydenham, south London and reopened in 1854 to host an eclectic array of events. A serious fire had destroyed the tropical (north east) part of the nave in late 1865, which had later to be rebuilt, but in April 1866, 'No more delightful locality exists' the *Daily Telegraph* assured its readers.

The cricket ground where the games would be held was 'one of the best and most favourite in the neighbourhood of London'. The Crystal Palace facilities were known to Ernst Ravenstein, as the basement included, besides a skating rink, a gymnasium, opened in 1865 like his own in St Pancras. Ravenstein appears to have been responsible for the NOA booking, as the forthcoming events, instead of listing National Olympian Games, trumpeted (among the assemblies of Odd Fellows, Druids and the Temperance League, and the Great Gathering of the Tonic Sol-fa Association), 'a great Gymnastic Gathering, including the German Turner-Verein'. This description probably explains the disappointing turnout of under 10,000 spectators for the athletics (comparable with that at Wenlock at this time) on 1 August 1866.

The previous day, the National Olympian Games had begun with swimming races in the Thames above Teddington Lock. On Wednesday, at 11am, over a hundred competitors marched out of the Crystal Palace down to the cricket ground where an enclosure was formed using chairs. Bunting abounded and the day was 'delightfully fine'. Hulley, true to eccentric form, appeared 'dressed as a Turk to present the East' – sadly it was as near to international participation as the games got. The crowds were disappointing, there being onlookers enough only to encircle the ground, two or three deep. Many ladies attended, perhaps a reflection of Ravenstein's recent creation of a class for them at St Pancras. Nevertheless, *Sporting Life* adjudged the arrangements to be 'as perfect as they could be for the first attempt at holding a festival of such dimensions'.

The entries for the events were strong enough, though there was a noticeable absence of gentlemen amateurs. Chambers was to let it be known that anyone competing at future NOA

Games would not be eligible for the AAC's nationwide championship. Some, however, defied these warnings, notably C.G. Pym, C.G. Emery, and E.G. Boor. Most of the successful competitors were from Ravenstein's German Gymnastics Society of London, the City Amateur Athletics Club, Southampton Athletics Club, Winchester, Hulley's Liverpool Athletics Club, King's College Running Club, Thames Running Club, and Norwich Athletic Club.

The programme was familiar to those that knew the Wenlock Games and the Shropshire Olympian Games: running races of 100 and 200 yards, half-mile, one-mile and two miles, 'steeplechase (which afforded much amusement, as an almost impossible water-leap was placed in the course)', hurdle-races, long leap (running and standing), high leap, pole leaping (vaulting), javelin, putting a 36lb shot, rope climbing, wrestling, boxing, and military exercises.

There were two truly outstanding athletic performances at the National Olympian Games. H.W. Brooke (no relation) of the German Gymnastic Society at St Pancras was second (out of 43) in the high leap, and second in the running and standing long leaps, besides winning the half-mile race (36 entries) and the half-mile steeplechase. Brooke, only 18 years old, had won the GGS Challenge Cup when only 15, and would become a familiar competitor at Wenlock, thrilling the crowds from 1869 until 1872 (plate 18). Also from the GGS and enjoying success at Crystal Palace were H. Landsberger, J.R. Hartley, A. Seeley, J.G. Elliott, E. Landsberger and J.C. Rathgel.

More remarkable even than Brooke's performance was that of the 18-year-old W.G. Grace in the 440 yards hurdles over 20 flights (plate 15). Fifteen men entered, and both Emery and Collins of the AAC were defeated by Grace. Remarkably, though, Grace was technically simultaneously competing in a cricket match for England against Surrey at the Oval, in which he scored one of his earliest huge innings – 224 not out – to help England to a total of 521 runs, beating Surrey by an innings and 296 runs. Besides running an extraordinary 431 runs in all, Grace's winning time at Sydenham was one minute 10 seconds over 440 yards. Grace (later, like Brookes, a doctor in general practice) recalled little of the day except 'Mr V.E. Walker the captain of the England team being kind enough to let me off the last day to compete in the National Olympian Association meeting at the Crystal Palace'.

There was some criticism. *Sporting Life* noted that the officials were 'sorely overtasked, and the affair at times seemed to be doomed by its own success. No doubt next year there will be improvements made, such as a telegraph-board with the numbers of starters and winners displayed, and perhaps the management will take the hint to allow none but actual competitors in the inner enclosure.' After Thursday's competitions and displays at the German Gymnasium at St Pancras, 'where all sorts of daring and healthy feats were gone through', *Sporting Life* concluded that the NOA had 'risen out of insignificance to…great importance'.

The event brought Brookes's cause to national attention – it was even parodied in cartoon. When Lord Robert Montagu failed to show up in the Handel orchestra of the Crystal Palace to present the prizes, Brookes got his break, was put in as chairman, and stood up to make 'an able address'. He took a swipe at the AAC – both its success in winning large numbers of subscriptions and at managing to put off probable NOA competitors with threats of disqualification. 'In Great Britain we look to public opinion for support, and if our institutions, therefore, like our native oaks, are slow in their growth, like our oaks, too, they take the deeper root (loud cheers)'.

He regretted that some were prejudiced against athletic meetings, particularly since the ban of any pastime drove it underground, leading men to beerhouses and vice. Brookes displayed his knowledge of the development of gymnastics, invoking the German innovators, J.C.F. GutsMuths (1759–1839) and Friedrich Ludwig Jahn (1778–1852). He mentioned that the *New York Herald* had a few years earlier noted the physical degeneracy of the North Americans 'for want of athletic exercises' and that military subscription in France in 1863 had revealed that 731 out of a thousand young men had been rejected as 'physically unfit to bear arms'.

This, he felt, justified his warning against complacency in Britain now that the majority of her population lived in towns and cities. The events of the Crimean War and the American Civil War had demonstrated the need for readiness at all times. At the 1864 Welsh Eisteddfod it had been remarked that the age of physical force 'and with it the olympic games' had passed, a comment which he characterised as a 'dangerous delusion'. Rising to a rhetorical climax, he foretold that if the British people gave up manly games for 'the delicate amusements of the drawing-room and the croquet lawn – then, I can tell you, what will assuredly and rapidly pass away – the freedom, the long-cherished freedom, and with it the power, the influence, the prosperity, and the happiness of this great empire (much cheering).'

Brookes foresaw obstacles for their Olympian Games, 'but obstacles, be it remembered, when rightly handled, are often great aids to success. Let us continue, then, to persevere, in the hope that the inhabitants of all the great towns in England may follow our example, and that the Government of the country may at last see that, in a nation like Great Britain – great, it is true, in its energies and resources, but numerically weak – the maintenance of the physical stamina of the people is an object not unworthy the attention, the patronage, nay even the support of the state'. Brookes resumed his seat 'amid several rounds of applause and waving of flags.'

Exposure on the national stage did Brookes and his cause no harm. *The Oxford Journal* pronounced him 'the father of the Olympian movement', acknowledged that 'through the exertions of this gentleman, the athletic societies of the country have now become connected in one grand body', and announced that the NOA's annual festivals would be held in London, Southampton, Norwich, Birmingham, Liverpool, and Bristol.' His words were quoted on the other side of the world, in Tasmania, one of whose periodicals, 'We' had urged its athletic societies to join up with the NOA.

The AAC and the NOA were now in open competition. The initial popularity of the AAC must have been galling to Brookes, but if well-being for all was truly his deepest aim, he had to concede that the AAC's national championships were open to all. In 1867 John Chambers himself would see his title in the seven-mile walk taken from him by half a yard by J.H. Farnworth who worked in a Liverpool bar. The runner up in the four miles for three years running in 1871–73 was London cart-driver Alfred Wheeler.

However, the same was not true of membership of the AAC. In the same year that Farnworth was striking a blow for the working man, the AAC tightened further its definition of the amateur, adding to its bar on those who had earned their livelihood in PE anyone who '…is a mechanic, artisan or labourer', a loathed display of outright snobbery, which became known as the 'mechanic's clause'. And this in the year that the second electoral reform act was passed, making workers the majority of voters in most boroughs in Britain. In 1868 the Club went further and rewrote the opening to read that an amateur was 'any gentleman who…' so excluding most of Brookes's athletes. The AAC, though, in hauling up the drawbridge, was retreating into a siege from which there could be no escape.

Brookes would have been undaunted, having already encountered this type of metropolitan exclusivity, faced it head-on, and overcome it. The Royal College of Surgeons of the late 1840s had proposed the foundation of a new and inferior College of Surgeons and General Practitioners, to set the London Surgeons apart from their provincial counterparts. In urban London, where medics were abundant, the surgeons could specialise in theatre work, but the provincial surgeons had, of necessity to engage in all branches of medicine, including the dispensing of medicines, and midwifery (which the Council regarded as beneath its dignity and for which it affected 'a great contempt').

Brookes had spoken out through Thomas Wakley's *The Lancet* on behalf of his fellow surgeons in the provinces against being shovelled into a lesser college, describing them as an 'insulted and indignant profession'. Something similar had been tried before with a National Association, and Brookes described the new proposal as 'Rhubarb Hall re-decorated and metamorphosed'. He had also spoken out in *The Lancet* against the College's refusal of admission to its governing committee to anyone who lived 'more than 5 miles from the General Post Office in St Martin's le Grand', London. 'That infatuated body, the Council of the College of Surgeons' was obliged to take note, and, after Brookes had likened its members to the pre-1832 electors of the former Rotten Boro', Old Sarum, reform was indeed instituted along the lines that Brookes also dared to suggest.

Brookes held no truck with the exclusion from athletics of working men on the grounds of class. The Wenlock competitors were not professional runners, as they worked for a living. The programme for the second NOA Games (in Birmingham) in 1867, included its own definition of the amateur, remarkably like that of the AAC in its original form, provoking perhaps the tightening up by the AAC of its definition, to try to exclude NOA competitors:

'The Competitions are strictly confined to Amateurs.

Persons who have competed for Public or Admission Money, or for a Prize with Professionals, or have ever made Gymnastics or Athletics a means of livelihood, are ineligible.'

A man like Wenlock's William Roberts, for example, a painter and publican, would remain eligible to compete in the National Olympian Games, while his hurdling rival from Gateshead, Jack White, who had regularly competed professionally would be excluded – a distinction made with all the precision of a surgeon's knife.

One result of Brookes's triumph at the 1866 National Olympian Games was that at the Wenlock Olympian Games the following June, the attendance in 'scorching heat' was 'decidedly larger than has ever before assembled'. Francis Richards, the Judge for the events (a boot and shoe-maker from Barrow Street), presented Brookes with the Wenlock Olympian Society's Nike first-class silver medal, and looked forward to the forthcoming NOA Games at Birmingham. Musing on the growth of their little, contentious event into a national and, if Tasmania was to be believed, an international association, Brookes reached for two prophetic metaphors. 'Drop a stone into the middle of a lake,' he said, 'and the little ring first formed will go on gradually increasing in circumference till, at length, the distant shores are reached.'

Ever the botanist, he continued, 'Sow a single seed of a rare plant in the most secluded spot and if the soil and other conditions are favourable to its germination, it will grow up and bear other seed, and, in time, produce plants sufficient to cover the length and breadth of the land.' Just before the tilting at these games, Wenlock's photographer, James Laing, stepped forward to capture a panoramic view of the event (plate 6).

A fortnight after the 1867 Wenlock Games, Brookes was in Birmingham for the second of his National Olympian Games, held with the help of Birmingham Athletic Club at its Portland Road ground. As at the Crystal Palace, the Games were spread over three days, Tuesday to Thursday 25–27 June. Tuesday was filled with tilting and athletic competitions for boys and men, and Wednesday with the martial events, including fencing, boxing, broadsword, sabre and bayonet competitions. On Tuesday evening a team competition in gymnastics was held, and on Wednesday evening, an assault of arms. The swimming was on the morning of the last day at the Kent Street Baths. After that, all returned to the festival grounds, for a grand cricket match, the distribution of prizes (silver and bronze medals, and some art works) and in the evening, the event would be rounded off with an Olympian Ball at the Town Hall.

After the crowning of Thomas E. Jukes of the Coates, Much Wenlock, as victor in the tilting on day one, Brookes addressed the audience. He once again spoke of how such events were frowned upon by some for a lack of refinement, 'which they fondly hail as the distinguishing mark of an advancing civilization, but which, if carried to excess, I look upon as the sure forerunner of a national decay. These sickly sentimentalists shrink with a painful sensitiveness from everything which, however sound at the core, is not highly polished on the surface; they think, therefore, that there are but two classes in this country that can be trusted to meet together in large numbers for amusement without misbehaving themselves – viz. the upper and middle classes. Experience has led me to a very different conclusion.'

He also stepped up his campaign for the provision of PE in national elementary (primary) schools in Britain. Indeed, one of the stated aims of the NOA games at Birmingham was to support 'all efforts made to introduce bodily exercises into schools as a regular branch of education', one not listed at the time of the formation of the NOA at Liverpool Gym in 1865. Brookes spoke of the sadness of doctors facing 'much suffering, and some fatal cases of brain disease, the result of excessive mental application'. He complained of schools' grant funding being awarded according to examination results during visits by inspectors. Brookes claimed that this led to 'mental forcing on the part of the schoolmasters, in order to secure a liberal grant, which is very injurious to children'.

Again prophetically, Brookes looked to Prussia, the rising region of Europe, 'where bodily is combined with mental education'. Prussia had been completely overrun by Napoleon in 1806, when she enforced only dress and drill on her soldiers. After defeat, a complete system of PE in schools in Prussia had been established, followed by three years' service in the line. And the result? Prussia had 'only the other day' (June–August 1866) overrun the Austrians in the Austro-Prussian or Seven Weeks War, which had brought Prussia to dominance in a future Germany which excluded the Austrian states.

Looking at Britain in 1867, Brookes concurred with John Ruskin's view (a friend of James Milnes Gaskell's son, Charles) that 'we manufacture everything [in our new cities] except men'. He believed the Birmingham gymnasium would benefit all classes except perhaps the medical profession, yet they would find doctors among its most liberal supporters, 'because their missions are missions of benevolence; their lives, lives of self-denial and devotion to the interests of humanity'.

In the boys' events at Birmingham, pupils of King Edward's School (where Joseph Hubbard taught) predominated, including R.H. Smyth who won the 100 and 200 yards races on day one and the half-mile race on day two, all for under-14s, and A.T. Barney, C.A. Heath, F. Lewis, J.G. Chamberlain and C.E. Williams. In the men's athletic events, competitors came from London, Gloucester, Bristol, Leeds, and Norwich, as well as Wenlock. J. Duckworth of Haslingden AC won the high jump, clearing 5ft 5in, with P.A. Brindley of Leeds a close second and J. Plowman of London third with a 5ft 3in jump. Brindley was more successful in the long jump, leaping 17ft 9in, beating Duckworth into second at 17ft 2in, with Plowman third again at exactly 17ft. Also on the opening day, Ravenstein's GGS from London had much success, the General Prize and Wenlock medal being awarded to H. Lansberger.

The middle day was one of cloudless skies with a slight breeze. Of the athletes' performances, 'the running of Mr [J.E.] Duckworth was much admired, and he carried everything before him in the races in which he took part'. These included wins in the 100 yards flat race in 10 and a half seconds, followed by the 200 yards in a notable 20 and a half seconds, the hurdles and the standing high jump (4ft 8in). M.E. Jobling of Northumberland Cricket Club, who also rowed, belonged to the LAC and the Civil Service, was noted for 'showing great promise' in his running. He won the half-mile (two minutes 15 seconds), the mile (four minutes 47 and a half seconds) and the half-mile steeplechase, after a close race 'right at the end' of which Jobling overtook J. Edmonds to win by three yards. Despite the rumblings of the AAC, Jobling had formerly competed at Liverpool's Olympic Games, and in 1866 competed in the AAC's first national championships.

On the final day, at the Kent Street Baths, the three swimming races, 116 yards, 290 yards and 870 yards were dominated by the GGS, their William Tyler winning the first race, and Walter Long both of the others. In the afternoon, back at the BAC's Portland Ground, King Edward's School played the Birmingham Gymnastic Club in a friendly cricket match and beat the adults by 5 wickets and 3 runs. The Birmingham Daily Post concluded that the Games had been 'very successful' and that they had 'given a new impetus to the cultivation of manly and athletic accomplishments in the town'. BAC membership had risen to 238 and it held its first highly successful meeting in 1868. The editorial said that 'The golden age of athletes is about to be restored, and men are learning that they have bodies which need training and culture as well as the mind.' It called for gymnasia not just for men, but for women as well.

The NOA committee resolved that its next Games would be held at Manchester in 1868. However, this did not come off, probably because the venue for the event, Pomona Gardens, changed hands that year, being bought by James Reilly. An event that should have been held in the teeming city of 'cottonopolis' fell instead to the market town of Wellington, which had hosted the Shropshire Olympian Games in 1861. The two-day event was hosted by St John Charlton on his land at Spring-hill, close enough to the town for a procession to be made from the town centre. Despite the modesty of the location by comparison with Manchester, many local grandees including the Earl of Powis, Lord Berwick, Earl Granville, and Viscount Newport supported the committee. (Newport was away shooting over the event itself, but forwarded a basket of grouse for the dinner.) Many of the national clubs were represented on the organising committee, including George Henderson of Liverpool Athletic Club, John T. Murray of GGS in London, R. Margetson of Westmoreland Wrestling Society, and W.E.S. Thompson of the Thames Rowing Club.

The Wellington National Olympian Games were held on Tuesday and Wednesday 25 and 26 August 1868, the first day being for amateurs only and the second for locals who would run for money prizes – counter to the founding terms of the NOA but presumably at Brookes's insistence. Included in the programme were track and field competitions for all-comers, tilting at the ring, a General Competition (with 'rising at the horizontal bar' in place of the rope climb), boxing for light, middle and heavy weights, single stick, fencing, broad sword and bowling. On Wednesday morning, Ravenstein delivered a talk on 'Physical Education' which was 'not so well attended as it deserved to be' attributed by the reporter to its being a morning lecture which 'do not, as a rule, "take"'.

The afternoon brought the local competitions, the more unusual including under-14 boys trundling a hoop 200 yards, a race for Rifle Volunteers in uniform and a two-mile walking match. The programme specified that with regard to dress, 'Competitors must wear Clothing from the Shoulders to below the Knees'. There would be a dinner for members of the Association and friends at 7pm on the Tuesday evening at the Town Hall, chaired by the Tory MP for North Shropshire, John Ormsby-Gore, the future Lord Harlech. Thursday's competitions consisted solely of a brass band contest, which nevertheless attracted a crowd of 2,000 who enjoyed (or were subjected to) fully four hours of music. The winners were Wednesbury Band.

In the event, Brookes was unable to attend the Wellington NOA Games 'through illness', but his old friend T.W. Jones as Secretary (now a member of BAC), was much in evidence, and at the dinner, he thanked Ravenstein and Clement Davies (Vice-President of BAC) for their help. The first day had drawn an estimated 3,000–4,000 spectators, and the second day, about 2,000, the 'upper 10 percent' being notably absent. Also on the second day, Joseph Bowen of Wellington broke a leg after falling at a hurdle and had to be taken to hospital by train.

The Wellington NOA Games were hailed as a success, but in reality, they were a disappointment. On the amateur day, competitors came from Manchester Athenaeum Gymnastic Club, Birmingham Athletic Club, the GGS from London, from Gloucester, Shrewsbury and Bristol only, Liverpool being notable by its absence. Ravenstein, in his closing remarks, hoped that when the games were next held 'there would be more competitors'. The

Association was losing ground to the AAC, whose threatened exclusions were keeping away the best athletes, making competition less appealing in general, although Brookes would not yet admit defeat.

Between the 1867 Birmingham Games and the Autumn games of the Wenlock Society, Brookes had fallen ill, quite seriously so, and his absence from Wellington might have been a recurrence, for it was reported that he had decided to hand over the management and Presidency of the Wenlock Games. The *Shrewsbury Chronicle*, though, was shrewd to add 'nominally at any rate'. Brookes was back in the chair for the Society's next meeting in November 1867 and re-emerged in Spring 1868, keen to push forward his agenda of PE for primary school children.

After a 'heated' meeting of WOS members on 31 March, Brookes drew up a petition to be sent up to Parliament through J.M. Gaskell their MP. He hoped that a clause demanding PE in elementary schools might be grafted on to either of the education bills then before Parliament. Some members of the Society may have felt that they were straying into propagandist waters, away from the founding purpose of giving local men beneficial recreation. Brookes was as forceful as ever, saying that he had not found that farmers paid too little attention to education, but that they took too little notice of the physical demands on their future employees. He observed bluntly, 'It is too late to straighten the tree when it is grown up'. Brookes, however, was to find Parliament more difficult to sway to his will than the WOS committee, and the petition was unsuccessful.

After the disappointments at national level, Brookes turned his gaze from the larger-scale games, back to Wenlock. There were three notable innovations at the June 1868 Wenlock Olympian Games. First, the tilting competition was spiced up by making the tilters jump two hurdles with the 10ft lance under their arm, before piercing with the lance the tiny ring. The new contest was 'watched with immense interest', the skill of the riders eliciting 'the repeated acclamations of thousands of spectators'. After 40 minutes, William Ainsworth of Spoonhill, despite having taken his first ring only to have it slip off the lance and count for nothing, was the first to succeed three times. He was crowned by Miss Christian Warren of the Towers, Market Drayton, as a choir sang the Prize Ode composed by Willie Brookes.

The second innovation of 1868 was the invitation of a guest of honour as President, that year Sir Henry Harnage. He had been President before in 1861, but that had been an exception. The President since 1850 had been Brookes or a committee member. From 1868, dignitaries — usually local landowners or the MP — were invited. Harnage, of Belswardyne Hall, whose father had been an old friend of the Brookes, was met at the edge of the town on the Harley road by a mounted deputation from the Corn Market. The horsemen accompanied Harnage back past the Gaskell Arms, up the High Street and Spital Street en route to the Windmill Field. This provided the inspiration for forming up the procession at the Gaskell instead of the Corn Market, as they had since 1854. From 1870, the format of the Whit Tuesday event (one day only after 1868) became set. The procession started from the Gaskell Arms at around 11am, and the Games ran from about midday until 6.30pm, sometimes with a luncheon in the middle of the day, sometimes with dinner in the evening.

The final and most significant innovation of 1868 was the addition to the Games themselves of the 'General Competition', or the Pentathlon – a feature of the ancient games comprising running, jumping, discus, javelin and wrestling. Wenlock's five disciplines were climbing a 55 foot rope, the running high leap, running long leap, putting the (36lb) shot, and the half-mile foot race. Three competitors fought for the prize in 1868, Messrs Warren, Cross and Snead. Snead won the shot put and the foot race, but Warren won the climb and two leaping contests, so claiming the crown and the first Nike medal.

The 1868 Wenlock Olympian Games stretched into a second day, when a local General Competition was staged, incorporating foot racing, hurdling, standing long leap, javelin and throwing the hammer. It was won by William Lawley. Lawley was the younger brother, by four years, of Henry, victor in the under-14s' foot race at the first Games, of the jingling in 1855, and the archery in 1859. Like Henry, William had been brought up at the Post Office on Wilmore Street neighbouring the Brookes. William was to occupy a unique position in the professional/amateur debate. In mid-July 1862, a month before the Games that year, the *Wellington News* reported that a 140 yards footrace had been run the previous Monday 'for six sovereigns', between William Tonkinson a shoemaker from Bridgnorth and known as 'The Star', and William Lawley.

Each was accompanied by numerous supporters and they met on flat ground on the Bridgnorth road, opposite Wenlock racecourse. Lawley took the lead from two to three yards out, and kept it till within 40 yards of winning line, when the Bridgnorth man drew level. After a severe struggle, Tonkinson came in the winner by a yard and a half, to the great joy of his Bridgnorth friends. Everything passed off with good humour on both sides, both parties retiring to Mrs. Yates's, the George Inn, for a merry evening. 'It was one of the best contested foot-races ever witnessed in the neighbourhood of Wenlock'.

Technically, under the emerging distinctions, this made Lawley a professional runner, yet he was to win the amateurs' General Competition at the Wenlock Olympian Games six years later, and come second in the hammer in 1870 (left and right hand throws totalling 56 feet), and third in 1871 and 1872. He did not get away with it, though in the NOA Games at Wellington in 1868 when, after winning the final of the 100-yard race he 'was disqualified'. Nevertheless, Lawley was a judge at the Games in 1872, which would no doubt have added to the metropolitan view of Wenlock as the wild-west of athletic sports.

Henry Lawley became a railway station manager at Longwood, Yorkshire, so after the death of her husband, Jane Lawley & Son took on the running of the printing business, which usually produced the programme for the Wenlock Olympian Games. In 1871, this included the rule 'Professional Athletes are excluded from all amateur contests'. Nevertheless, Lawley was, like Roberts, one of the best servants of the Wenlock Olympian Society, first competing, then as the supplier of the programmes and posters, also as an official, singing glees at the dinners, and finally as the Society's Secretary (for which he won high praise) from 1879 until after Brookes's death.

At the 1868 Games, on the second day, just after William Lawley won the local Pentathlon, Henry Harnage gave the toast to the Games at the 4pm dinner at the Gaskell Arms. Harnage praised Brookes's 'indomitable energy' for resulting in their most successful meeting yet. He noted pointedly that there was 'nothing with which the clergy could have found fault'. Brookes responded that 'I have done no more than my duty as a member of a benevolent profession…from motives of philanthropy, to prevent, as far as possible, those diseases and infirmities to which the human frame is liable, and many of which are under our control.' He said that next in importance to food and clothing, clean air and water, cleanliness and temperance, 'I rank bodily training for the young, and out-door recreation and athletic exercises for the adult'.

Two months later, Brookes was ill for the Wellington NOA Games but he must have spent some valuable time with Willie before he went back up to Christ Church, Oxford at the end of August 1868. Willie was now 23, and a post-graduate in medicine, having attained first-class honours in his BA the previous year (plate 14). He was tutoring undergraduates and working closely with one of the great Victorian pillars of the university, Henry Wentworth Acland (1815–1900) the university's Regius professor of medicine, physician to the Radcliffe Infirmary, reviver of Oxford's medical school and founder of the Oxford University Museum (1861). This was the man whose 'entire confidence' Willie had won, for being 'Cultivated, gentle, industrious, punctual'.

By late November 1868, Brookes and Jane were looking forward to Willie's return for the Christmas vacation – he was due to 'go down' on Wednesday 16 December. Then, on Monday 7 December, Willie went missing. The porter said he had seen him leave through Tom Gate as the cathedral clock struck half-past seven but he had not seen him return. Willie's friends were asked – nothing. Willie's parents were alerted, and Brookes arrived at Oxford on Tuesday. By then the City and County Police were actively searching: 'Height, 5ft 7in; age, 23; slight build, fair complexion, slight auburn moustache, wore a black pot hat, overcoat of Oxford mixture'. He was 'A gentleman of very punctual habits, and, as a rule, had but little to say to anyone.' All information to the University Police Station, Broad Street.

Then, on Saturday 12, the *Pall Mall Gazette* learnt 'by telegram…that the body of Mr Brookes of Christ Church…was found by [James] Beesley, a fisherman this morning, in [six feet of water in the middle of] Louse Lock, near Hythe Bridge', opposite the back of Worcester College 'where the river leads into the canal.' Beesley had hauled Willie's lifeless body into a punt, before it was removed to a stable at 'the Running Horses' pub. There, William was identified by Christ Church's Dean Henry Liddell who had the body taken to No.4 Tom Quad, Christ Church. The Coroner F.P. Morrell's inquest was held in No.3, Tom Quad, on Saturday afternoon. Willie was described as having been in his usual health 'if anything…rather more cheerful than usual' when he left college on Sunday evening. No more was heard of him until his hat (bought that term) was spotted by Beesley on Monday who, not learning of the disappearance until Friday, only then dragged the lock.

Liddell was present to hear a verdict returned, after 20 minutes' deliberation, of 'Found drowned', with its implication that suicide could not be ruled out. Several of the jury afterwards inspected the spot where Willie died 'and the impression that the deceased had met with his death by accident…was much strengthened'. He was believed to have been crossing the lock gate, when his hat blew off. Distracted, and being 'rather near-sighted' he probably walked into a dangerous cross post and fell in. Willie's staircase scout reported being told by his father that 'he could swim but little'.

On Monday evening, William's body was 'removed from the lecture room' at Christ Church and taken by train to Shropshire for burial, each heave of the departing engine like an irrepressible sob. In Oxford, 'The cathedral bell tolled'. Much Wenlock, in early December, had been celebrating the restoration of the church bells by the former Mayor R.T. Davies. Now they tolled for one of her most promising sons, each muffled strike rocking Brookes's house to its foundations. 'A sense of sadness prevails in Much Wenlock and district', reported the *Shrewsbury Chronicle*, 'in consequence of the irreparable loss by the family of W.P. Brookes Esq.'

Acland and Liddell (father, himself, of Lewis Carroll's 'Alice') clearly thought highly of William. Liddell wrote 'I can never sufficiently testify to my esteem for him. From the day on which he first came to the day of his unfortunate end, he never ceased to improve himself; and I believe a useful and distinguished career was in store for him'. Liddell continued 'Dr Acland…is inconsolable for the loss of a Pupil from whom he expected very much'. Acland's letter confirms that this was no exaggeration.

'I have been for many years waiting for such a person to work with me at the Hospital… I had been fitting up my room in preparation for [a project that they were to do together] & was to have all ready for the end of this vacation & he is thus suddenly taken. I have no prospect of such another companion. All this I say that you may at least know that I also in my poor & remote degree suffer with you, I am in some sort smitten also.'

Brookes and Jane must have been crushed by the loss of their second son (and Jane was to lose her father, and Brookes his mother in the coming months). Letters came, of course, testifying to Willie's great promise and exceptional qualities. Perhaps the most moving, touching on the powerlessness of even the surgeon in such a case, was one from the doctor at Broseley, Frederick Hartshorne who had buried his own son a week before. 'Both your son and mine, in youth passed from this life, without a call for their father's help…and we are dumb and open not our mouths because the Lord has done it.'

Two months later, the Olympian Society's Annual Meeting was held at the Talbot Inn, Much Wenlock. The Treasurer, mercer Henry Price asked the meeting what they thought it right to do about the Society, 'decidedly one of the most popular in the kingdom', given 'the great affliction which has befallen Mr Brookes's family, and which renders him incapable of exerting himself as he has hitherto done.' They decided to press on. Edwin Yardley admitted that he had proposed to retire as Secretary, 'but knowing that not one iota could be expected from one who heretofore had done so much, he would be putting heart and soul into the institution this year, and trusting that all others would do likewise.' At the end of the sombre meeting, the health of Brookes and his family was 'drunk almost silently, yet with intense sympathy and respect'.

Brookes was not a man who, by the nature of his profession and because of the need to be an example in the community, could sit for long mute and motionless in mourning. For the Society's meetings of 13 April and 15 May 1869, he was back in the chair, perhaps thankful for the minutiae of organising the games. The precise wording of a declaration to be signed by competitors to state that they had not competed for money since 1 January was settled, Miss Wadlow was to be asked to be Queen of Beauty, with four maids of honour of her choosing.

The 20th Wenlock Olympian Games were held on Whit Tuesday 18 May 1869, for amateur competitors, with a one-mile hurdle race over 15 flights, and a one-mile steeple chase included for professionals. It seemed appropriate that rain should fall all day. H.W. Brooke of the GGS wowed the crowds and took the Pentathlon crown, their own Thomas P. Everall beat William Lawley in the hammer, (Everall's left and right-hand throws combined added up to 61ft 2in). Brookes, of course, was absent, although the *Wellington Journal* was previous in asserting that he had 'ceased to take any part'.

Despite being such a difficult time for Brookes, significant improvements were made to Windmill Field in 1869. A new turf track was laid around the perimeter, the centre of the Field was levelled at some expense, and in October 1869, various members of the Society, including Thomas Jukes senior and junior, Edward Stroud the schoolmaster, Thomas Evans, Thomas Edwards, Henry Price, George Wheeler and Brookes 'spent a very pleasant day' planting trees and shrubs. These included two *Cedrus deodara* and two *Cedrus deodara* 'Robusta', one at each corner of the bowling green, the gaps between them filled appropriately with 200 laurels, the gift of Thomas Jukes. This would protect the green for most of the year, but on Games day, the sward was sacrificed to the feet of dancing couples, so they were also creating a romantic bower.

The same day in 1869, the group planted 42 lime trees in a single row to the north and east sides of the ground. These were donated by Brookes, and are deeply symbolic of many aspects of his life, and might even represent a memorial to his son, though this is nowhere mentioned. The lime was reputed to have medicinal properties; for a botanist like Brookes the lime also recalled the father of botany, Carl von Linne, or Linnaeus, whose name reputedly derived from a lime near the home of his ancestors; the Society's Reading Room was evoked by the fact that its inner bark was used to make paper, so called 'liber', giving us the word 'library'; its relatively light timber was used to make ploughs and yokes symbolic of Wenlock's agricultural economy; in Greek mythology Philemon and Baucis were turned into an oak and a lime respectively in reward for giving shelter to Zeus and Hermes – the former of course connected with Olympia and the latter's winged heels particularly appropriate for a running field. The two trees grow well together, and Brookes was later to plant oaks for the royal family and for Coubertin on the Field. The heart-shaped leaves of limes were always connected with love – filial certainly, but also the erotic love of the young women spectators admiring the competitors at the Games. For a field that would be used year round for recreation, an avenue of limes would make a romantic walk. The row became known as Linden Walk. From 1872, after the relaying of the running track and other improvements, Windmill Field was renamed Linden Field.

A 'large and convenient grandstand' was also built in the north-west corner of the Field in 1869, with room next to it for the orchestra, to entertain the grandstand's occupants. On Games day, grandstand admission was by payment. The judges, the secretary and the newspaper reporters occupied the front shilling seats, and the elite the rest. Members of the Society's committee served as its Stewards. The grandstand was initially open to the sky, but after 1873's

Games day began in 'duck's weather', the *Wellington Journal's* reporter suggested that it might be covered in. It was in front of this focal point that the champion tilter threw down his gauntlet and was afterwards crowned by the Queen of Beauty. The tilting stand, from which the tiny rings were hung, doubled up as the finishing post for the races, right in front of the grandstand.

The field events took place in an enclosure beyond the track, facing the grandstand. This appears by 1867 to have been delineated by white posts and chains. A rope climbing event was introduced at Windmill Field from 1868, and became part of the Pentathlon competition. The rope was suspended 'from a gaily painted pole some 55 feet in height', but Isaac Nevett got to the top at the first attempt. The pole doubled up as a flagstaff, though, so the effort was not entirely wasted. In 1869, W. Horton of Stanway Manor donated a new pole 83ft long and 5ft 7in in circumference at the base. With the help of 25 volunteers, it was erected on 19 September 1869, in time for the autumn amateur games. It stuck 73ft out of the ground and measured 81ft to the top of the flagstaff. To judge competitive climbs, it was painted with white rings every 10ft. On the crossbar at the top was painted 'Excelsior', an allusion to Longfellow's highly popular poem, which set to music was a favourite parlour song. Given the poem's metaphor for urging oneself to greater effort (foreshadowing the Olympics' 'faster, higher, stronger'), Excelsior was a theme song for muscular Christians.

Another feature of the Linden Field on Games days were the entertainment stalls. In 1859 there had been 16 of them, and in 1862 they had included 'a photograph establishment… promising a perfect likeness for a nominal sum, a few nut and gingerbread stalls, and our old popularity "Aunt sally"'. Four years later they had expanded further to include 'roundabouts, shooting galleries, orange stalls' and others. By 1867, there was a 'long line of shooting galleries, boxing booths, shows, and publicans' tents' – the latter well patronised in the 'scorching heat'.

By 1868 there was a sense that the stalls were detracting from the sporting events, and lowering the tone. At the committee meeting in March, it was resolved to limit the number of booths to just four, that they be let by public auction and, to keep the benefit local, 'that no person be allowed to bid unless he be a member of the society and a parishioner of Wenlock'. The reduction was seen by the reporters as an improvement, and these, plus 'about half a dozen cake stalls' were felt to be adequate for the 3,000 people present in 1869. 'Aunt Sally' and other 'attendant nuisances' returned in 1870, but at a distance from the enclosure, 'whereby the probabilities of personal injury from an unskilful thrower are materially lessened'. Jasper More alluded in his speech of 1872 to 'the booths on the course, which the clergy said placed temptation in the way of the people, and made them take only a lukewarm interest in the games. He would tell the strangers present that it was the object of the people of Wenlock to show that they could provide a people's holiday without privileges being abused.' In 1869 it was also decided that spectators should be charged. '1d entrance to the ground on the day of the games, and horses 6d, horse and 2-wheeled carriage 1s; 4-wheeled carriages 1s 6d; no waggons to be allowed on the ground.' Horses taking part in the procession came free.

The Games of 1869–72 saw consolidation. Their acceptance as an appropriate amusement for the labourers is confirmed by the levity with which the *Wellington Journal and Shrewsbury News* joked of the 1871 Games that 'extreme good order prevailed throughout the day...There was not a solitary fight to vary the entertainment throughout'. However, one man fell from the climbing rope, 'sunstruck', and a riderless horse 'bolted [from the field] down the principal street'. In 1871 the local mercer, James Bodenham, a committee member, showing an early flair for product placement, donated a yellow silk velvet fringed sash to be worn by the victor in the tilting, bearing the motto 'Honour my guide'. Brookes's investment in the Field was rewarded with the attendance of several athletes from the GGS in London in 1869-71. Most notable were Henry Brooke who had been outstanding at the Crystal Palace Games, and Robert Clement. Brooke was victorious in the Pentathlon again in 1870 and Clement in '71.

The Liverpool athletes stopped coming to Wenlock after their gymnasium fell out of fashion and the annual athletic festivals ceased. This occurred after John Hulley married, against her parents' wishes, Georgiana Bolton, the granddaughter of a former Mayor of Liverpool. Hulley was jilted at the altar of the Ancient Unitarian Chapel in Toxteth Park, on Thursday 15 July 1869, when his bride was locked in her bedroom. Being no longer a minor, Georgiana took matters into her own hands and, allegedly 'cut off without a shilling', went to the chapel the following morning by cab with neither wedding gown nor parents. The two were married in the company of some supportive friends.

Hulley's apprentice, Alexander Alexander recalled that 'The gymnasium received the full force of the shock'. It was sold off by 1871, and by 1882 belonged to the Young Men's Christian Association. Alexander departed on somewhat picaresque wanderings around the UK until returning in 1882 to run the gym until 1896. Hulley spent several winters on the continent for his health, but died on 6 January 1875 at his home at 91 Grove Street, Liverpool aged only 42. His efforts in the cause of physical recreation were acknowledged in 2009 by the renovation of his grave in Smithdown Road Cemetery, Liverpool, to which both the International Olympic Committee and the British Olympic Association contributed.

Brookes's campaign for PE in schools meanwhile, continued unabated. In March 1870, Brookes drew up another petition to be forwarded to G.C.W. Forester of Willey, the Conservative MP for Wenlock, for presentation to the House of Commons, asking for the introduction of PE into the National Elementary Schools. Ralph Benson was also asked to write a letter to the same effect to the Liberal MP William E. Forster who was revising the Code of Regulations in his current Education Bill to try to form a system of national education in Britain.

Brookes's petition said that 'no system of education...can be considered complete which does not combine with the cultivation of the intellectual powers, some care for the development and conservation of the physical health and strength of the young. That such discipline is especially important to the children of the poorer classes who are destined to earn their living by laborious occupation'. It was signed by almost 80 members of the Society. However, if Brookes hoped for a sympathetic result from a Liberal government, he was disappointed. Education for all children at elementary level became compulsory in 1870, but PE did not, although Article 24 stated that 'Attendance at drill, under a competent instructor, for not more than two hours a week, and 20 weeks in the year, may be counted as school attendance.'

Edward Stroud, the schoolmaster at Much Wenlock, forged ahead regardless. At the WOS May 1871 meeting it was proposed by Brookes, seconded by Edwin Yardley and unanimously carried, that a beautifully illustrated copy of Longfellow's *Hyperion* be presented to Stroud 'as a slight token of their appreciation of his valuable services in promoting the health and strength of the Wenlock National School Children by Drill and Gymnastic exercises.' This school was one of the first in the country to provide PE for its pupils. At the same meeting, Thomas Jukes, who for years had organised the procession, was presented with a 'coloured photograph' of the crowning of the tilting victor in 1867 'as a mark of their respect and gratitude for his untiring exertions'.

Events on the European continent now provided an unexpected and sobering vindication of Brookes's calls for PE in schools. In July 1870, a coalition of German states led by Prussia invaded France, beginning the Franco-Prussian War (19 July 1870–10 May 1871). The rapidity with which France was beaten in the war caused a realignment of the continental powers and the victory ultimately enabled the unification of Germany. The *Illustrated Times* noted, during the siege of Paris, 'the wonderful marching power and general capacity for enduring fatigue exhibited by the German infantry soldiers, and especially by those of Prussia…This need excite no surprise, however, when we remember that athletic exercises form a regular portion of school and college training in Prussia…' Too late for Forster's Education Bill, it begged 'Let a *g* be added to the three *rs* – gymnastics to 'reading, 'riting, and 'rithmetic' – in our school curriculum'. More helpfully, the School Board Chronicle recalled that Brookes's speech at the Crystal Palace NOA Games back in 1866 had highlighted the difference between France and Prussia in terms of PE.

The failure of the Society's petition was mentioned by Edwin Yardley, the Society's Secretary, when he delivered Brookes's opening address to the 1871 Games. 'Drill alone,' he said 'may be a good preparation for military manoeuvres, but will be found insufficient for that complete muscular development which conduces to health and strength…The superiority in manliness which early discipline and gymnastic training give to a nation has been so clearly manifested in the late war between France and Germany, that the neglect of this branch of education by any Government will henceforth be regarded as highly culpable.' Col Corbett, the invited dignitary acknowledged that 'the victory of the Germans has been attributed to the athletic training of their soldiers'.

Brookes was absent from the 1871 Wenlock Games, mourning once again the loss of a child. This time, the youngest of his daughters, Isabella had been taken from them, from her husband Charles Great Rex and from three little children, Arthur, Gertrude and Talbot, all under seven. Further sadness was to follow. Mary, the Brookes's eldest child would die in 1874. By 1875, William and Jane Brookes had lost all but one of their five children, Adeline only being left to them. Isabella's children gave some hope for the future, but Talbot was to pre-decease his grandfather, dying at the same age as Willie, 23.

Chapter 4

'I beg to assure you of my cordial concurrence in the principle that physical training, by manly sports and otherwise, is a matter at all times deserving of careful attention, and that no education can be considered complete from which it is excluded.'
W.E. Gladstone (as Chancellor of the Exchequer) to W.P. Brookes, 3 November 1862

When education at primary level (to the age of 12) became compulsory nationwide in 1870, Brookes acquired a real framework upon which to hang his campaign for physical education. Furthermore, the issue of PE in schools was gaining influential support. In 1871 William Hepworth Dixon, a writer and historian, who sat on the first School Board for London from 1870, stated that he would like to see PE adopted in schools, not merely military drill, a motion passed unanimously by the London Board. Elizabeth Garrett Anderson, the first woman ever to gain a medical qualification in Britain, began to raise the issue for women, making the point that anyone looking for the impoverished in regard to PE 'would have to begin with the young ladies'.

Herbert Spencer, the philosopher and sociologist, had written four essays on education in 1859, of which one was entirely devoted to physical education. Other men of influence such as John Ruskin and Matthew Arnold (son of the Rugby head, and a highly influential poet, thinker and critic) though neither of them fans of the new 'athleto-mania', pleaded for its introduction for the well-being of children. Arnold said that for little boys, carefully taught gymnastics would be better than games. Edwin Chadwick, the great public health reformer, pointed out to the Newcastle Commission of 1859 that a child could not stand more than three hours' teaching a day without some exercise or manual work. Through the Royal Society of Arts and the National Association for the Promotion of Social Science he raised the cause, and led deputations to government.

Sensing that opinion was turning his way, yet seeing that governments were timorous, Brookes decided that some statistical evidence might give individual Members of Parliament the confidence to back PE in schools over drill. With the help of Edward Stroud, Brookes set up an experiment at Much Wenlock National School. On 21 August 1871, he picked a dozen of the schoolboys, and took physical measurements of their chest, upper arm and forearm. Over the following six months, six of the boys practised drill and gymnastic training, including Indian Club, vaulting the horse, and work on the horizontal and parallel bars, while the other six did only the drill currently suggested for schoolchildren.

Drill (exercises performed in unison involving marching and coordinated actions, often to music) had been a part of Britain's military training since at least its introduction in the 16th century by the Dutch Prince Maurice of Orange, in an attempt to bring efficiency to the army when fighting in formation. For its combination of physical and disciplinary benefits, drill had been introduced into public schools after a concerted effort by Lord Elcho in 1860. However, because drill and gymnastics were taught in public schools by sergeant instructors (of lower social status) they were always seen as inferior to team games which also taught team spirit and group loyalty. In the army, in addition to drill, gymnastic courses had been introduced into military and naval training establishments in 1822 by P.H. Clias, a Swiss Army officer and disciple of the great German teacher J.C.F. GutsMuths. Donald Walker, a pupil of GutsMuths and Clias, in his book *Manly Exercises* (1834) had tried to adapt the German approach for the British public. His book ran into 10 editions by 1860 and gymnastics started to gain ground, as seen from the opening of the Liverpool and St Pancras gymnasia in 1865, and the Birmingham AC gymnasium that opened in 1866 at Bingley Hall.

The Education Department (in whose formation in 1839 R.A. Slaney had played a significant role) had always shown an interest in PE. Exercise was considered useful for reasons other than health, such as extending the moral influence of the teacher. Her Majesty's Inspectors stressed the importance of providing a closed exercise ground for the children. By 1860, however, aspirations were not matched by results. Of the 35 British Society schools inspected in the Metropolitan District that year only three had playgrounds. In 1862, Lord Elcho lobbied for the introduction of drill into other schools, but it was turned down on the grounds of expense. Mathias Roth also campaigned for the Swedish system of gymnastics to be introduced into schools, but despite growing concern for children's physical welfare, little was done during the 1850s and 1860s.

Beyond schools, until 1870, the development of educational gymnastics was being undertaken primarily by the influential Archibald MacLaren at Oxford, with the support of the military (the gym at Aldershot was to be based on MacLaren's) along the lines of GutsMuths and Clias. Elsewhere, followers of P.H. Ling from Stockholm were introducing the 'Swedish system', which required little equipment. MacLaren (*c*.1819–1884) was a Scotsman who had studied in Paris and settled in Oxford, opening a fencing school and gym in Oriel Lane, and in 1858 building his own gym at the corner of Alfred Street and Bear Lane (patronised by William Morris and his undergraduate friends). MacLaren and his wife also founded the boys' school Summer Fields, Oxford, in 1864.

It is intriguing to wonder whether, perhaps accompanying Willie to Oxford, Brookes might have visited MacLaren's gymnasium. The two men were of one mind on exercise for children, seeing it as a necessity to produce men fit for purpose in life. In his *A System of Physical Education, Theoretical and Practical* MacLaren wrote, 'Yes, it is health rather than strength that is the great requirement of modern men at modern occupations…it is simply that condition of the body, and the amount of vital capacity, which shall enable each man in his place to pursue his calling'. Brookes was evidently influenced by MacLaren, not least as MacLaren was a pioneer of anthropometry – the name given to using bodily measurements to show the effects of particular exercises.

In February 1872, Brookes returned to Much Wenlock School with his tape measure. There was little difference in the arm measurements of both groups of boys. The results in the chest measurements, however, were striking. Whereas the drill-only boys' chests had almost all expanded by half an inch, the drill plus gym boys had all increased their chest measurement by at least one and a quarter inches, and one boy by an astonishing two and three-quarter inches. All 12 of the boys had grown about the same in height. This was significant when, as Brookes was to say in 1882 (recalling Thomas Beddoes in *Hygeïa*) 'In a cold, uncertain climate like England's, with its pulmonary diseases, it was important that a man should have a good large chest.' Brookes had the results printed and sent them to interested parties. Once again, Brookes was showing that he was right at the forefront of his field. In time, scientific measurements of every kind would become a daily feature of athletics training.

Not surprisingly, the Wenlock Olympian Society's programme for the 1872 games added to the children's prizes Indian Club, Horizontal Bar, and Vaulting Horse competitions. The programme also included, for the only time, a demonstration by the children of drill and gymnastics on the day after the Games at the Schoolhouse, to which other Managers of Schools were 'specially invited'. Games President Jasper More of Linley was the children's Guest of Honour. Also impressed, was 'Professor' Joseph Hubbard of the Birmingham Athletic Club, who offered to come down another day and 'teach them some new movements'. (The title Professor was sometimes adopted by coaches to denote their expertise and professional status.)

At the Games themselves Brookes could and did speak with renewed confidence on school PE. He assured his listeners that drill alone, as currently required by the Committee of the Council on Education, though a move in the right direction, 'will be found quite inefficient as regards the development of the muscular system'. He invoked the Franco-Prussian War reports on the physical condition of both sides. The *Daily Telegraph* said that the hospital authorities 'were struck with the remarkable difference between the bodily development of French and German soldiers – describing the French as under-sized, thin, slightly-developed men,' while the Germans were 'thick, powerful fellows, well filled out, hard and muscular'.

The inclusion of the children was not the only reason that the 1872 Wenlock Olympian Games were important. The grass track had been taken up and completely re-laid 'and is now really a credit to the society'. The Duke of Cleveland had generously supplied timber to rail in the whole course, the work almost finished by the date of the June Games. This was to prevent people wandering on to the course, causing accidents and damaging the new track. The programme for 1872 stated for the first time that 'Horsemen are particularly requested not to ride along, or across the running course, except at those places which are covered with tan'. Visitors were also asked not to touch the trees and shrubs that decorated the field. Finally, in 1872 at a special committee meeting on 23 October, the cricket section of the Society was allotted a pitch south of the Bowling Green 'to be kept in order by themselves'.

The crowds in June 1872 were immense, an estimated 6,000–10,000 people, 'the most gratifying feature' of which 'was the presence of so many of the fair sex'. People still came 'in vehicles of every description, some crowded to an astonishing extent, and returning home even still more crowded'. It was the railway, though, that brought the majority. Great Western (now operating the line) did their utmost but no doubt wished for a second line for the day. In 1870, carriages made for eight were carrying 15, and before they had come to a halt 'the living mass was pouring through the doors, utterly regardless of the voices and gesticulations of the officials.' Returning home that evening, before the 7.10pm arrived, the platform and waiting rooms were 'closely packed' with 'a good-tempered crowd'. The station-master Mr Ruscoe kept order.

Once on the train, the newspaper reporter, sharing a first class carriage with 14 others, had first the pleasure of 'two individuals [who] attempted to amuse the occupants by singing'. Having got rid of these 'we were troubled with the hunting reminiscences of a local farmer, and it was not without a feeling of satisfaction that we found the train had arrived at Wellington.' In 1871, special trains 'had to be put on with double steam power'. In 1872, specially long trains ran continually, 'yet these were insufficient, for…crowds were left behind, compelled to be satisfied with the prospect of 'waiting for the next train,' although as many as from 15 to 20 positively packed themselves into each compartment.' And in the evening, instead of two trains between Wenlock and Wellington, five were needed to get everyone away, the last at 11pm.

The GGS did not send any competitors in 1872, or as the newspaper put it 'The cockneys…were conspicuous by their absence', probably because Ravenstein had resigned as President in 1871. Joseph Hubbard's Birmingham AC was out in force and its athletes were very successful. Four of them competed in the General Competition, John Anderton, William Oldfield, B. Wareing and S. Harris. Anderton, 'in every respect a perfect athlete' was victorious. The crowds were impressed when he climbed, as did Wareing, to 'within a few feet of the top' of the new pole. Having descended, Anderton then went up again about 25 feet.

More amazing still was the Society's own man clearing up after the event. Like the competitors, he used the rope to climb to the top, then got on to the iron supports of the Excelsior cross piece, unhooked to rope and let it fall, then plucked out the flag. Now he had to descend unaided and carrying the flag, 'which he succeeded in doing without any assistance, to the surprise and admiration of those who witnessed it, as they testified by their applause.' Another noteworthy competitor was William Rowlands of Homer, third in the labourers' flat race, who was described in the newspaper as 'one-armed', though in the census as 'one-eyed' though not from birth (more likely, given his occupation as a 'land drainer' for which digging would be essential). In 1870, aged 20, he had won the quarter-mile handicap.

Brookes was dashing about as usual, 'and, with his well-known hospitality, invited numbers to his house where they were courteously and liberally entertained.' He was wearing a cluster of medals, presented to him by the NOA, WOS, the GGS, BAC, and Liverpool Gymnasium. He reflected on progress with PE in schools in his speech at the dinner on the second day. 'It is a very difficult matter, as we all know, to give a direction to the national mind on any subject, more especially to one which has received but little public attention.' He credited Ravenstein, Hulley and Clement Davies of Birmingham with labouring long in the cause of PE. 'If we have not accomplished all that we desired, we are not…disheartened, for we well know that the seed we have sown will produce fruit abundantly.'

He was often asked what was the good of PE. 'The use…of physical education is to develop, to strengthen, and to perfect, as far as possible, those bodily powers given to man for the performance of the active duties of life, for his enjoyment, and for his intercourse with the world in which he moves'. He observed that many admired and might work hard to protect a fine building from destruction or decay. 'But who, except under the influence of personal attachment, stops to admire that most glorious of all edifices, the palace of the human soul?... Were a knowledge of the structure of the human body more general, it would be more valued and better cared for; we should encounter less opposition or indifference to the physical education of the young in our national elementary schools or to health-giving recreation or invigorating athletic exercises for the adult in the open air.'

To crown a highly successful year at Wenlock, a 'Wellingtonia Gigantea' (*Sequoiadendron giganteum*) was planted in Brookes's honour at the renamed Linden Field, in the south-west corner of the ground (where it flourishes still) which would be seen as competitors (running clockwise round the track) entered the home straight. Members of the Society carried the tree to the field 'with great ceremony', the schoolchildren following a 'spirit-stirring drum'. After the tree was planted, the children sang a song composed by Edward Stroud:

...Flourish for ages,
Wonderful tree:
When the storm rages,
Firm may'st though be.
Tell of the gatherings
Thou wilt have seen.
Of the games and rejoicings,
The dance on the green.
Of the dash of the tilter,
The speed in the race,
The strength of the climber,
The disc-thrower's grace;
Of the bright eyes that glanc'd
From the tournament stand,
As the victor advanc'd
With banner and band....
And now we have planted thee,
Watcred thee, welcomed thee,
Let us proclaim to thee
What henceforth thy name shall be.
Thy name shall be 'Brookes's tree;'
That name may'st thou bear
For many a century
For many a year.'

Francis Moreton reminded them that 'about 25 years ago we could scarcely muster a hundred persons to witness our games, but now we can command thousands.' He listed Brookes's achievements besides the Games – the laying out of the grounds, the Corn Market, the library, and the railway. 'We heartily endorse the name given to the tree, and sincerely hope that it may flourish, and ever be remembered…as a memento of Mr Brookes's family, which has ever been an honour to our town and neighbourhood.' In response, Brookes said he felt their compliment deeply. He hoped that they would see 'the tree just planted, at present small, but destined to become a gigantic one, as an emblem of a great movement'. He hoped that the children would grow in grace to 'possess strong and healthy bodies' mindful of the words of the psalmist, 'I will praise Thee, for I am fearfully and wonderfully made'.

With the Linden Field in top condition, and with the cause of PE showing signs of gaining ground, Brookes decided to hold a meeting of the NOA at Much Wenlock. The 1873 Wenlock Olympian Games, in any case, attracted athletes from London, Birmingham, Ormskirk, Liverpool, Hereford and Manchester, so it represented a relatively small step. The Earl of Bradford, of Weston Park, Shifnal (owner of 10,500 acres of Shropshire) whose wife Selina was a sister of Lord Forester, agreed to be President, and a fund to raise £300 for prizes was established. The date was fixed for Monday and Tuesday 25 and 26 May 1874.

Meanwhile, in 1873 came confirmation of Brookes's success in propagating athletics nationwide, with a backlash by the novelist, Wilkie Collins. Collins' 1870 novel, *Man and Wife*, considered the position of contemporary woman within marriage, but also attacked 'Athleto-mania' in British society. One of Collins's characters, Geoffrey Delamayn was caught up in the 'present rage for muscular exercises' while inwardly becoming increasingly brutal. In other words, while becoming outwardly strong, he became morally weak.

While apparently unhelpful to Brookes's aims, this, in fact, played into the hands of Brookes's continued inclusion of tilting and its attendant pageantry in his Games, at a time when they increasingly appeared eccentric. No other athletic meetings had such an element. Yet the chivalric ideal of mediaeval literature that Brookes was promoting was the antithesis of Collins's character. Courtly literature made precisely the point that brute force was nothing without moral courage, and that the strength of the individual should not be put to selfish ends, but used for the good of all, and it set this within a Christian framework, just as Brookes always did in his speeches.

The *Globe and Traveller* of 31 March 1873 entered into the debate, acknowledging the phenomenal growth of sport. 'What,' it asked, 'has been the effect of all this?' The answer, 'A development of bodily vigour among the youth of the upper classes which could have been produced by no other means'. The question of whether any injury had been caused had to be asked. Ironically, it was an eminent surgeon, Mr Skey who had claimed that the boat race caused 'violent strain' to the heart and nerves and was possibly 'dangerous to life'. Yet Mr Skey was now dead, and the rowers of former crews were found supporting their university on the towpath every year, still pictures of health.

The other complaint, as suggested by Collins, was that sport 'debases and degrades the mind' making participants 'ignorant, coarse, and cruel'. To rebut this, the *Globe* pointed to the Greeks, 'the least ignorant, most civilised, and most *spirituel* people of antiquity'. Wilkie Collins, the *Globe* claimed, 'knows about as much of athletics as he does of the Athenians'. Rather, it pointed to the dons of Oxford and Cambridge who had initially been against sports, but seeing that it had no adverse effect on academic results, 'have long ago admitted in its most practical application the doctrine of *mens sana in corpore sano*'. Finally, the *Globe* gloried in the fact that unlike horse racing, 'it is really refreshing to turn to an arena where there is not even a suspicion of unfairness' – a vindication of the efforts to clean up athletics.

In preparation for the fourth (Much Wenlock) NOA Games, Brookes beefed up the aims of the NOA, the programme stating that its goal was 'to promote Physical Education generally, but especially, by gymnastic exercises, in our National Elementary Schools, under the authority of the Committee of the Council on Education'. He also drummed up an impressive Council of titled men and MPs to bolster his cause. Besides Bradford they included his oldest supporter Lord John Manners MP, General the Hon Sir Percy Herbert KCB MP, Sir Henry Harnage, Colonel Corbett MP, C.C. Cotes MP, Jasper More, Col Bradney Gilpin, and from neighbouring Herefordshire the philanthropist and MP James Rankin.

In addition, he drafted in Hepworth Dixon of the London School Board, and Thomas Hughes, the author of *Tom Brown's Schooldays*. Brookes's co-Secretary for the 1874 NOA Games was Ernst Ravenstein, whose GGS colleague R. Schweizer was a 'genial time-keeper', while Joseph Hubbard from Birmingham judged. As Brookes acknowledged with gratitude, they came to help entirely at their own expense. The other judges included Evan Davies of Patton, Davies' neighbour Edward Wadlow, T.W. Jones of Wellington and Francis Moreton, maltster and publican of the Talbot, and a Wenlock Councillor (who had family in both Liverpool and Manchester). Brookes's committee also drew in J.B. Hillkirk, President of the Manchester Athenaeum Gymnastic Club, W. Player of Birmingham, and William Waddell the Secretary of the London Athletic Club, who was soon to give great annoyance to the AAC of London. Among the regulations, besides being covered from shoulder to knee it was stipulated that 'If tights are worn, loose drawers round the loins must be worn'.

The choice of Much Wenlock for a national event seemed as unlikely as ever, but even *The Field* had to acknowledge that the prizes offered were 'of unusual value, amounting in the aggregate to £270, and the muster of competitors was a fair one: Birmingham, Manchester, London, Newcastle, Hereford, and other towns being represented.' Indeed 1874 was to be the year of greatest turnover for WOS under Brookes, over £165 (equivalent to about £6,650 today). *The Field* further judged that Linden Field was 'one of the finest playgrounds in the kingdom'. The tilting competition elicited further comment, being 'unique', which drew a detailed description, perhaps from Ravenstein (it was signed 'GGS'). It dubbed Brookes 'the soul of the National Olympian Association', a description echoed by the *Wellington Journal*, which called him the 'county Nestor of Physical Education', and Linden Field 'the prettiest recreation ground in England'.

Monday opened with the usual 'Percession' from the Gaskell Arms at 11am. The two days' sport began with the Pentathlon, won by William 'Tiny' Oldfield of BAC. Over lunch, the Earl of Bradford spoke, followed by Ralph Benson, vice-President, 'one of the best after-dinner speakers it was ever our lot to listen to', who gently teased Lord Bradford about his racehorses 'in a speech replete with witticisms'. Lord Bradford had lately been attending the Czar of all the Russias; he would see 'a few more 'rushers' when he witnessed the tilting.' That came after lunch, and was won by John Webster of Stanway.

Then came a two-mile flat race, one-mile hurdles and a quarter-mile hurdles for farmers. The tilting ceremonial was followed as usual, Webster rising afterwards and bowing as low as he dared in his olive crown. Oldfield did not receive his Pentathlon medal from Mrs Benson, because the previous year, instead of bowing, he had scandalised polite Wenlock society by kissing the lady's hand 'in a way that made the prudes shudder and all others vastly entertained.' At a concert in the evening, Brookes's niece Edith (Andrew's daughter from Shrewsbury) played the harp and sung in the glee songs. Ernst Ravenstein also gave a lecture on the benefits of PE.

The second day began with 100 yards flat race, won by Oldfield again, hotly pursued by John Thomas the Sergeant from Wenlock police station, who was otherwise on duty for the Games. Then came quoits, the half-mile and then the one-mile flat races, in which the appropriately named E.G.S. Corser of Hereford Football Club came first and second respectively. The quarter-mile hurdles, won by H.V. Thomas of Hereford Football Club (and Hereford Rowing Club), were followed by the running high leap (C.B. Oldfield of Birmingham AC and W.M. Tilley of Liverpool second), single stick, running long leap (won by F. Wilding, also of Hereford FC, jumping 19ft 5in), the 120-yard hurdles (H.T. Thomas of Hereford, intriguingly described as 'namesake of the famous bone-setter', with William Roberts 'the old Wenlock favourite…without exception one of the best county runners' second), and the flat tilting. Finally came the quarter-mile flat race (H.V. Thomas first and George Geyden of BAC second) and a two-mile walking race (J.W. Goldsworth of Hereford first, C.S. Jackson of Hereford second).

In the middle of all this, another lunch was held, chaired this time by Brookes. He noted that in 1872 there had been 1.945 million children in education as inspected by the Government. He then looked forward a century and a half to 2022 to their descendants. 'What might we behold? On the one hand, should we have attended to the health and cultivated the bodily powers of the young in our National Elementary Schools, we might see women as beautiful as at present, for we could not wish them more so, but healthier as we would all desire…and in the men a stalwart, noble race, strong in body and in mind…On the other hand, how mournful might be the spectacle, that of a stunted, puny, miserable race, deficient in strength and courage,…a luxurious, effeminate, wealth-adoring, degenerate people.'

Brookes followed up these games by sending a commemorative medal to Lord Bradford, and by planting a 'Picea Nobilis' (*Abies procera*) on Linden Field opposite the grandstand the following March, to be called the 'Bradford Tree'. Lord Bradford, Orlando Bridgeman, had been the MP for South Shropshire from 1842 until he inherited his title. He had also served as Lord Chamberlain, Master of the Horse and a Privy Counsellor. The tree was planted with an almost super-abundance of wishes; for the health of their benefactor and his wife; prosperous growth to the tree; success to the National and Wenlock Olympian societies, and for the cause of physical education. Despite these burdens, it grew up unbowed.

After hosting the 1874 NOA Games, Much Wenlock celebrated the 25th Wenlock Olympian Games in May. Instead of being at the celebratory Games, Brookes was once again in mourning, this time for his eldest daughter Mary. Lord Forester had also died in 1874, having been the greatest supporter of the Games since that first afternoon on the racecourse in 1850. The year before that, in 1873, J.M. Gaskell of the Abbey had died. A Tory in politics, Gaskell had always worked closely with Brookes towards the success of the Games, and Brookes had appreciated the work done by Gaskell on his estate to improve the labourers' cottages in Wenlock. In 1875 a Picea Grandis was planted to his memory at the north-eastern corner of Linden Field.

Edwin Yardley, one of the Society's greatest servants, was also lost now. Originally a cooper but by 1870 an 'attorney's clerk', Yardley had been either the Treasurer or Secretary in almost every one of the 25 years since the Games began. In 1870, on Games day, Yardley had acted as the starter, and, noted the *Shrewsbury Chronicle*, 'bore the hard work and various little annoyances of his office with a good humour that surmounted every difficulty', an appropriate epithet for his contribution as a whole. He died in 1875, and his wife Esther, herself an asset to the Games, the year after. Yardley was succeeded in his roles by Thomas P. Everall, a hammer throwing competitor in the late 1860s and early 1870s, the President of the labourers' autumn Games in 1867 and 1868, and by 1880, the publican at the Raven.

Despite these losses, the familiar Wenlock programme unfolded in 1875. Thomas Jukes mustered the procession at the Gaskell at around 11.30am, it proceeded to the Field where a 'Picea Nordmanniana' (*Abies nordmanniana*) was planted in memory of Lord Forester. Lyde Benson deputised for Brookes at the dedication and opening of the Games. Richard Webster won the flat tilting and Charles Ainsworth beat eight others to the hurdle-tilting title, and was crowned by Miss Poyner. Three Birmingham men competed for the Pentathlon, C. Smythe beating J.W. Keeling and R. Spong. Over lunch in the marquee, Benson spoke again, alluding with feeling to Brookes's absence. In the afternoon's 200 yard foot race Oldfield beat Keeling, the mile hurdles was won by T. Childs of Ruabon, and the mile flat race by Edward Finch, a sawyer from Rushbury, who had made the competition his own, winning almost every year since 1869. Finally the bowling green was sacrificed to the boots of the young who danced to the Benthall Works Brass Band under Mr Bevington.

Benson's speech alluded to forthcoming games in Manchester, in fact a sporting spectacular staged at the Royal Pomona Gardens by the 'Northern Counties Olympian Association for the Promotion of Physical Education' a trumped-up title to lend gravitas to what was a profit-making show. The Pomona Gardens were where the third NOA Games in 1868 should have been held, but the Gardens had been bought that year by James Reilly. Located in the wealthy suburb of Old Trafford the Gardens had been developed in the 1830s and had hosted, among other events, the Manchester and Salford Regatta on the River Irwell, and from 1857, the Manchester Cricket Club until it moved to the nearby Warwick Road Old Trafford ground, becoming (by joining with others) in 1864 Lancashire Cricket Club.

Brookes had called a public meeting in the Mayor's Parlour at Manchester Town Hall to propose holding NOA Games in the city in 1875. However, jealousy of Brookes's efforts by local handicappers and others involved in northern athletics, and rivalry between two new sporting journals in Manchester meant that a second meeting was needed at the Clarence Hotel. Reilly was present and managed, allegedly by packing the hall with his own supporters, to win a vote to put the event into his hands, squeezing Brookes out. Nevertheless, Brookes sent his tilters, and shortly after noon on Wednesday 16 June, eight Wenlock men 'peregrinated the town on horseback and in costume, preceded by their Herald'. The *Sporting Chronicle* thought that 'the formality of the opening and closing of the tilting will appear 'somewhat ludicrous' to matter of fact people,' but John Webster emerged victorious, beating Charles Ainsworth, the victor the month before at Wenlock.

All athletic feats of the summer of 1875 were eclipsed though, when on 25 August, Matthew Webb, son of the surgeon at Coalbrookdale, achieved world fame by becoming the first man to swim the English Channel. Webb was quite the 'hero of the hour'. After sleeping at the Hôtel de Paris and being cheered through Calais, he was taken back to Dover. In London, he was feted at the Alexandra Palace and received promotional offers of all kinds. His reputation was further burnished when it was revealed that he had, in 1862, jumped into the Atlantic attempting to rescue a fellow seaman who had fallen from the rigging, for which he received the Royal Humane Society's medal. Here, then, was a patron-saint for the muscular Christians, with physical and moral strength in equal measure. He received official welcomes at Ironbridge and Dawley. However, after turning professional Webb was to die in July 1883 attempting to swim across the whirlpool rapids below Niagra Falls.

These events may have encouraged the next development at Linden Field. Certainly by 1875, Randall's Tourists' Guide to Wenlock noted of the field that it featured 'a reservoir; excavated for a swimming bath,…which will be completed as soon as some generous benefactor shall be found to supply the requisite funds.' This must have been a particularly sensitive project for Brookes after the drowning of Willie, although the tragedy might also have provided impetus for its installation. It is unclear whether the swimming bath was completed, though Coubertin in 1890 made reference to a swimming pool used in 'la belle saison'. Certainly no swimming events took place at the Games in Brookes's lifetime.

At the March 1883 meeting of the Society at which the annual report was delivered, William Lawley noted that 'Great improvements' had been made at the recreation ground. 'The space excavated for a swimming bath has been greatly extended, measuring now 44 yards in length. For its completion, however, a considerable sum will be required.' The financial decline of agriculture that began to bite now probably explains why the money for the pool was elusive. In July 1889, a walk of Linden Field was made by members of the Olympian Society, where the proposed bath, 45 yards long by 23ft wide was inspected. The party adjourned to the Raven for their meeting, at which Lyde Benson introduced 'the most important subject of the evening…It had long been felt that a swimming-bath was necessary on their ground, and, if that were accomplished, it would make their ground very complete. Owing to the difficulty of obtaining the necessary funds, they had been unable to complete the swimming-bath.'

Benson then proposed that, as Brookes would accept nothing for himself for his 80th birthday 'but was willing to accept anything which would be for the good of Wenlock and its inhabitants, and as he had set his heart upon the swimming bath, he considered it would be a good thing for them to complete the bath, and present it as a kind of testimonial to their old and beloved friend Dr Brookes. (Applause.)' Brookes responded 'I accept, gentlemen, with the warmest gratitude, the dedication to myself of your proposed undertaking.'

The pool would have been a more pleasing testimonial to Brookes than that which was generously made to him at the end of October 1875. The presentation was supposed to have taken place at the 25th Games, but Brookes had been absent. Instead, as autumn set in, Ralph Benson chaired a dinner at the Gaskell Arms. Here Brookes was presented with one large and two small silver epergnes or table centres, and a silver tea service, including an engraved salver, after £250 had been raised by subscription. After dinner Benson proposed Brookes's health and read the address with which the 230 subscribers presented him. This mentioned his unselfish devotion 'to works of public utility and social improvement'. The Wenlock Olympian Society had become 'the parent of a more universal and national association…no inefficient instrument in popularising and fostering the great cause of physical education for the people'. There is something uncomfortable about this occasion – delayed because of Mary's death, at which Benson dwelt rather too long on the cause of the delay before introducing the gift 'as an heirloom' to this man who had just buried the fourth of his five children. In the light of Brookes's earnest desire for a swimming pool, it seems a slightly unfortunate choice, albeit typical of the times.

Never a man to rest on his laurels, Brookes introduced a further innovation at the Wenlock Games of 1876 – bicycle racing. The first cycle races in England were held in 1869 and the first championship by the AAC in 1871. Pierre Michaux's pedal-powered bicycle (or 'boneshaker') had appeared in France in the 1860s, but its development was impeded by the Franco-Prussian war. The attachment of the pedals to the front wheel meant that the larger the front wheel, the greater the distance travelled with each turn of the pedals. In 1870, James Starley of Coventry had added spokes and mounting steps to the French design, and his 'Ariel' bicycle was the first product of the British cycling industry, nick-named the Penny-farthing, after the coinage of the day. The first bicycle with wheels of similar sizes was designed by Starley's nephew John K. Starley who in 1885 marketed his revolutionary Safety Bicycle called the 'Rover'.

It is therefore entirely appropriate that it was a Coventry man, Tom Sabin, who dominated the first three years of bicycle racing at Wenlock (plate 20). In 1876, the only race was the three miles or eight laps of the course. There were four entrants, Sabin, about 23 years old, of Allesley, Coventry, J. Fieldhouse of Birmingham, J.O. Richards of Bridgnorth and J.E. Cox of Wolverhampton. Richards retired on the fourth lap, having only 'a small steed', and Cox dropped out in the fifth. This left just Sabin and Fieldhouse, and a 'very exciting' race ensued, the newspaper reports sounding surprisingly modern with their references to Linden Field's 'Quarry Corner' and 'Station Corner'. In the end, 'Sabin won among loud cheers from the excited crowd.' Another annual feature of the Wenlock Olympian Games had been discovered.

At the pre-games meeting at the Raven in March 1877, it was decided that the bicycle race should be reduced to one mile. In the event, the three-mile race stayed, and a one-mile was added. The three-mile race was contested by four cyclists, Sabin, G.W. Corbett of Wellington, W.H. Cooper of Birmingham and W.R. Stretton of Kidderminster. Sabin won easily, but 'The plucky performance of Cooper, who is quite a lad, was much applauded.' They had time to regain their breath during the hurdle tilting and the crowning of John Webster by Miss Sparrow of Church Preen, before Sabin, Corbett and Cooper competed in the one-mile race and came home in that order.

In 1878 the same two races were held, and were fought by Sabin and W.G. Worthington of Manchester ABC. Sabin was handicapped yet still 'soon made up his leeway, notwithstanding that he had a fall and won easily' – a detail that demonstrates just how much faster than the competition Sabin was. The 5ft 11in tall farmer's son, at just over 10 and a half stone, was described in December 1878 as 'the first bicyclist in the Midlands', of perfect build for cycle racing. Sabin had bought his first bicycle in 1873 to get him in to Coventry from Allesley and his first public race had come in April 1874. He was no stranger to falling off and remounting, as he did at Wenlock, the same having happened at Leeds in 1876, when he had come second. His first success at Wenlock in 1876 was repeated all over the country that year. He came first in 15 out of his 19 starts, and second three times. Sabin's only training, he said, sounding like a true gentleman amateur, was 'leaving off smoking'.

In the local games, other developments of the 1870s included the recording of some of the times and distances jumped and thrown. The 1870s saw some memorable long jump and high jump results. These had always been the least-well rewarded of the athletic events, for no apparent reason. Their outstanding exponents were H.W. Brooke of GGS in 1869–71, and Harry Sproston of Birmingham AC who won both in 1872. The highest recorded jump at Wenlock was 5ft 5½in by Brooke in 1871, equalled by Ernest Edwards of BAC in 1876. (For comparison, in 1876, 6ft was cleared for the first time by the Hon. Marshall Jones Brooks, who shortly afterwards cleared 6ft 2½in.) In the long jump, F. Wilding of Hereford jumped 20ft 6in in 1873, and Gerard Fowler of BAC 20ft 4in in 1876. (In 1869, Alick Tosswill was the first amateur in Britain to clear 22ft.)

Pole leaping or vaulting came in at Wenlock in the mid 1860s, as it did nationally – the Lake District being a centre of excellence. Before this, pole leaping was done for distance, not height. In the early days, the hands could be walked up the ash, cedar or hickory pole once it was vertical, and the bar taken in a sitting position. The magic target here was 10ft, crossed by J. Wheeler in 1866. At Wenlock, two men from Brewood, Staffordshire, John G. Wilson and R.B. Mole tied for first place in the 1874 NOA Games, clearing 10ft 4in. Ernest Edwards of BAC equalled that in 1877. W. Gough of Shrewsbury leapt 9ft 2in in 1882.

Hammer throwing was a discipline that produced some fun at Wenlock. In May 1866, just before he took part in the AAC Games in London (despite being the northern representative for the NOA games) William Mitchell of Fearns Hall, Rossendale, was a guest at Wenlock. He and his three brothers had competed at the Liverpool Games from 1862, dominating the 1865 Festival. In 1863, Mitchell, a great runner, recorded a cherished 'evens' time of 10 seconds in the 100 yards – the four minute mile of the day. After joining the Wenlock procession and addressing the spectators 'on physical education', a talk deemed 'too clever, too refined, for nineteen-twentieths of those for whom it was intended', he watched the sports. After the hammer had been won by George Kidson of Wenlock, Mitchell grabbed the hammer, and 'to the astonishment of the crowd, threw it 17 yards 2 feet [53 feet]; 2 feet 6 inches further than

Kidson had thrown it.' William Lawley managed 56ft in 1869. By the early 1870s, the 16lb hammer with a 3ft 6in wooden handle was launched from a scratch line after an unlimited run up, but from the middle of the decade a 7ft throwing circle came into use. Thomas Everall and Lawley were the best throwers from Wenlock. In 1871, Robert Clement of GGS threw the hammer 63ft 2in, and Everall 62ft 2in.

Shot put distances at Wenlock were sometimes composed of the total of a left plus a right-hand throw, and sometimes of one throw only. The weight of the shot was also 32lbs instead of the 16lbs used today. In 1871, Robert Clement of GGS threw 18ft 5½in, in 1872 H. Grimstone of Manchester AGC managed 40ft, increasing it the following year to 41ft 1in. In 1876, Louis McCann of BAC threw 20ft.

At the other end of the reward scale at Wenlock, the hurdles races of the 1870s changed from 200 yards in 1872–75 to 120 yards from 1877. The height of the hurdles was standardised nationally at 3ft 6in in 1866. The year before this, Clement Jackson set a national record of 16 seconds, which was not beaten for 26 years. Straight leg hurdling was pioneered by Oxford student Arthur Croome in 1886. Wenlock's outstanding figures in this discipline in the 1870s were H.V. Thomas of Hereford Rowing Club who won in 1872 and '73, and Ernest Edwards of Birmingham AC who won in 1875–78. Unfortunately, times in this discipline were not recorded.

The half-mile is the only flat race for which times survive. H.W. Brooke managed 2 minutes 14 seconds, and Robert Clement 2 minutes 32 seconds in 1870, and J.W. Keeling of BAC managed 2 minutes 35 seconds in 1875. To break the two minute barrier was the aim, and the first to do so was the Hon. Arthur Pelham, a 6ft 4in tall Cambridge undergraduate with an enormously long stride who recorded 1 minute 59.8 seconds in 1873. That was on cinder though, whereas at Wenlock, the track was the slower grass.

F.B. Harrison (plate 16) was the outstanding home-grown competitor of this period, winning the hurdles in 1879, but also the 200 yard and quarter-mile flat races the year before, the former won by him 'easily' and 'in splendid style'. In 1877 he had come third in the 200 yard flat race, described as 'a brilliantly contested race'. He seems to be of the same family who in 1851 owned land in Barrow, the village near Lord Forester's home, Willey Hall, and he played for Willey Wanderers cricket team. Harrison was voted straight on to the committee of WOS in 1877, the first time that he appeared at all in the minutes, and later the same year was Starter and Secretary of the local men's Autumn Games. He drummed up 20 new local competitors in 1877 and was a great asset to Brookes, serving as President of the Autumn Games in 1878. Harrison was handicapping the local races at the 1880 Games, the year when he also long-jumped 19ft 10in. He was the only man to have his own stand at the debt-liquidating bazaar to be held in the Corn Market that year. Sadly, by 1882, the minutes noted that he had 'left the neighbourhood'.

One runner who was to become a nationally-known figure for reasons good and bad, who first entered the Games at Much Wenlock in 1877 (quarter-mile flat race for under-18s) was William Snook (1861–1916) competing for Pengwern Boat Club (founded in 1871 on the River Severn opposite the Quarry where the Shropshire and NOA Games were held). Snook (plate 17) was Shrewsbury-born and in his early years, rowed, cycled and ran. In 1879 he ran again at Wenlock and won easily the half-mile. F.B. Harrison was responsible for the handicapping, and he lined Snook up at 'scratch', but he nevertheless came through and beat F. Yates, J. Harley and B. Ainsworth. That year, H.M. Oliver of Moseley Harriers, who had competed at Wenlock himself in 1877 and 1878, and who was to return in 1880 as handicapper, invited Snook to join his Birmingham club. In 1880, therefore, Snook competed in the blue and yellow colours of Moseley Harriers in a remarkable 49 races nationwide, from Southport, Crewe and Widnes to Brecon, Bridg water and Birmingham, being placed first to fourth 43 times, mostly at half-mile, one and two-mile distances. In the 1881 season, he tried cross-country for the first time, and in July travelled to Paris where he ran a seven-mile match in the Bois de Boulogne against M. Duplay, and won.

On his return from Paris, however, Snook was hauled before the AAA (as the AAC had become) for allegedly conniving with the entry of a professional runner posing as an amateur entered under a false name in the one-mile handicap at Southport earlier in July. The AAA suspended him from competition until 31 December 1882. Snook continued to compete in non-AAA affiliated competitions, from Ilkley to Lurgan, until the AAA made it clear that athletes competing against him would also be liable to suspension. Despite the ban Snook competed 50 times in the 1881 season at non-AAA events, 'cocking a snook' at the authorities (though the phrase was not coined for him, being in use almost a century earlier) winning 24 races, and being placed second to fourth a further 17 times.

After kicking his heels in 1882, Snook returned to athletics in 1883, and at Much Wenlock won the half-mile handicap by 10 yards, despite starting from scratch, beating J. Carver of Wellington and James Cleobury of Broseley. In the two-mile handicap, once again running off scratch, he beat F. Potham, although the runners ran a lap short 'owing to a blunder by the officials'. In July at Hadley Institute Athletics Club Festival, held in conjunction with the NOA, the *Shrewsbury Chronicle* described him as a credit to Shropshire. This seemed justified indeed in 1885 when the 'king of running' was unrivalled after his old adversary, Walter G. George had turned professional. At the AAA Championships that year, he won the one, four and 10 mile events, as well as the steeplechase.

However, on 6 March 1886, Snook unexpectedly lost the National Cross Country Championship at Croydon to J.E. Hickman of Godiva Harriers, whom Snook had beaten the month before. He was accused of deliberately 'roping' to let Hickman win (because of betting) and he was suspended permanently by the Southern Counties committee of the AAA at a meeting on 30 April. This was the first permanent suspension of an athlete and caused a sensation in the world of athletics.

Snook appealed on 22 May 1886, but the decision was upheld. He tried again in February 1887, with the backing of the Midland Counties AAA, but he lost again. Notably 'a Mr Oliver who certainly ought to know a bit about Snook's form', reported *Sport and Play,* a Birmingham journal, 'stated that a more deceptive runner never stepped on the path and he defied anyone to know when he was beaten and when he was not'. Snook turned professional, but by now it was much more difficult to make a living as a professional runner. He married in Toxteth, Liverpool in 1884, but his wife petitioned for divorce in 1892, claiming mistreatment, and adultery with a relation of hers. From about 1890 Snook moved to Paris and trained athletes, but during World War One fell on hard times and returned to die in Birmingham Workhouse Hospital in December 1916.

Finally, in the 1870s, as has been seen, a new name entered the tilting lists, that of Charles E. Ainsworth, the younger brother, by 10 or 11 years, of Joel, who had won in the second year of the competition, and of William who had won in 1868. In 1875, the boy who had been nine when Joel died, entered the same competition aged 22, to try his luck against eight horsemen. He emerged victorious, and was crowned by Mrs E. Wadlow. Ainsworth then hit a run of being beaten by John Webster of Stanway, or William Braithwaite (of Droitwich) at Wenlock and at the Shrewsbury NOA Games in 1877. In 1878 he won again, though, and was described as a 'very popular winner' when he was crowned by Viscountess Petersham. Ainsworth's father had died by the end of the decade, and Charles had taken on the tenancy of the 250 acre Spoonhill Farm near Wenlock. He was living with his widowed mother, his older brother William having taken a farm of his own at Bourton. Charles was always a popular Wenlock winner, perhaps because he was the town's auctioneer as well, at Smithfield market near the railway goods station. The Websters were another great Wenlock tilting dynasty, three brothers, John, Edward and Richard having competed at Wenlock from the late 1860s until 1889.

The Secretary of the Society after Edwin Yardley (a role he combined with that of the Treasurer for five years) Thomas Everall, who at 4 Wilmore Street had been a neighbour of Brookes, asked to be excused his responsibilities in 1879, when he was succeeded by William Lawley. Everall's resignation came probably because of the pressures of giving up his grocer and butcher business and taking on the Raven in Barrow Street. The inn was a large establishment, having besides the assembly room, bedrooms, the neighbouring butcher's shop, and loose boxes, so that farmers coming into town could leave their horse safely while they conducted business, and make the inn their base for correspondence and refreshment while in town. The 39-year-old Everall, also a Town Councillor, and his wife Eliza had three daughters, Anne, Isabelle and Kate, and a son Stanley.

This tale of upwardly-mobile aspiration, however, suffered a major setback on 26 June 1880. In a case reminiscent of that of Brookes versus Beddoes in 1863, Everall had become suspicious of the relationship between his wife Eliza and one of their regular clients at the Raven, farmer Edward Parr of Aston Eyres, about four miles from Much Wenlock towards Bridgnorth. One Sunday afternoon, Everall rode over to Parr's farmhouse, and after sitting with Parr for a while, without warning, leapt up, and (bearing in mind Everall's hammer-throwing capability) hit Parr a back-handed blow across the face with the metal handle of his whip.

Parr got up and ran for the door, only to be followed down the passage by Everall who punched him and hit him further with the whip. Outside, 'It was life or death with me', thought Parr, 'and he looked at me straight in the face and said, "I'll kill you —— ——-"'. Parr grabbed the whip, both men fell over, and Parr managed to escape. He hid around the end of the stable until Everall, having searched within, left the yard. Dr Thursfield was called, and testified to the extent of the injuries. The doctor had to 'elevate' Parr's nasal bones. There were further blows to the back of his head.

1. William Penny Brookes (1809–95) surgeon of Much Wenlock, who started the Olympian Class in 1850 despite facing discouragement and derision.

2. Wilmore Street, Much Wenlock. The figure (centre) is in front of Brookes's house. Next (nearer the camera) are Lawley's print shop (which housed the original WARS library), the Lawleys's home, and the Stork Hotel, home of William Lawley's wife, Helen. Far left is the half-timbered Guildhall of 1540.

3. Spital Street, Much Wenlock showing the Corn Exchange (left) home of WARS. Opposite is one of the lamps erected after Brookes helped bring gas to the town. At the end of the street next to the Guildhall is the draper's shop of James Bodenham (WOS committee-member). It was up this street that the first-ever Olympian Games procession set out, in 1850.

4. Thomas Yates, the Herald of 1887 in the costume of the Tudor court, as advised by Covent Garden Theatre. On its first outing, in 1860, it 'excited universal admiration'.

5. Tilting at the Ring was introduced in 1858 and rapidly became the highlight of Games day. Hurdles were added in the run-up in 1868. In this image of the 1887 Games, John Webster is successfully piercing one of the rings that were less than one inch in diameter. The tilting judge that year (left) was Edward Wadlow.

6. Windmill Field on Games day, 11 June 1867. 'The tilters, the band, and the officials were arranged in front of the elevation ground; and a photograph of the whole was taken by Mr [James] Laing. The spectacle was a most picturesque and pleasing one'. This is the earliest known photograph of an athletic meeting.

7. The Raven Hotel, Barrow Street had close links with the Wenlock Olympian Games hosting meetings and dinners, including that attended by Pierre de Coubertin in October 1890. Of its landlords, Robert Hartland was on the committee and T.P. Everall was Secretary and Treasurer in the 1870s.

8. Tilting at the Ring on Bicycles at the Liverpool Gymnasium, 1869. It was at the Gym's opening in 1865 that the National Olympian Association was formed by Brookes, John Hulley (probably standing, centre) and Ernst Ravenstein. Wenlock's influence is clear in this competition, won by Ralph W. Leyland (founder of a shipping company in 1875) who speared a ring six times out of 10.

9. The German Gymnasium or Turnhalle, St Pancras, London, founded by Ernst Ravenstein who brought many members to the Wenlock Olympian Games until his retirement in 1871. It was a venue for the National Olympian Games, 1866.

10. Joseph Hubbard, 'one of the best athletes England possessed' and founder in 1866 of Birmingham Athletic Club. He judged at the Wenlock Olympian Games and was Secretary of the National Olympian Association in 1878, also supporting Brookes in his attempt to get PE on to the curriculum.

11. William Roberts (1841–1910), a notable home-grown talent and servant of the Wenlock Olympian Society. He competed at the third Games in 1852 and acted as starter until after Brookes' death. 'The old Wenlock favourite', he was the outstanding competitor of the 1860s, a hurdler, high- and long-jumper. Professionally he was a painter, plumber and publican of the Plough and Royal Oak on Barrow Street.

12. The officials, herald and tilters in 1887, Jubilee year. The tilters are (back row left to right) John Webster, Richard Webster and Charles Ainsworth. Thomas Yates is the Herald on the grey pony, to the right of which stand Brookes (wearing the medals of the Liverpool and German Gymnasia, NOA, WOS and Birmingham AC) Lyde Benson, and Lord Forester of Willey. Left of the pony is probably Thomas Jukes. The other officials that year included T.H. Thursfield, T.R. Horton, S.C. Meire, Thomas Barnett, and William Lawley.

13. The Wenlock Olympian Games Pentathlon medal, awarded 1868–79 and 1881. It depicts Nike, Greek goddess of Victory, and includes words from one of Pindar's ancient Olympic Odes. For Wenlock winners the medal was cast in silver.

14. William Brookes (1845–68) Brookes' younger son, a first-class Oxford medic, who drowned in the canal on a December night, after falling into Louse (Isis) Lock.

15. W.G. Grace at the Crystal Palace Cricket Ground, Sydenham, London, where in 1866 he won the 440yd hurdles in the National Olympian Games.

16. F.B. Harrison of Barrow, near Much Wenlock, a runner and hurdler of 'splendid style' in the late-1870s. He also drummed up new members and was the only man to have a stall at the bazaar in 1880.

17. William Snook (1861–1916) a Shrewsbury runner of national standing. Spotted at the Wenlock Games in 1879, he joined Moseley Harriers and then Birchfield Harriers. After his superior rival, W.G. George turned professional in 1885, Snook became the 'king of running' but was controversially permanently suspended from competition by the AAA the following year. He was to die in Birmingham workhouse hospital.

18. Henry W. Brooke (1849–1929) of the German Gymnastic Society, London. Brooke was an outstanding all-round athlete, winning the Wenlock Pentathlon in 1869 and 1870. He went on to become a Director of music publisher Novello & Co., with responsibility for the printing.

19. The crowning of the Champion Tilter, Charles Ainsworth at the 1887 Wenlock Olympian Games by the Queen of Beauty, local rector's daughter Miss Serjeantson. Superficially eccentric, the chivalric code that this represented stressed the principles of amateurism, including truth, courage, justice, honour, and fair play, in contrast to professional athletes who ran for financial reward. It was one of the elements of Wenlock that most struck Coubertin when he visited the Games in 1890 and is reflected in the modern Olympic medal ceremonies.

20. Tom Sabin of Allesley, Coventry, the outstanding cyclist at Wenlock 1876–78. Described in 1878 as 'the finest bicyclist in the Midlands' (he could fall off, remount and still win) his only training, he said, was 'leaving off smoking'.

21. The silver cup donated to the National Olympian Games, Shrewsbury by the Greek monarch, George, King of the Hellenes, in 1877 – jubilee year – for 'the man of the Pentathlon', J.G. Wylie, who played for Shropshire Wanderers FC and for England in 1878. King George, grandfather of HRH Prince Philip, the Duke of Edinburgh, presided over the first IOC Games in Athens in 1896.

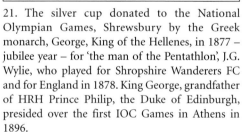

22. Joannes Gennadius (1844–1932) Greek Chargé d'Affaires in London, who oversaw the dispatch of the silver cup to Brookes. Brookes corresponded with Gennadius from 1877–93, repeatedly urging the Greeks to revive their ancient Games.

23. Baron Pierre de Coubertin (1863–1937) first Secretary of the International Olympic Committee, from the photograph that he sent to Brookes. Wishing to discuss the role of sport in education, he visited Brookes in 1890 and saw an autumn Olympian Games. In under two years, Coubertin would propose the revival of the Olympic Games.

24. Much Wenlock Railway Station, where Coubertin first arrived in 1890. He likened it to a 'delightful cottage'. Brookes was a director of the company that brought the line in 1861, and the station was built at the gates to the Games Field. This would prove invaluable, as trains on Games days were packed.

25. The grandstand on Games day around the late-1890s after Brookes' death. Mr & Mrs Lyde Benson (centre) prepare to present the prizes. Standing, centre front holding his hat is probably Lord Wenlock, and second from the left with the watchchain appears to be William Roberts.

26. A postcard of Linden Field in 1931 showing the separate tracks for running and tilting (and cycling) the railings (donated by local landowner the Duke of Cleveland) and the bowling green.

27. Spyros Louis winning the marathon at the first IOC Olympic Games at Athens in 1896. This represented Brookes's lifelong dream, but he died 17 weeks before the Games.

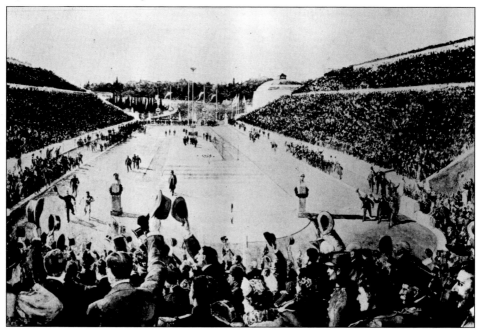

28. Harold Langley, winner of the Pentathlon at Much Wenlock in 1923. He was the first Wenlock medal winner to compete also in Olympic Games – the Paris *Chariots of Fire* Olympics the following year. He went on to be a Field Judge at the London post-war 'austerity' Games of 1948.

29. Alison Williamson became the first Wenlock Olympian Games medallist to win a medal at the Olympic Games. In 1981, aged 10, she won Wenlock silver in the archery. At the Athens Olympic Games of 2004, she won bronze, surely the fulfilment of Brookes's dream.

30. The Wenlock Olympian Games 2010 received a visit from the London 2012 mascot named after the town, in recognition of Wenlock's contribution to the Olympic movement. Wenlock is seen on the state-of-the-art athletics track installed at the newly-renovated William Brookes School adjoining Linden Field. Wenlock's Games continue to be held annually in early July.

Under questioning, Parr claimed to have no idea why Everall should have done what he did. However, it became clear that Parr had been writing to Eliza Everall at the Raven, addressed to 'Mr Smallwood'. They had planned to run off to Leeds, and Eliza had given Parr a pipe, wrapped as a gift, in the Raven's bar. At the Grand Quarter Sessions in Shrewsbury, Mr Plowden acting for Everall, testified to his good character and 'quiet demeanour' and claimed that 'The assault was committed from the most honourable and most natural of motives…could any of them doubt who was the injured man, who was the best man, and who was the worst, and that if the fullest and best justice could be done to both, Parr would be where Mr Everall now stands'? Considerable applause followed, and the Chairman remarked that 'if there was any noise of that sort he would have the Court cleared.'

Evidently there was strong feeling locally that Everall had, like the tilters at the Wenlock Games, let honour be his guide. The court, however, found Everall 'guilty of a common assault, and recommended him to mercy on the ground that he had received great provocation'. Everall was given one week's imprisonment without hard labour, and a fine of £50. The following year, Everall was living at the Raven with only his daughter Anne as Barmaid and his son Stanley, plus staff. Eliza was boarding in the Wolverhampton house of wood turner Thomas Proudman and his wife and their three sons at 4, Herriet Street, (Mrs Proudman hailed from Much Wenlock) with Gertrude, a one-month-old daughter. At the 1882 Wenlock Games, young Stanley Everall was third in the under-12s' 200 yard race, and in 1884, second in the under-15s' 220 yards to Henry Roberts, son of the old Wenlock favourite William, whose inn was just along Barrow Street from the Raven. Sadly in 1885 the Society noted that Thomas Everall 'had left England'.

Lawley became Secretary and Brookes took on the role of Treasurer for three years, until Lawley felt able to combine both, as Everall had done. Lawley oversaw the introduction of one other new sport at the Linden Field now, lawn tennis, though it did not feature at the Olympian Games. At the 1881 Games, Brookes announced that their guest for the day, Alexander Brown, the Liberal MP for Wenlock, of Richmond Hill, Liverpool, had donated £5 for the introduction of 'a lawn tennis ground on Linden Field, which will be a great boon…especially when we consider the importance of promoting healthy, agreeable, and appropriate outdoor recreations for the fair sex. (Loud cheers.)'

The game had been invented in neighbouring Montgomeryshire by Major Walter Wingfield 11 years earlier, and patented and marketed from 1874. The All England Croquet Club in Wimbledon held the first championships in 1877. Wenlock's first court came four years after that, in the same year that the first women's championship was held in England, in Bath. In May 1882, Lawley reported to the Society that a 'Tennis Lawn, 60 yards by 15 yards had been laid out' by Mr Bowdler, the costs met after the donation from Brown had been matched by Lord Forester, and £1 added by Brookes. In 1883, the same year that the swimming bath had been extended, Lawley announced that 40 yards had been added 'to your tennis lawn' making it now one hundred yards long, 'and rendering it thereby suitable for archery, a contest which your committee hope to see introduced into your programmes.' The tennis lawn was just inside the running track, between the bowling green and Windmill Hill.

With a new herbaceous border along the south side of the Field, making floral displays on three sides, Linden Field had now reached its greatest extent of development. It had the finest turf running track in Britain, tilting and bicycle courses, cricket, bowling, archery, lawn tennis and quoit grounds, a swimming pool under excavation, and an area for gymnastic exercises – all in 'perfect order' (plate 26). Beyond the Games days, the Field was a superb addition to the town, not just for exercise, but for recreational walks. As a public amenity in 1883, the field was an astonishing achievement for a small town in rural Shropshire, as indeed was the national reputation of the Wenlock Olympian Games.

Despite appearances, the mid-1870s were not a period of unqualified delight for Brookes. The NOA was losing ground to the AAC; Greece had been consumed by political problems, although a glimmer of hope for Brookes's Olympic dreams dawned in 1875, when Ernst Curtius finally began his archaeological project at Olympia. Between now and 1881 he would systematically excavate the whole of Olympia, publishing annual reports. On a personal level, Brookes lost Mary in 1874, and Roger Blakeway had died in August 1875 – an ally against Wayne for the Games in 1860, practical help during the Beddoes case in 1863, the backbone of the efforts to bring the railway, and besides, a great companion who, as Brookes's mother wrote for example in 1860, called in and 'drank tea'.

In 1877, Brookes staged the fifth NOA Games, this time in Shrewsbury, the county town, described by American novelist Henry James this year, as 'most capital'. In an illustration of the weakness of the NOA, the athletics were combined with the local horticultural show in the Quarry, the races taking part on the cricket pitch. Bad weather was again a theme, the rain running on to the pitch until 'it seemed somewhat marvellous how, in such a puddle, the competitors were able to run at all'.

F.F. Downward of Shrewsbury School won both the half-mile and the one-mile races. From further afield, the most notable competitors were H. Crossley of Stoke Victoria Athletic Club (founded in 1868) second in the 100 yards, C. Hazenwood from Manchester Athletic Club, F. W. Todd of London (second and third in the half-mile race), Ernest Edwards of BAC who was runner-up in the Pentathlon, S. J. Weale of London Athletics Club (second in the quarter-mile hurdles), and B. Marshall of Manchester AC (second in the one-mile race). Brookes was in muted form, expatiating on the delights of the vegetable kingdom, and only briefly mentioning the importance of educating the spirit, body and mind in schools.

The 1877 NOA Games were a shadow of what they had been at the Crystal Palace. Yet while the outlook for this movement appeared superficially bleak, in 1877 and 1878, the prospects for Brookes's NOA as the country's governing body for all sports and for hosting the national championship for athletics received an unexpected fillip. The Amateur Athletics Club, which had been holding the national championships at Lillie Bridge in London since thwarting the NOA's Crystal Palace games in 1866, began to fragment. This gentlemen's club had been established to preside over rather than to run athletics. It staged no athletics meetings, for example, other than the national championships.

Much more 'hands on' – as it turned out, a significant difference – was the London Athletic Club (LAC) which was run from 1870 by the rather less gentlemanly Waddell brothers, William (who had been on the 1874 NOA committee at Much Wenlock) and James. The energetic LAC held several meetings a year, and in 1869 moved its events to the AAC's multi-purpose stadium Lillie Bridge (which hosted the FA Cup in 1873 and Middlesex Cricket Club's home games) and held athletics meetings there until 1876. By the mid-1970s, Chambers and his AAC had become dependent on the LAC for much of their income. Chambers pressed LAC for a larger percentage of its takings, which the Waddells were obliged to supply, but in response, they opened a subscription for their own ground, which opened as Stamford Bridge in 1877 (today the home of Chelsea Football Club) right under the nose of the AAC.

This put Chambers in a difficult position, just as he was under pressure to move the national athletics championship from its spring date to high summer. Spring had been suitable when most of the competitors were university undergraduates with all day to practise, but working men now made up many of the entries, and with a five and a half day working week, they would be obliged to practise in the dark to compete at Easter. The AAC refused to accommodate these men, but the LAC was only too happy to oblige. So, in 1879 rival national championships were held, the AAC's in spring (all Oxbridge and a re-run of the Varsity match) and the LAC's in the summer (all London athletes).

Into the middle of this, once again, the NOA intruded, in an *Athletic World* article of 24 May 1878, in which the case for the NOA as the arbiter of sport in Great Britain was renewed. Quite apart from its (slight) seniority of foundation, the eminent experience of Ravenstein and particularly Brookes (whom it praised highly) in running sport, and the backing of the Earls of Bradford and of Powis to act as trustees for the prize fund, the article thundered that the NOA was 'thoroughly representative which the Amateur Athletic Club is not'. To the committee of every club in the kingdom, 'we say, lose no time in becoming subscribers to the National Olympian Association of Great Britain.' The magazine committed itself to 'help the association by all means in our power to attain the eminence of its noble objects, and become the ruling power in the athletic world.'

CHAPTER 5

'Our work is not yet finished: we shall have more appeals to make...ere we see gymnastic training
generally introduced into our national elementary schools; but we shall work on, encouraged by the
conviction that energy and perseverance in a good cause seldom fail.'
W.P. Brookes, speech at the Wenlock Olympian Games, 1873

It seemed, by the late 1870s, that the southerners could not organise a contest in a capital, and the provincial clubs were brassed off. There had been a boom in the growth of northern clubs in the 1860s and 1870s, remarkable when it is remembered that although some skilled workers had Saturday afternoon off from the 1870s, and the Bank Holiday Act of 1871 had given all workers a few paid holidays per year, the weekend was not born until the 1890s, when most workers finally gained a Saturday half-day. Huddersfield Cricket and Athletics Club was established in 1865, Burnley Cricket and Football Club two years later, Stoke Victoria Athletic Club in 1868, and Southport AS Sports in 1869. The management of these clubs' competitive meetings varied, but Huddersfield and Southport in particular were considered highly efficient.

The 1870s proliferation of clubs made consolidation as necessary here as in the south, to regulate the rules and standards for competition and to combat unfair practices. On Saturday 14 June 1879 10 representatives of northern clubs met at the Prince of Wales Hotel, Southport and formed the Northern Counties Amateur Athletic Association, though they had been holding their own regional competition for over a decade. Among the observations about 'unsportsmanlike conduct' and 'abuses', they expressed the need for 'the provinces to look after their own interests in the matter of a Championship meeting', with unfavourable reflections on past AAC meetings at Lillie Bridge, London.

The following year, 1880, the Midland Counties Amateur Athletic Association was formed for similar reasons. Unfortunately, Brookes was in no position to take a lead, as the Wenlock Olympian Society hit financial problems now. Brookes seems consciously to have withdrawn, not mentioning the developments in his speeches at Wenlock, nor inserting relevant material into the Minute Books of the Society. He might have been feeling his age, and glad to let younger men take the movement forward, particularly when he had such a capable and reliable conduit, for example, as Joseph Hubbard in Birmingham.

Besides the championship frustrations, differences between the regional organisations and the AAC in the nuances of the word 'amateur' had become apparent. To the northern and midland Associations, the word referred to an athlete not competing for monetary prizes, and to keeping gambling and malpractice out of track and field sports. As at Wenlock, it implied playing clean. To the AAC, 'amateur' had all the class connotations of the high Victorian age, when there was a place for everything and everything should be in its place including the gentleman and players. In cricket (in which sport a gentlemen's team had been playing a professionals' since 1806, revived in 1819, and perpetuated until 1962) it was common for amateurs and professionals of the same team to use separate doors to enter the pavilion, separate facilities, and separate gates on to the field.

North and south seemed remote from consensus, yet a common desire was keeping money out of athletics, a sentiment with which three young men from Oxford University concurred. Recognising that the formation of the Northern and the Midland Associations posed threats to the AAC and to metropolitan control of athletics, Clement Jackson (a don, 33), Bernhard Wise (President of the University Athletics Club, 21) and Montague Shearman (a recent graduate reading for the bar and running competitively in London, 22) took charge of the situation. They felt (like Brookes) that athletics should be open to anyone so long as they did not compete for money. They spotted a solution and summoned a meeting at the Randolph Hotel, Oxford on 24 April 1880.

With finesse worthy of bridge club, they pacified the northern and midland delegates with the offer of a rotational annual championship, kept the LAC and the Waddells happy by proposing that the championship take place in the summer and by the inclusion of two events that they particularly wanted, and got Chambers and the AAC on board by making it clear that any rival championship would be boycotted by all other parties, and that when the championship was held in the south, the venue would be Lillie Bridge. However, they insisted that the AAC's mechanics' clause be dropped. Chambers conceded and offered to hand over the AAC's national trophies to the new organisation. With that, the Amateur Athletic Association was formed.

The first championships were held in the rain three months later, but those at Birmingham in 1881 were a great success, drawing crowds of 12,000 who saw two Americans, E.E. Merrill and Lawrence 'Lon' Myers challenge Britain's best. Thus the first international meeting went to the AAA and not to the NOA. As Shearman later recalled of the 1881 meeting that returned a profit of £325, 'it put us in funds and it made the country and the world at large respect us for the way in which we conducted our championship Meeting, and from that time until now I do not think we have ever gone one step backwards.'

Brookes's attempts to perpetuate the moribund NOA now in the light of the success of the AAA assume pathos. In February 1882, Brookes addressed a meeting of Hadley Athletic Society, near Wellington, who were considering holding their next athletic meeting in conjunction with the NOA (not the other way round). He swayed his audience, and the Games were staged in July 1883. At those Games, Brookes asked rhetorically of his work for physical education 'What chance is there of its success considering how long you have been working for it, and how little you have been able to accomplish.' Well, I do not despair, for I often think of a remark of [Daniel] O'Connell's that 'There are but two classes in the world; one to hammer, and the other to be hammered at.' So I shall hammer on in the belief that others will succeed me who will strike with more effect, and that what is right in itself and good for the nation will ultimately prevail.' To quote the late Irish Nationalist leader at the height of the Home Rule debate illustrates the heat of Brookes's passion for PE for children.

In September 1882, Brookes went to Ludlow, as he had to Hadley, to suggest that the town host a sixth NOA Games. Brookes misjudged the meeting and dwelt more on his desire for PE to be introduced into schools and on the pedigree and aims of the NOA than on the practicalities. After he spoke, the question of funding, particularly of fitting up the ground and purchasing the prizes was immediately raised, and a figure of £500 or £600 was estimated. Brookes confirmed that the NOA had no funds with which to help. In the light of this, Arthur Salwey, an influential local landowner, proposed that Ludlow should not offer to host the NOA Games. Salwey was seconded by H.T. Weyman, and the proposal was carried. For Brookes, it must have been a long journey home.

The following year, in 1883, Brookes approached the 50-year-old British army hero, moderniser of the infantry drill book, and Gilbert and Sullivan's 'model of the modern Major-General', Sir Garnet Wolseley, about supporting the NOA, probably by patronage. Wolseley declined, writing that his responsibilities prevented him from taking 'any active part in your association which has done so much in furtherance of the physical education of the people.'

After the death of old supporters (Francis Moreton of the Talbot died in 1879), rejection by those from whom he hoped for help, no movement on PE in schools, no word from the Greeks, and a triumphant AAA, Brookes was at a low ebb. Sport was steaming ahead, yet he seemed becalmed. What had been said of the Shropshire Coalfield in 1871, which had seen others all over the country overtake it, using methods first tried there, now seemed true of his Society. 'Shropshire was somewhat in the position of a man who, while conscious that his own best days were past, regarded with pride the race of giant sons which had grown up around him'. So, for the first time, in 1884, Brookes gave in, and the Wenlock Olympian Games programme for 3 June announced that the Games would be held 'under AAA rules'. Even this admission of surrender did not prevent Brookes from asking Shrewsbury, in 1886, to become the British base for the NOA, an offer that it declined.

Contemporaneous with these disappointments were significant problems with his Wenlock Olympian Games over the decade 1876–86. Although the Linden Field reached its peak of development in 1883, there was nothing that Brookes could do about the weather. It poured on the 1877 Shrewsbury NOA Games – the year that American novelist Henry James visited the Gaskells at the Abbey, Much Wenlock, and described it as 'too brutally pluvial. This is a rather big thorn on the Wenlock rose, which, however, on my first day, bloomed irreproachably'.

In 1878 the Wenlock Games day was 'simply wretched', and the following year it rained until 11am, deterring many spectators. To add to the soggy mood, Brookes was disappointed when, at the amateur games in the autumn of 1878, 'an act of poaching' was committed on the ground, which, as a borough magistrate, he assured his audience would be fully investigated. In 1881 it again rained all morning, and in 1882 there were showers. The newspaper reporter observed that 'the Wenlock Games had become associated with wet weather.' No wonder that in 1884 it was noted with acclaim that the day was 'beautifully fine'.

Unfortunately, over the 20-year period from 1874, there were only about half a dozen good summers. What made for poor returns for WOS, made for financial disaster for local farmers, particularly those in the Wheatlands. Tenant farmers laying out capital every year for fertiliser, labour, and seed corn, only to have the crop ruined the following summer, began to give up the fight and leave their farms, in turn, leaving landowners with reduced incomes. Wheat imports, particularly from the mid-west of the newly-United States began to pour in through Liverpool docks, driving down prices for UK corn, and ruining those tenant farmers that had managed to harvest a crop and were hoping for a high price owing to scarcity.

Brookes depended upon the local farmers and landowners to support the Society. The apparently unassailable landowners were now hit hard, despite endeavouring to keep up appearances. Deer parks were left unstocked, jewels and paintings taken to sale rooms, and wine cellars auctioned. The larger local farmers, Brookes's other primary supporters, watched crops fail and livestock die while frozen meat from Australia began to arrive in new refrigerated ships. As a result, WOS finances were hard hit. In 1875 there was a shortfall of Receipts against Expenditure of £5, but in 1876 it amounted to £55 (subscriptions had fallen from £82 in 1873 to £67 in 1876). By the end of 1877, although the Games of that year had broken even, the Society was carrying over £82 debt. This grew the following year to £127 (subscriptions had fallen to under £60). In 1879 the *Wenlock and Ludlow Express* was deploring the lack of pecuniary help for the Society and asking for a good turn-out at the Games to ease the situation.

By 1880, the Wenlock Olympian Society's debts were £130 and no Pentathlon was contended for at the Games, to save the cost of the Hunt & Roskell medal. The doctor's remedy was a bazaar at the Society's Reading Room on 11 and 12 October 1880. Patronage was secured not only from local gentlemen, but from their wives, who again donated an impressive array of items. Four stalls were set up among the book cases and displays of curiosities and fossils in the Reading Room. Adeline Brookes and her cousin Edith, Mrs E. Wadlow, F.B. Harrison and Mrs R.T. Davies of Walton Grange worked hard and realised £88 which, with a £1 donation from the Earl of Shaftesbury, went some way to curing the ailing patient.

In 1881, despite an estimated attendance at the Wenlock Games of 3,000–4,000, the newspapers discerned 'a considerable falling off of attendance', which it attributed to 'the distress which has so long prevailed in the districts whence so many patrons of the sports are usually drawn'. In contrast to the burgeoning go-ahead cities, mines, steelworks and manufacturing towns, the agricultural regions of Britain appeared beleaguered. The landowners' power was further diluted by the third Reform Act in 1884 by which most working class men were finally given the vote. Many young people now exchanged muddy fields for gilded streets.

At the pre-Games tree-planting (to Charles Milnes Gaskell, his daughter Evelyn and Ralph B. Benson) in 1882, Brookes struck a reflective note. He hoped that the 'Wellingtonias Gigantea' and the 'Picea Nordmanniana' would flourish and be friends of the games 'which though not so important in their scope as I could wish them to be, will nevertheless, I trust, rival in duration those of ancient Greece'. At these Games, almost symbolically, occurred the only serious injury to a horse, which appears to have been fatally staked in the brisket jumping one of the hurdles in the tilting competition. The same year, as Brookes would have noted dolefully, the British army suffered defeat at the hands of the Boers in the Transvaal, southern Africa, in the first Boer War.

The Wenlock Olympian Games were scaled back now. Taking the Pentathlon as one event, there were 16 events in 1878, which had fallen to about a dozen – a 25 per cent fall – by 1886. The Pentathlon, put on hold in 1880, was competed for once more in 1881 and won by Fred d'Escofet, of Birmingham before it was phased out for good in 1882. There were still some notable performances. The outstanding sportsman of the 1880s was probably Edward Sandalls, second in the 120 yards hurdles and high leap in 1882, and the latter again in 1883. He won the high leap from 1884-86 inclusive (clearing 5ft 2in in 1886), was second again in 1887, and third in 1889. He went on to become a grocer in Much Wenlock, living with his Cheltenham-born wife, Lucy, at 5 Mardol Terrace.

Sandalls's high-jumping crown passed to Edwin Pritchard of Broncroft near Craven Arms. The son of a lawyer, it was the 18-year-old Pritchard (who become a carpenter) who beat Sandalls in the running high leap in 1887, and won the 'high jump' as it was called for the first time, in 1888. In 1889 he was beaten into second place by d'Escofet of BAC. Pritchard combined high jump with pole leaping (vaulting) winning that in 1886 with a vault of 9ft 2in. The following year he shared first prize in the pole leaping at 9ft 10in. He won the pole leaping again in 1888 and 1889 with another 9ft 10in leap.

Pritchard's pole-leaping bête noir was W.H. Gough, a consistent pole leaping competitor at Wenlock, winning in 1882 and 1887 and second in 1886 and 1888, described as being from a variety of different home towns. In 1882 he was 'of Shrewsbury', in 1885, of Crewe, and in 1886 of Brownsover, Rugby – all places with strong connections with the railway, which suggests his likely profession. There are references to a W.H. Gough as Superintendent of the line for Cambrian Railways Company, based at Oswestry, in 1899.

Of the youngsters coming through, a couple of Scoltock boys, sons of a bricklayer and later mason, and a dressmaker, living on the High Street, Wenlock appear prominently in the results. At the 1885 Games, George Scoltock aged eight, came third in the 120 yards boys' race, and was second the following year. His older brother William was second in the under-15s' 200 yards race in 1882 when he was 13. George went into the grocery business, as an apprentice by the age of 14, while William was, by 1891, living in the household of a Plumber and Gasfitter at Sale in Cheshire. Scoltock is still a Wenlock name today.

Cycling at the Wenlock Olympian Games was to produce some notable winners in the 1880s, including R. Chambers of Birmingham who won the three-mile and one-mile races in 1883, and the three-mile in 1884. Frank Frehock Sharpe of Wolverhampton began coming to Wenlock, aged 17 in 1886, when he too did the double. In 1888 he returned and easily won the half-mile handicap in just over one minute 56 seconds, won the mile and two-mile races too, and was placed in each of these events up to and including 1890. In 1891, he collided with C.F.G. Boyes in the mile handicap and came home a poor second.

Sharpe's 1888 clean sweep was repeated in 1889 by W.M. Robins of Dennis Park, Stourbridge, but against a 'poor field', certainly in the one-mile handicap. When Sharpe and

Robins went head to head in 1890, Sharpe won the one and two-mile handicaps, with Robins victorious in the half-mile. When he first won at Wenlock, in 1889, William Robins (or Robbins) aged 22, from Wollaston, Worcestershire, was a solicitor's clerk, a career that he went on to pursue. In 1888, Robins came second in the half-mile, one-mile and two-mile handicaps, the latter producing 'an exciting finish'. He returned to Wenlock the following year and came first at all three distances. In 1890, Robins won the half-mile, was second in the two-mile and third in the mile handicaps. Other cyclists coming through were W. Travers also of Wolverhampton, who took the one and three-mile doubles in 1892, and R. Trow of Bradmore who did the same in 1893.

Both Coventry and Wolverhampton were important centres of bicycle manufacture. In Coventry, Singers' employees formed a football club that would become Coventry City FC. In Wolverhampton, cycle racing, watched by up to 20,000 people, took place at Molineux Hotel and pleasure grounds, which later became Wolverhampton Wanderers FC's ground. Given the proximity of both to Wenlock, it is not surprising that many of the competitors came from these towns, and from Kidderminster and Birmingham. Other notable cyclists include J.T. Mein of Kidderminster, E.H. Guest of West Bromwich, and C.A. Halmer of Moseley.

Despite the Duke of Cleveland's railings, there were some accidents at Wenlock, which added to the excitement. In the 1885 games in the two-mile race, F.J. Turnbull of Bridgnorth took a fall, but fortunately suffered only the 'total collapse of his bicycle'. In 1887, in the one-mile race, an unnamed rider 'fell soon after the start through colliding with a lady who got on the track, and got his machine doubled' – the outcome for the lady is not recorded. In the 1892 mile, G.A. Henson of Edgbaston 'who was leading in this race, came to grief in the last lap, owing to a foolish fellow crossing the path. The man was knocked down, and severely bruised; fortunately Henson, although he lost the race, was able to re-mount his machine, and came in a good third.' In 1883 it was the officials who caused havoc. The two-mile race was run a lap short, owing to their error.

The outstanding tilters of this period who joined the Ainsworths and the Websters in the honours, were Tom and Charles Rudd of Chetton, near Bridgnorth and the Bishop brothers of Oxenbold. Tom, a farmer's son, of Harpsford Mill near Much Wenlock, won the flat tilting in 1888, and was second in the hurdle tilting in 1885, 1886, 1889 and 1892. He finally won the hurdle tilting in 1890. 'Trooper Rudd' also competed in one of the new equestrian events, tent-pegging, in which the rider had to skewer ground targets with a sword or lance from his speeding horse. In the 1892 Wenlock Olympian Games Tom Rudd was 'undoubtedly the best tenter', but was disqualified for not performing in his regimental uniform, a most unpopular decision. In 1893 he won another new equestrian 'very humorous' event, the Victoria Cross Race. Tom went on to become a family butcher and lived at Lower Forge, Eardington, south-west of Bridgnorth.

Charles Rudd was among Tom's closest rivals in the tilting in these years. The two might have been cousins, although Charles' parents are obscure, and he seems to have lived with an uncle and aunt at The Downs, Chetton near Bridgnorth. He competed in the flat tilting in 1881 and came joint second with Viscount Petersham. Rudd won the flat tilting in 1885 and the same year was equal second with Tom in the hurdle tilting. W. Bishop competed in the flat and hurdle tilting from 1886–84, coming second or third, but never winning. His younger brother competed in the hurdle tilting in 1895 only, and won. Viscount Petersham, Charles Stanhope (1844–1917) was a bright light for Brookes in 1881, and the antithesis of snobbery. In his mid-thirties and a great horseman, having served in the Earl of Chester's Yeomanry, Petersham, of Elvaston Castle, Derby and Gawsworth Hall, Macclesfield, Cheshire, 'entered the lists to try his skill against the veteran tilters of Wenlock'. Stanhope had served in Malta, where he had learnt to play polo, so probably fancied his chances, but William Ainsworth of Bourton was too good for him.

Brookes asked Petersham (a friend of agriculturalist T.H. Thursfield of Barrow) to be President the following year. By then, he had inherited from his father, and become eighth Earl of Harrington. In a warm speech, Harrington said how pleased he was to be present, and he wished landlords would take part with their tenants, especially at a time when 'certain unprincipled men' were trying to stir up inter-class animosity. When he had first come to Wenlock, 'he was struck with the presence therein of a very remarkable boy…who seemed to be always in the midst of any mischief or fun that was going on…Dr Brookes'.

Harrington was the only President of the Games who also participated. In 1882 he had another go at the flat tilting. Unfortunately, he did not manage to take a ring, and was beaten by Charles Tully of Martley. Lady Harrington crowned William Ainsworth victor in the hurdle tilting for a second year. After champagne had been passed round in the Forester Cup, Harrington joined Ainsworth in a demonstration of tent-pegging for the crowd. In 1883, he sent a prize for the flat tilting. Harrington kept thereafter to polo, invented papier mâché goalposts, was President of the County Polo Association and founded the Polo Pony Stud Book. Another notable President, in 1887, was Capt. James Foster, whose home was Apley Park, Bridgnorth, later P.G. Wodehouse's inspiration for Blandings Castle.

Harrington's glamorous support was welcome in the difficult 1880s. In 1888, the decorations in the town 'were by no means so profuse as in former years', but those between Robert Hartland's ale and porter warehouse and Cecil Tart's butcher shop opposite (in Sheinton Street) were admired and 'considerably enhanced by the charming display of plants upon the ledge of Mr Hartland's shop front.' The decorations were also noted at the Plough Inn (William Roberts) and at the Raven Hotel. In 1889, the town decorations were 'profuse and pleasing', decorations by Hartland (a magnificent triumphal arch by the railway station) and Tart were again noted. Of the grounds themselves the newspaper reported that 'they have now reached a degree of perfection seldom, if ever, found in public grounds connected with provincial towns.'

In 1889, two turnstiles, for 6d and 13d were installed at the entrance to Linden Walk, after discussion at a meeting of the Society in May. Thomas Cooke proposed the motion and was seconded by Edward Deakin, proprietor of the Talbot. It was put to a vote (there were 18 on the committee) and carried by a majority of seven. It is highly unlikely that Brookes would have supported such a move. It is surely his voice that comes through in Lawley's report after the Games of 1889 when it was noted that the extra made on the gate that year over the last was £2 18s 3d, 'so that the turnstiles, which cost £4 had really resulted in a loss'.

To add insult to financial injury, Wenlock Borough was hard hit by the Reform Act of 1884. Besides extending the franchise, this Act took Parliamentary seats away from many rural constituencies and gave them to the new urban areas. Wenlock had been one of the first boroughs permitted to send a Member up to the House of Commons in 1468, but now it was stripped of its MP altogether and the county divided into North and South Shropshire instead. Brookes seemed almost personally affronted. Planting a Wellingtonia in September 1885 in memory of Lord Wenlock, whose ancestors had secured from Edward IV the borough's representation 420 years before, Brookes said 'We regard this treatment as a violation of our rights.' He returned to the theme at the planting of a tree to mark the silver wedding of the Prince and Princess of Wales (the latter described as being of 'almost matchless beauty') in March 1887. Brookes believed that instead of losing their MP, the neighbouring districts of Buildwas, Leighton, Cressage, Harley, Kenley and Preen should have been added to Wenlock, to enlarge the constituency.

Over this period, Brookes was increasingly frustrated at not making ground with his campaign for PE in schools. In 1878, after lunch as the rain poured down outside, Brookes said 'I cannot understand why' the Education Department had ignored the Society's petitions, displaying 'indifference to that physical development which contributes so much to health and strength as well as to inclination and aptitude for labour'. The following year, 'I am disappointed but not disheartened…I cannot believe that the Committee of Council disapprove of physical education.' The debate over the Education Act was becoming so cumbersome that he believed that it would soon need 'pruning', at which point, PE might be 'engrafted'. Brookes used humour to make his point. 'Would you have the qualifications for a farm labourer, and the passport to the ranks of the army, the navy, the merchant and civil services consist of a smattering of geography and the ability to make a bad drawing of an old teapot?' Just as the *Illustrated Times* had suggested that the three Rs have a G added to them – Gymnastics, Brookes called for another three Rs, 'running, riding and wrestling', not literally of course, but they 'represented what was aspired to'.

At the 1880 Wenlock Olympian Games he stepped up the emotions by referring to the 'indifference' of the governments of both hues, and the year after he went further still, attacking the 'short-sighted system of education which neglects that early bodily training which is so essential to the welfare of the individual'. He described the present education system as 'injurious to the country, and so unjust to the children of the working classes'. In 1883, at the Hadley (and last) NOA Games Brookes had vowed to hammer on. A couple of months later, his frustration became clearer still, at the St George's Amateur Sports day. 'Unfortunately, the Committee of Council on Education seem neither to take any interest in the bodily development of the young, nor to recognize the truth that the collective strength of a nation depends on the strength of its individual citizens'.

Just as he had at Birmingham in 1867, Brookes complained that tax payers were not getting good value from the present school system which under-exercised the body, and over-taxed the brain, resulting in 'pumpkin heads upon pigmy bodies…I consider that payment for results acts as a temptation to teachers to overwork the brains of the children…Like a blight on a beautiful flower just beginning to unfold itself, the relentless strain upon the minds of our young school children robs them not only of the sunshine of the morning of life, but too often of life itself'. The children were 'our young martyrs of education'.

A few days before the 1884 Wenlock Olympian Games, Brookes broke his arm, so did not join the procession. Instead, it stopped outside 7 Wilmore Street, and Brookes addressed it from the steps of his home, his arm in a sling. 'Of the seed which you have sown of…physical education, much, I regret to say, has fallen upon stony ground, and much, without effect, upon the half cultivated soil of the Education Department, a soil choked with the weeds of official prejudice, so difficult to eradicate, and producing only one kind of crop where others are required…I am glad, however, to observe that under the powerful and fertilizing influence of public opinion, and through the earnest and able advocacy of several distinguished persons…[including] Mr Edwin Chadwick…some of the seed is beginning to germinate, and, if the harvest is slow in ripening, as often happens with truth, you may rest assured that it will come to maturity and produce fruit abundantly.'

The reference to Edwin Chadwick, the social reformer more usually linked with the Poor Law and water and sanitation for inner-cities, came four months after their first correspondence. It appears that Brookes sent Chadwick information about the Wenlock Games and his campaign for PE in elementary schools. Chadwick derived 'particular pleasure' from learning of Brookes's work 'in the cause of physical and intellectual improvement of the population, of whom and whose proceedings…it so happens that I had never heard before.' This is a vivid reminder of the difficulty of coming into productive contact with others in the same field at this time. R.A. Slaney had worked with Chadwick drafting the report of the Health of Towns Commission in 1843–44, which ultimately led to the 1848 Public Health Act. Despite differences in their methods, Slaney found Chadwick 'an able' and 'humane' man whose 'excellent' Sanitary Report of 1842 had convinced many of the need for 'remedies'. Brookes had been a disciple of Slaney, yet only now were Chadwick and Brookes connected.

Chadwick's response to Brookes was to forward papers of his own, to draw his attention to a paper by Dr Richardson, and to pledge efforts 'to make a push' in the direction Brookes proposed. In a postscript, Chadwick asked whether 'in your neighbourhood you have had any examples of satisfactory physical training in the schools'. Brookes immediately forwarded the statistics from the National School at Much Wenlock, which Chadwick acknowledged 'to be very valuable for quotation'.

In 1883, the year before this exchange with Chadwick, Brookes had made a similar approach to Lyon Playfair, a Liberal politician known to Lord John Manners (President of the Wenlock Olympian Games that year) as his predecessor as Postmaster General in 1873–74. Brookes had sent Playfair reports of his Olympian festivals. Playfair replied. 'I entirely agree with you that physical training in our Schools is a subject of great importance.' This was a useful admission, as Playfair was to become the vice-President of the Committee on Education for five months in 1886, but too briefly to take forward Brookes's cause. Brookes also claimed, in 1884, to have the support of Sir Francis Peake, an early exponent of the benefits of walking, and of outdoor life.

The final area of thwarted hopes in 1876-86 was in the revival of the Olympic Games in Greece, towards which Brookes worked hard over this period. Brookes's contacts with Greece had gone nowhere since the flurry of contact around the 1859 Zappas Games, mainly because of further upheavals within the young Greek state. By October 1862, King Otto, who had attended the Zappas Games, had been removed from the throne. He was replaced, in June 1863 by King George, a teenage Danish prince, brother of the Princess of Wales, the future Queen Alexandra. In 1869, the Prince and Princess of Wales visited Athens. (King George's fourth son, Andrew was the father of HRH Prince Philip, the Duke of Edinburgh.) After initial wobbles, the situation had stabilised sufficiently by 1869 for the government to announce the staging of a second Olympiad in November 1870. However, there were to be 21 different governments between 1864 and 1874, presenting challenging circumstances, to say the least, in which to organise international games.

As in 1859, the 1870 Games in Athens came a poor second to the agro-industrial competitions, receiving only six per cent of the overall budget, despite Zappas's money being used. This time, though, the ancient stadium near Athens was excavated (as Zappas had wished), so the spectators could at least see. Serious work was done by the sub-committee for the Games, who paid the travel expenses of poorer athletes, and covered the costs of their uniforms and accommodation in Athens. About 40 athletes of all classes took part. The programme was not as elaborate as Wenlock's at this time, but track and field and gymnastic contests were included, and they attracted over 30,000 spectators – a crowd that outnumbered almost any of the IOC's Olympic Games held from 1900 until 1920. They were an astonishing popular success, and King George attended and crowned the victors with olive.

Further Games were held in 1875 in Athens, but by now Greece, like Britain was adversely affected by the class-related issues of the amateur/professional debate, with complaints that in 1870 a butcher, stone cutter and manual labourer had won their competitions. It was deplored by some that more well-educated youths had not taken part. Thus the 1875 Games lasted two and a half hours, only 24 athletes took part, royalty did not attend, the track was uneven and the seating poor. After this fiasco, an anti-athletic circle came to prominence in Greek political life, holding back progress for years. It believed that war, dependent now on mechanical weapons instead of physical strength, no longer required high levels of fitness in young men. Brookes was to call this 'A mistaken notion' in July 1891 in the *Shrewsbury Chronicle*. 'Warlike weapons require men to both carry and use them...It...will not be an easy matter to induce armies, however brave, to stand still and be shot down by thousands'.

In 1877, to mark 40 years of Queen Victoria's reign, Brookes, encouraged by the 1870 and 1875 Athens Games, renewed contact with the Greeks through His Excellency Joannes Gennadius, the Greek Chargé d'Affaires in London (plate 22). (Gennadius was later to found the famous library that bears his family name in Athens.) Through Gennadius, Brookes secured a beautiful silver cup for the Shrewsbury NOA Games in 1877, engraved 'George I King of the Hellenes' for 'the man of the Pentathlon' (plate 21). It was won by law student John G. Wylie, who played for Shrewsbury Wanderers FC and the following year scored for England in a friendly against Scotland.

Brookes's attempts to make further progress were unsuccessful. Indeed, in Greece there were no further national Games, despite hopes that some might take place in October 1888. King George's sons sustained their support attending displays by the Panhellenic Gymnastic Society in May 1891 and 1893, the former just a few months after Crown Prince Constantine, heir to the throne, announced a resumption of the Greek Olympic series from 1892. Once again, though, political turmoil thwarted the plans, and Athens's renovated stadium remained redundant until the first IOC Olympic Games were staged there in 1896, and the intercalatory Games (between Olympic Games) in 1906.

It is disappointing that Greece was held back now, because contemporaneously, the possibility of holding international athletic meetings was increasing. The Germans had for decades staged a quinquennial Turnfest featuring gymnastic displays and individual events. These had become international and had grown until in July 1880, 18,000–20,000 competitors gathered in Frankfurt. Joseph Hubbard, the regular Wenlock judge took 10 of his BAC athletes including Fred d'Escofet. Hubbard demonstrated boxing at Frankfurt, his gloves described as 'a novelty' to the Germans. Brookes's other friend, Ernst Ravenstein of the GGS acted as tour guide, chaperone and translator to the British athletes in Germany.

This must have given Brookes renewed hope that his dream of international Olympic Games in Greece was a real possibility. Some time in 1880, apparently through the medium of Gennadius (who was made an Honorary Member of WOS in November) Brookes made contact with Socrates A. Parasyrakes, to try to agitate in the Greek press for his international Olympic Games in Athens. Parasyrakes, editor of the *Panhellenic Annual*, was receptive to the idea, though Gennadius warned that 'the present troubled and critical circumstances of the kingdom' made it impossible.

On 21 January 1881, at the Society's annual meeting, Brookes reported that 'Your committee has suggested the holding of an International Olympian Festival at Athens, when the present critical state of affairs in Greece is ended, as her friends earnestly hope it will be, speedily and satisfactorily. The proposal has been favourably received by Greeks resident in England, and will, no doubt, be cordially responded to by...the principal Athletics Societies of Great Britain'. Many of their members would, he felt, welcome an opportunity to visit Greece, meet the Greek people, and see 'the interesting and important archaeological discoveries recently made at a great cost, by [Curtius for] the German Government and nation.'

In June 1881, an article initialled SAP (Parasyrakes) appeared in the Greek Newspaper *Clio*. It gave a detailed account of the Wenlock Olympian Games, of Brookes's foundation of them, and of the £10 prize for the Zappas Games in 1859. 'Dr Brookes, this enthusiastic Philhelline, is endeavouring to organize an International Olympian Festival, to be held in Athens, from which much good will arise in many respects, and we have no doubt that the Greek Government will give every facility for its realization.' This was the first time that the ambition to stage an international athletics festival in Greece, emanating from abroad, had appeared in print in Greece. However, Parasyrakes's optimism was premature. Greece was pre-occupied with making territorial gains from the settlement of the Russo-Turkish War (1877–78). That year, after the Conference of Constantinople, Greece expanded her territory to include the plain of Thessaly, to the north of the Peloponnese.

After the 1883 Wenlock Games, with the Linden Field at its loveliest, Brookes forwarded on 5 October an account of the events to Gennadius, hoping to sustain momentum. Gennadius was now based in Vienna, another factor that conspired to thwart Brookes's ambitions. Gennadius wrote courteously that he fully appreciated Brookes's objective of getting athletic sports into schools and added that 'as a Greek I can but feel indebted to you that you combine with this idea the project of a revival of the Olympic games. I heartily hope and wish for the realization of your double object.' There was little more to be done for now.

Therefore, by 1885, with so many of his life's objectives thwarted, Brookes was feeling his age. In 1881, he had taken on a partner in his medical practice, Dr Allan Mackenzie, so that he could think about retirement, which would follow in 1891. The same year, his brother-in-law in London, Thomas Wilkinson died, and Brookes was at Hackney old church for his burial, to support his sister Anne. The sense of belonging to a passing generation was compounded in 1885 by the death of his wife Jane who had endured with him their family tragedies and humiliation, and who had contributed so much to his endeavours, both financially and practically through letter-writing and bazaar organisation. The precious churchyard plot that he could see from his windows now enfolded his wife, two daughters and two sons. His only surviving daughter, Adeline remained with her father, only marrying (aged 62) George Fyfe, a doctor formerly of Wellington, in June 1901, after Brookes's death.

Early 1886, then, probably represents the lowest point of Brookes's indomitable spirits. In mourning, he would not be able to attend his own Games. The Wenlock Olympian Society's meeting in May 1886 was chaired by George Meredith of the Grange, Much Wenlock, a new member of the committee. Meredith moved to Much Wenlock in 1882, and remained on the committee until the family left, after Brookes's death. Brookes must have welcomed the support of this erudite, cultured gentleman and his wife, the daughter of surgeon Walter Scott.

Meredith was the father of the future novelist Mary Webb (1881–1927) whose works (*Gone to Earth, Seven for a Secret* etc), portray Shropshire life in market town and countryside at precisely this time. In *Seven for a Secret*, we meet a malevolent Elmer. In *Gone to Earth*, Webb's male protagonists, Reddin and Marston seem to reflect the two elements of muscular Christianity, the former all brute physicality, the latter moral rectitude and gentleness. The heroine, Hazel Woodus's untutored femininity flutters between the two. In 1912, Mary was to marry Henry Webb, a nephew of the Channel-swimmer, Matthew Webb.

Despite Brookes's frustration, with hindsight, his importance to sport at this time is clear. From 1871 until 1882 (the year the BAC resolved to restrict its activities to gymnastics alone), Joseph Hubbard, a driving force in sport in Birmingham had acted as handicapper of the races at Wenlock. He was succeeded in his Wenlock role in 1883 by Harry M. Oliver, editor and part-owner of *Midland Athlete* magazine, who assisted Brookes until 1887. Oliver was Secretary of Moseley Harriers athletic club, Birmingham (founded *c.*1874), and an important early scout for talent in the West Midlands at this date, as has been seen from his recruitment of Snook at Wenlock. Oliver, like Snook, fell from grace after he was convicted of embezzlement and imprisoned for two months. He had been 'borrowing' funds from the bank that employed him to produce his magazine, then repaying the sum before the month-end, so evading detection. Within three years Moseley Harriers had disintegrated. From 1888, Brookes turned to Oliver's rival W. W. Alexander, who handicapped the runners at Wenlock until at least the mid-1890s and became the leading figure in midlands athletics.

Alexander was for over 45 years, from 1882, Secretary of Birchfield Harriers of Birmingham, (founded in 1876). The club would supply British competitors at every Olympic Games (bar 1932) from London 1908 to the present day. Like Oliver, Alexander saw his role at Wenlock as an opportunity to buy up youngsters by offering to pay them to come to his club, contrary to a strict interpretation of amateurism. Nevertheless, so important was Alexander's contribution to athletics in Birmingham (including encouraging women to train and compete at this early stage) that when Birchfield bought its 12-acre ground in 1926, it was named after him. The club's new stadium built in 1975 (updated with £12.25 million from 2010) was called Alexander Stadium in his memory. Birchfield Harriers remains one of the most important athletic clubs in Britain today, its recent athletes include Denise Lewis, Ashia Hanson, Mark Lewis-Francis, Kelly Sotherton, Du'aine Ladejo and paralympian Mickey Bushell.

Wenlock was therefore an important nexus for leading figures who were laying down the foundations of athletics in the West Midlands, the North West and London. To Brookes, though, appearances were very different in 1886. He had had the brush off from Gennadius and from Wolseley in June and July 1886, and his meeting in April to persuade Shrewsbury to take up the NOA had produced nothing. The Wenlock Games on 16 June attracted no competitors from beyond Birmingham or Leamington. There were just nine events, plus two children's races. The only consolation came from an appreciation of his efforts by Stanley Leighton, the MP for Oswestry, and President that year. Leighton had for many years espoused the cause of education in the House of Commons and was therefore a knowledgeable commentator.

Leighton assured his listeners that their absent friend was 'proving by experiment what can be done, what ought to be done, and what will be done in making our English system of education a true development of the human faculties…All reform begins with the enthusiasm of some few individuals'. Leighton knew well the workings of governments. Reforming individuals had to battle with states, and within that, with departments. 'The Education Department might be young, but it has got into grooves, and Dr Brookes is trying to get it out of one of its grooves.'

Leighton confirmed that there had been a number of deaths in elementary schools attributed to 'overpressure'. The Department had 'as usual, resisted enquiry as long as it was possible to do so'. At length, however, the medical profession 'proved that nervousness, brain diseases, headaches, and failing eyesight are becoming chronic in our elementary schools. The state-educationists are in fact conferring knowledge at the expense of health. Against this state of things Dr Brookes had long ago raised his voice. He was right all the time, but people, especially State departments, would not pay attention to him'.

Leighton's insightful and considered appraisal must have been extremely welcome, but Brookes longed for real results not lip-service. Now some promise of that finally came. In 1886 the National Physical Recreation Society was established under the Presidency of Herbert Gladstone MP, son of the Liberal Prime Minister, William Gladstone, himself a keen exponent of physical exercise. The Prime Minister's favourite pastime at his Hawarden estate in Flintshire, North Wales, was to wield an axe in the woodland, his study housing an impressive collection.

The founding committee of the NPRS promised real hope for PE in schools, having several ingredients for success besides the ear of the Prime Minister; popular sportsmanship in the form of its Treasurer Arthur F. Kinnaird, who was to play in nine of the first 11 FA Cup Finals, was President of the Football Association for 33 years, and a director of Barclays Bank; military clout in Col George Onslow, Her Majesty's Inspector of Military Gymnasia; dash and popularity in Lord Charles Beresford, of the Prince of Wales's Marlborough House set, the original John Bull of popular imagery, a naval commander and MP, known generally as 'Charlie B' who was usually accompanied by his British bulldog; sporting ability in the Hon T.H.W. Pelham a cricketer and brother of the record-holding mile runner; and rowing backbone in T.C. Edwards-Moss, the Conservative MP for Widnes, former President of Oxford University Boat Club and winner of the Diamond Challenge Sculls at Henley. The Secretary was Alec Alexander, whom Brookes had known as apprentice to John Hulley at Liverpool Gymnasium, of which Alexander was now Director.

The stated objective of the NPRS was 'the Promotion of Physical Recreation amongst the Working Classes', which could have been lifted from the founding objectives of WOS 36 years before. Also lifted from the NOA was its motto, as Alec Alexander recalled. 'Dr Lyttelton asked me if I could remember anything suitable. Whereupon I quoted Juvenal's maxim, '*Civium vires civitatis vis*' – 'The strength of the citizen is the strength of the State.' This was agreed to amidst applause, and I rose in the estimation of the meeting.' On 1 September 1886, Alexander wrote to Brookes to inform him that at Monday's meeting, with Herbert Gladstone in the chair, 'you were unanimously elected a Member of our Council. Knowing your warm interest and great work in all that pertains to the health and strength of our people, I hope to hear from you soon accepting this office.' Brookes was on his way again, but this time with influential political support, a metropolitan presence, public profile, and youth on his side.

The NPRS held festivals and displays nationwide to popularise PE. Brookes found an outlet in the Journal of the Society, writing an article on 'National disaster, the penalty for National Degeneracy' in March 1888, and another on tilting that May. Of much greater benefit were the opportunities for communication with influential men of shared aims. Lord Beresford became President of WOS in both 1888 and 1889. Beresford failed to be present at either meeting, but he had warned Brookes that his commitments meant he was unlikely to be there. In June 1889, this might have been just as well, as Beresford was, at precisely that time, involved in a scandal surrounding his affair with Daisy Brooke, future Countess of Warwick. The affair had just broken and was becoming public gossip, after Daisy had threatened Beresford's wife.

Brookes and Beresford were to sustain a warm correspondence from 1888 until the end of Brookes's life. In May 1888 Beresford regretted his enforced absence from the Whit Tuesday Wenlock 'tournament', but wrote of his certainty of the 'benefits of exercise'. He had put down a motion in Parliament for the provision by County Councils of a gymnasium for every 100,000 inhabitants. 'There is no doubt that physical education is as necessary as mental & as essential for the well being of body & mind.' A couple of days later, Beresford wrote from his 100 Eaton Square address having forgotten to add, poignantly, 'how necessary I think it is that swimming should be included…for not only may that knowledge be the means of saving one's own life, but also…that of saving the life of another'.

In September 1888, after Brookes had again asked him to be President in 1889, Beresford accepted, 'as I should so much like to help one who has done so much for the object we all have in view meaning the manliness and health of our people by means of physical exercises.' The Prince of Wales, with whom Beresford had toured India in 1875–76, began himself an affair with Daisy in 1889. Queen Victoria took a very dim view of the Prince's Marlborough Set as being too 'fast', so perhaps it was fitting that the tree planted for Beresford on Brookes's 80th birthday, 13 August 1889, a 'Picea Nobilis Glauca' (*Abies procera* Glauca), 'the noble sea-green Picea', was dug in between the Queen's Jubilee oak and that of her son.

Beresford's charm is evident in his correspondence with Brookes. Two of his replies were written from HMS *Undaunted*, at Malta and Alexandria, expressing thanks 'for your letter and also for thinking of me though so far away', and his desire to go to Wenlock 'and see myself all you have done'. He forwarded his photograph on request, which was added to the Society's minute books, and he was made an honorary member in February 1891. After Brookes had described Beresford's tree in his speech at the planting ceremony, as 'representing the noble character and profession of his Lordship…the emblem of a service which is ever ready, resolute, and strong enough to defend our Sovereign', Beresford wrote to 'thank you most warmly for the far too flattering remarks you made…If in after years I can do as much for my country as you have locally for Wenlock I shall die a very happy man.' Dr Brookes must have swelled as Daisy Brooke had swooned.

Having the Navy with its requirements for fit young men now in his camp, Brookes also ensured that he had the Army covered. In 1888, he renewed his correspondence with Sir Garnet, now Lord Wolseley, who similarly sent thanks for reports of the Wenlock Olympian Games. Brookes wrote to compliment Wolseley on an address that he gave at Oxford in May 1889. In his reply, Wolseley a supporter of the NPRS, sincerely trusted that 'the time may soon arrive when the physical education of the young becomes accepted as a national necessity'. Wolseley too had a tree planted in his honour in June 1892, a 'Picea Nobilis', was made an honorary member of the Society in February 1891, and forwarded his photograph for the Minute book.

Herbert Gladstone made slower progress with the NPRS than Brookes would have liked. Time was not on Brookes's side, after all. In 1890, Brookes sent Gladstone, too, the report of the Wenlock Olympian Games. Gladstone confirmed that he believed the cause of both the WOS and NPRS to be 'of national importance, & I sincerely hope that before long the subject may be taken up & dealt with by the Govt in a practical manner.' He wrote with similar thanks the year after, but his postscript was less formal. 'My father I am glad to say is practically well again'. It was another two years, though, before he felt able to reassure Brookes, in a letter marked 'Private', that 'Physical Education is bound to come – the sooner the better. Whether soon or late, you at any rate will have been one of its most vigorous pioneers...My Father is friendly to a proposal I ventured to make to him for a Royal Commn. to examine into the physical condition of the nation with a view to legislation & administrative action...Money is the obstacle – but I am not without hope that an effective step may be taken next year. At any rate any influence I may have shall all go strongly in that direction.'

Of most practical help, though, unquestionably in the drive to get PE made compulsory in elementary schools, was Reginald Brabazon, the 12th Earl of Meath (1841–1929) a prominent Conservative member of the House of Lords, and President of the NPRS who was finally to steer a bill to that effect through the upper House of Parliament. Meath, besides owning 14,500 acres in Ireland, owned nearly 700 acres at Eaton Court, near Leominster in Herefordshire, south of Shropshire. He had abandoned a diplomatic career to devote himself to 'the consideration of social problems and the relief of human suffering.'

In 1887, Meath edited a paper 'Prosperity or Pauperism?' about the dwindling health of city populations in the *Journal of the Royal Society for the Promotion of Health*. He called for the provision of gymnasia at schools and believed that 'Physical and intellectual education should go hand in hand.' He quoted Alexander of the Liverpool Gymnasium, and Brookes's figures from Much Wenlock School to drive home his arguments. The same paper included a piece by Edwin Chadwick who called for a half-day for schooling and a half-day for exercise. Prominent figures in the cause of public health were finally coalescing into a movement destined to bring about real change.

Meath corresponded with Brookes throughout the final push to legislation. In July 1888, he wrote to Brookes beginning 'You know how thoroughly I agree with you in regard to the necessity of introducing Physical Education into our Elementary schools', but he feared, correctly, that 'the Education Bill is doomed for this year...I hope we may get a better one next year.' True to his word, he tabled a motion in the Lords in favour of PE in May 1889, was trying to bring pressure on MPs in November 1890, and re-introduced a bill for the promotion of PE in elementary schools into the House of Lords in February 1891, which got a second reading in June. He turned to Brookes each time to 'please whip up any Peers to support me whom you may know to be in favour of some such measure'. It must have been a relief for Brookes, for once, not to be initiating efforts, but instead to be playing a supporting role.

Recognising Meath's dedication, Brookes made him an honorary member of the Society in February 1891. Yet the Earl of Meath seems to be the one glaring omission from the Linden Field arboretum, no tree having been planted in his honour. The *North American Review* of mid-1891 carried an article by Meath, in which Brookes's results at Much Wenlock School were again quoted. The article also mentioned the 14 rules regarding PE in national schools that Brookes had drawn up and proposed at the meeting of the NPRS, chaired by Meath, at Northumberland Chambers, Charing Cross on 17 July 1890. Wishing to give the legislators no wriggle room, Brookes made concrete suggestions for the requirements of PE in schools, including one half hour every day 'not too soon after a meal' for bodily training, practical suggestions of the precise exercises suitable for boys and for girls of differing ages, the exemption of children considered 'by Medical men too weak', suggestions for funding the apparatus, measuring the pupils to plot progress, and that schoolmasters or mistresses be instructed in Training Colleges to teach suitable PE.

In 1891, Meath's efforts were again unsuccessful, but in September 1892 he was again rallying Brookes to work on the Peers and MPs when he had 'another fling at the officials in regard to physical training when Parliament meets'. Meath's only caveat was, 'If God spares me', a sentiment with which Brookes must heartily have concurred. The news for which Brookes had worked for four decades finally reached him in the shortest of notes, from Alexander's successor as Secretary, George Onslow, on 31 March 1894. Addressed from the Cavalry Depot, Canterbury, it read simply:

Dear Dr Brookes,

I enclose you an extract from the new Education code which was only made public yesterday. I am sure you will be gratified to see that Phy-Education in Elementary schools is at last made compulsory. It has been a hard fight but one worth winning. Hoping this may find you in health, I remain yours very truly

Geo M Onslow'.

'Gratified' would hardly seem adequate to describe what Brookes must have felt on receiving that note. Entirely appropriately, it was Lyde Benson, always hitting the right tone with his speeches, who at the 1894 Wenlock Olympian Games properly summed up what it meant to Brookes. Jasper More first 'congratulated Dr Brookes on having lived to see the Legislature taking up his idea respecting physical education, which was to be put in operation in their schools.' Benson went further. 'I am sure it will be with unfeigned delight that one and all will learn to-day that those efforts in the cause of physical education which for these 44 years Dr Brookes has never for an instant relaxed have at last been crowned by a full and glorious victory...after August, 1895, physical exercises shall form a compulsory item in the Educational Code. Now that this effort of his unselfish philanthrophy has proved successful, I don't believe our old friend would change places with any crowned head in Europe.' Benson led three cheers 'for our dear old doctor'.

CHAPTER 6

'The object of the festival was chiefly to enlighten Baron Pierre de Coubertin, a French gentleman, who desires to introduce athletics more largely among his own countrymen.'
The *Wellington Journal and Shrewsbury News* Saturday 25 October 1890

At the 1894 Wenlock Olympian Games, Jasper More pointed to the remaining unrealised ambition of William Penny Brookes, in his 85th year. 'He and others had proposed that there should be international athletic contests, and if he lived to carry that out he hoped all nations would be induced to put down their armaments'. However, Brookes's communications with Gennadius (now back in London) had continued in the old frustrating vein. Once in 1886 and twice in 1887, Gennadius regretted his absence from the Wenlock Games. In 1887, he had the Greek king and his sons in London for at least six weeks over Queen Victoria's Jubilee. In 1888 he was in New York. Therefore, when, on 30 July 1889 Brookes received Gennadius's thanks for the Games report and compliments on his 'enthusiasm', followed by 'I may visit…' he might have been forgiven some scepticism.

Hope for a revival of his international athletic dream came in 1889 from an unexpected quarter. Since 1883, young French aristocrat, Pierre Frédy, Baron de Coubertin (1863–1937) had been researching the secret of England's success. Brought up in the searing humiliation of defeat in the Franco-Prussian war, the relegation of France in the European hierarchy of nations, and the loss of Alsace and Lorraine, Coubertin, like other contemporary French thinkers was looking for a cure for France's ills. Education had been identified as a possible force for change by the social reformer Frédéric Le Play (1806–1882) a powerful early influence on Coubertin.

Coubertin looked to England, with her immense empire and economic supremacy, for inspiration. By his own admission (during his visit to Much Wenlock in 1890) Coubertin on his first visit to England, 'hated the English' on historical grounds, England being the only European nation 'not subdued by [our] great Napoleon I'. Yet, his logic told him, there might be something in the education of the English leading classes that could be useful to France in regaining her position. When he looked to the England of the 1880s, Coubertin noted that every empire-building young leader received a public school education, followed by a spell at Oxbridge.

In 1883, Coubertin had therefore set out on a tour of English schools and colleges to try to identify the ingredients of success. He already had some inkling of what to expect. Coubertin had been traditionally schooled at the Jesuit college of St Ignace before trying and rejecting both a military training at St Cyr and the law at Paris's Faculté de Droit. From 1884, he attended the new, liberal Ecole Libre des Sciences Politiques in Paris, co-founded by Hippolyte Taine, a critic, historian and thinker. Taine had published in 1872 *Notes sur l'Angleterre* in which he described public school, particularly as seen at Harrow. To its French observer, such an education had seemed as horrific in its fagging as it was terrific in its sport.

As a schoolboy, Coubertin had enjoyed Thomas Hughes's *Tom Brown's Schooldays* and he read it again now in his early twenties, carrying his copy with him as he travelled. Coubertin discovered on trips in 1883, 1886 and 1887 to Harrow, Eton, Rugby, Wellington, Charterhouse, Marlborough, Oxford and Cambridge, the importance of sport to the public school boy. It was valuable, he noted (as had Taine) not just for its physical benefits, but because, being organised by the pupils themselves, it fostered responsibility, camaraderie, a sense of fair-play, mutual respect and dependency, self-discipline, loyalty to the institution, and alternative role models. It evidently had no monetary profit motive either, the school, the team, or the individual's honour supplying sufficient motivation. Furthermore sport took place in the fresh air beyond the school walls, somewhere that French pupils at this time were rarely encouraged to go.

Beyond sport, Coubertin noted that boys also discussed contemporary issues in debating societies and in articles for school newspapers (which they published themselves) and organised charitable societies. They were at liberty to go into town or wander in the countryside. Their study room was their own, to be decorated as they wished. All of these elements, combined with sport and learning, made the British public school education, he felt, a properly rounded preparation for life.

The headmaster held up as the originator of this system was Thomas Arnold, headmaster of Rugby from 1828–42, although similar changes were made, to a lesser extent, by Samuel Butler, headmaster at Shrewsbury School from 1798–1836. Beyond sport, they put boys in positions of authority over one another within the school, through a system of praeposters or prefects of which Butler was 'in all essential respects, the originator'. Ironically, Arnold, whom Hughes portrayed in his novel, had not felt any particular enthusiasm for sport for pupils. The cure of souls was his primary aim, moral development the second, and intellectual training third. Sport was useful chiefly as alternative to poaching or fighting with local boys. Butler thought that football was 'only fit for butcher boys', and believed the game 'more fit for farm boys and labourers than for young gentlemen', though it continued to be played at Shrewsbury.

Rather, both men approved of the requirement of the boys to organise themselves, to be self-reliant, through having, for example, to prepare the cricket grounds, and raise subscriptions, sport at this early stage not being a part of the school's curriculum, but a recreational choice of the boys themselves. It was not included in Rugby's curriculum until 1850, eight years after Arnold's death. Butler, a great classicist (educated at pre-Arnoldian Rugby) tried to suppress games at Shrewsbury, but his successor as head in 1836, Benjamin Hall Kennedy took the opposite view. Among his first acts as headmaster was to hire a cricket field, and in 1839 he officially recognised rowing and made the Captain of Boats directly responsible to him.

Similarly, at Eton, boating was developed and at Harrow, cricket above other sports, as its great school songs demonstrate. Changes at all three of these schools were underway before Arnold's tenure at Rugby.

By the 1860s, many British public school headmasters (often with Rugby connections) had followed Arnold's lead in giving the boys responsibility for their recreation and for the conduct of others, and many new schools were built on the Arnoldian model for the rising classes between 1830 and 1850. Among these influential heads were Charles Vaughan at Harrow School from 1845–59 (educated under Arnold at Rugby), George Ridding at Winchester (1867–84), Edward Thring at Uppingham from 1853–87 (who built the first gymnasium in an English school), and the heads of newer schools like Georges Cotton and Bradley at Marlborough from 1852–58 and 1858–70 (both formerly at Rugby), and Edward Benson at Wellington from 1852–59 (who had previously taught at Rugby). Annual school sports days were begun in 1856 at Rugby, 1857 at Winchester and in 1861 at Westminster and Charterhouse.

Thus it was that the system used as the backdrop for Hughes's novel, the Rugby system of an athletic education or, to use Coubertin's term, the 'pédagogie sportive', became Coubertin's model for French schools. On a visit to Rugby in 1886, when gazing on Arnold's tomb in the school chapel, he felt, suddenly, as if he were looking upon the very 'cornerstone of the British empire'. The PE penny had dropped and, after a somewhat erratic career hitherto, Coubertin had found his vocation. On his return to France, Coubertin wrote articles and books advocating in particular the introduction of PE into schools in France.

In May 1888 Coubertin formed the Comité pour la Propagation des Exercises Physiques dans l'Education, better known as the Comité Jules Simon after its Chairman, the Professor of Philosophy, Education Minister (1871-73) and Minister President in the French senate (1876–77) who shared Coubertin's passion for reforming French education and in particular for introducing athletic games into schools. 'The right which I demand back for our children is the right to play…I entreat for active games, what the English call athletic games', Simon said in 1887. In 1888, Coubertin published L'éducation en Angleterre, followed in 1889 by L'éducation anglaise en France (for which Simon wrote the preface). He wished to bring the public school system, available only to the élite in Britain, to all children in France.

However, Coubertin's advocacy of the adoption of English attitudes and practices in French schools aggravated many compatriots working in his field. Opposition to Coubertin's new Comité sprang up in 1888. The Ligue Nationale d'Education Physique was headed by Paschal Grousset (1846–1909) a man openly opposed to the import of English sport, particularly football which, if it must be played, should be called 'la barrette', not 'le football'. Grousset instead supported collective gymnastic exercises more akin to military drill. It was Grousset, though, who in 1888 first proposed a French Olympic Games as a modern national sporting festival, an idea that Coubertin, with great irony, publicly disparaged.

In 1889, Coubertin set off again on his travels, this time traversing from north to south, North America, studying the education system there, and the role of sport within it. The United States were of particular interest to the Frenchman (Coubertin was consciously following in the steps of Alexis de Tocqueville) the two republics having many parallels, and Coubertin was interested to observe the accommodation of Catholicism within the secular state. The US universities were undergoing reform and growth in number, including a broadening of the undergraduate curriculum and the development of post-graduate courses to produce a new intellectual élite, based not on class but ability. Alongside this change, sport was a rapidly growing phenomenon that Coubertin was keen to observe.

That trip (probably also influenced by Simon's interest in the American republic) resulted in his third book *Universités Transatlantiques* published in 1890. American sport had developed similarly to that in Britain, cricket (from 1809) boating and yachting being first to develop on the east coast in the 1830s and 1840s, the first America's Cup competition between the USA and Great Britain taking place in 1869. Cricket never really became established there. Baseball had become the 'national game' by the mid 1840s. American football had spread out from the Ivy League to other colleges and the Intercollegiate Football Association was formed in 1876. Athletics had become popular in the 1870s, the New York Athletic Club taking the lead in holding annual championships from 1876. An Intercollegiate Association of Amateur Athletes of America was founded in 1876, and three years later, the National Association of Amateur Athletics was formed, including, initially, 14 clubs. Overall, the trip confirmed Coubertin's observations about the English public school and university system: he wished to bring to French schools freedom and sport.

It was just before he departed for America that Coubertin came into contact for the first time with William Penny Brookes of Much Wenlock. As part of the Paris Universal Exhibition (which Jules Simon was organising) Coubertin had been asked to chair a congress on Physical Education. In early 1889, Coubertin sent a questionnaire round American schools and colleges about sport, and put a notice in the British press asking those with an interest in Physical Education to contact him. Brookes sent a small packet containing a pamphlet of his Crystal Palace speech of 1866, his statistics from Much Wenlock School, newspaper cuttings about the Wenlock Olympian Games, photographs and other printed matter.

Brookes had always been keenly interested in the welfare of France, whose tribulations he had so memorably shared as a student in Paris. He not only loved the country and its people (he took his wife there on honeymoon in 1835), but frequently held up the French as a model to the British establishment. In 1850, when the Royal College of Surgeons was trying to shovel the general practitioners off into a separate college, Brookes contrasted its attitude with that of medics in France. In an open letter, published in *The Lancet*, to Sir George Grey, Head of the Home Department, he explained that a congress of several hundred delegates from all over France had gathered at the Hôtel de Ville, Paris on 5 November 1845. They had passed unanimously a resolution that 'it was not expedient to have an inferior grade of medical practitioners'.

Five years later, Brookes sent another passionately-written plea to *The Lancet* asking Parliament to recognise adequately medical officers of the army and navy for their services during the recent campaign in the Crimea, after the Duke of Newcastle had failed to do so in Parliament. He contrasted this 'shameful ingratitude to our army surgeons!' with the view of the profession in France as one of 'honour, devotion and dangers, of superior courage'. Brookes's care for the welfare of France was further shown by his writing to the Emperor, after a visit, probably in the early 1860s, to express his concern at the physical weakness that he saw in the French people.

In 1866 Eugène Paz had built a gymnasium in the rue des Martyrs, Paris. As Brookes had mentioned in his March 1888 NPRS article on National Degeneracy, the highly popular French critic, Edmond About, had greeted the development by writing that 'succeeding generations of Frenchmen would be much healthier and stronger than the present.' Brookes noted, 'It was too late!' to save France in the Franco-Prussian war, an observation made with no shred of triumphalism, only sadness, and with foreboding for Britain.

Brookes had, of course, compared the French and the Prussian soldier in his 1866 Crystal Palace speech, and since 1871 he had attributed the defeat of France in the Franco-Prussian war to the physical weakness of the French, compared to the Prussian soldiers who had been doing physical exercises as schoolboys. He praised France for learning from this and for introducing some measure of PE into her schools, holding her up as an example of what Britain should do if she wished to avoid France's fate. At June 1881's Wenlock Olympian Games, he had even quoted Jules Simon: 'I beg you to assist me in introducing gymnastics [into schools]...a healthy child is better prepared by it for study, and especially for the battle of life'.

On 15 June 1889, Coubertin was able to give an informed speech at his Congrès International pour la propagation des exercices physiques dans l'éducation, as part of Paris's Universal Exhibition (for which the Eiffel Tower was erected and at which an archaeological plan of Olympia was laid out). These World Exhibitions, of which the first was the Great Exhibition in London in 1851 (called by the *Spectator* the 'Olympic Games of Industry') were another sign of the shrinking world in the late 19th-century – a factor that made the revival of the Olympic Games as an international athletics festival practicable.

During the congress, before he had ever met Brookes, Coubertin quoted from the doctor's Crystal Palace speech of 23 years before, describing Brookes as a perceptive speaker, 'un orateur perspicace'. Coubertin focussed on the Prussian victory and on French degeneracy, themes taken straight from Brookes's 1866 speech. The words that Coubertin notably managed not to utter in his 1889 speech (probably because of Grousset's proposal), were 'Olympian Games', despite Brookes's words being delivered at Britain's first National Olympian Games. It suggests that as yet, Coubertin had no intention of reviving the Olympic Games. After the conference, Coubertin set off across the Atlantic.

Brookes acquired cuttings from the French press about Coubertin's Congrès International (possibly from Coubertin himself) and pasted them into the Wenlock Olympian Society's minute books. On 1 November 1889, they appeared in the *Shrewsbury Chronicle*. Brookes made his first public allusion to the connection between himself and Coubertin in May 1890, at Wenlock's Games. Before the sports began, Brookes informed the crowds that 'I have had considerable correspondence with a most distinguished man in France, who is the secretary of the athletic movement in that country, and who intended to be present on this occasion, but was prevented, and who knows the example we have set in England, by our public sports, and is aware of the terrible consequences to France of the neglect of that physical education which we Englishmen have been equally culpable in neglecting.'

Coubertin's 'athletic movement' was a reference to the union that Coubertin was just forging in early 1890 between his Comité pour la Propagation des Exercises Physiques, and the Union des Sociétés Françaises de Course à Pied. The latter had been founded at the end of 1887 by George de Saint-Clair and comprised four school and three non-school sports clubs. It was modest, but their union meant that the movement for PE was joined with that for athletic sport in France, forming the Union des Sociétés Françaises de Sports Athlétiques (USFSA – its logo was a pair of overlapping rings). This organisation published a weekly journal *Les Sports athlétiques* which was a useful mouthpiece for Coubertin. The growth of the USFSA would help him both to consolidate his position on education and to overcome opposition.

Coubertin was also becoming more experienced in dealing with promoters of sports. He recognised that many wanted to push their own sport at the expense of others. He therefore looked to work with people who wished to promote sport in general – men like Brookes. Coubertin may also have taken to heart Brookes's passionate belief in sport for all people, not just the socially élite, for he was to make the USFSA's sports competitions as democratic as possible. This made the Union popular and helped its rapid expansion.

In late July 1890, Brookes sent Coubertin a copy of the resolution made at the meeting of the NPRS to favour compulsory PE in schools, and his 14 practical suggestions. He also sent Coubertin his photograph, a request for one of the baron, and a second invitation to Coubertin to come and visit Wenlock. In his reply, Coubertin noted that physical training had already been made compulsory in the elementary schools of France, and gave an outline of the current requirements of pupils of different ages. He acknowledged that 'the programme is not yet carried out everywhere as it ought to be…I quite agree with you that bodily training in National schools is of very great importance to the whole nation…I shall do my best to make Athletics popular amongst my countrymen, for I firmly believe that the wonderful "Expansion of England", the present "Grandeur of the British people" are the consequences of Athletic exercises…

'I will be delighted to talk the subject over with you when we meet in October. I must go to Birmingham & Rugby & intend starting towards the 20th of October, if it is convenient to you I can proceed at once to Much Wenlock, I leave it to your choice.' Coubertin had already sent Brookes a copy of his *Universités Transatlantiques* and that month's issue of the *Revue athlétique* containing the proceedings of his society's General Meeting held in Paris on 6 July 1890. 'You were kind enough to send me your photograph: I beg to return mine regretting that I have not a better one for it gives the idea of one much taller & stronger than I am.' (plate 23)

Thus it was that that 'most distinguished man in France' arrived by train at Much Wenlock, probably on Tuesday 21 October 1890, in time to attend the Games the next day. The sympathetic Francophile met the keen Anglophile on the platform at Much Wenlock and the two shook hands warmly in a premature 'entente cordiale'. Coubertin, keen to discuss PE in schools, must have dined that evening with Brookes. Brookes was determined to make an occasion of the Frenchman's visit, and he organised (at a cost of £37 11s 2d) an autumn games, such as had been held for the local men four times between 1869 and 1879. Brookes must have noticed that the 22 October was the date of his first ever games on the Racecourse, in 1850 – what more propitious date than 40 years exactly could he hope for?

Wednesday 22 October 1890, though, dawned wet. Unfortunately, 'from morn till eve rain fell, sometimes in drenching showers, almost incessantly'. Young Ralph B. Benson of Lutwyche was President for the event whose purpose was 'chiefly to enlighten Baron Pierre de Coubertin...who desires to introduce athletics more largely among his own countrymen'. Despite the weather, in the afternoon, the shopkeepers closed their shutters to show Brookes and the committee their full support. Notwithstanding the 'pitiless downpours', the event was staged in its entirety, so determined was Brookes to show his sports to his guest.

Richard Steadman, the retired Superintendent of Police, who had inherited the responsibility for the procession from Thomas Jukes, formed up the participants at the Gaskell Arms behind George Beard, the Herald on the customary grey pony. The marches were played by the Ironbridge Volunteer Band under George Beardshaw. Benson rode his horse behind the band, followed by Brookes and Coubertin, and the Society's Committee bearing their flags and banners. Behind them came schoolgirls with baskets of flowers, schoolboys wielding Indian Clubs, and the tilters and tent-peggers on horseback, each in his distinguishing colours bearing his lance. Bringing up the rear was the Shropshire Yeomanry Cavalry, both mounted and on foot, resplendent in their blue uniforms with scarlet facings and gold lace, under the command of the splendidly-named Sergeant-Major Bosher.

The procession moved along the High Street into Spital Street, turned right up Barrow Street as far as the Raven, doubled back, and along Sheinton Street, turned right past the station, and up to the gates of Linden Field. If Coubertin, despite dripping, were not yet aglow with the pageantry, he must have been delighted to find that since his arrival at the station the evening before, a floral arch of evergreens and dahlias had been erected over the gates to the Field. This said, in the red and blue letters of the French tricolour, 'Welcome to Baron Pierre de Coubertin, and prosperity to France'. 'So pleased' was he, the newspaper reported, 'that he requested that he should be allowed to take it home with him as a memento of his pleasurable visit to Wenlock, and of course his request was very readily complied with'.

Once at the Field, a circle formed up north of the grandstand at the foot of Windmill Hill around the sapling of a gold-leafed oak (*Quercus rubra* 'Aurea'), to be planted in Coubertin's honour. Brookes formally welcomed Coubertin, expressing 'the great gratification afforded to the members of the Wenlock Olympian Society by your visit to their Olympian Games and to this ancient town'. He then told (in best twinning-society fashion) how, 500 years before, a large group of Benedictine monks from La Charité sur Loire, had settled at Wenlock Priory, making the town's link with France a deep one.

Brookes wished Coubertin a pleasant visit and hoped that he might return for their Whitsuntide Games, since the short days of the autumn precluded them from carrying out their full programme of sports. Coubertin would, though, see their tilting and tent-pegging competitions which, Brookes hoped, might 'lead you to introduce them into France'. He then explained the choice of a golden oak as symbolising one of the 'golden days' of the Society. As he liberally doused the roots in champagne, he spoke of 'the sparkling wine of your sunny land' – a particularly welcome thought to Coubertin, no doubt, as the rain ran down the back of his neck. 'May this tree flourish for ages', Brookes said, 'and always be looked upon with feelings of pleasure, and of respect for Baron Pierre de Coubertin, the earnest and eloquent promoter of all those athletic sports which help to build up a manly and a noble race'.

In response, Coubertin thanked them for this kind gesture, which he hoped would 'cement the friendly feeling between the two countries, which ought to be everlasting', before suggesting that they call it the French oak. After the national anthem and much cheering, the sports began. The seven events that Coubertin actually saw on that wet afternoon were: flat tilting (in which 14 men competed, Tom Rudd emerging victorious over D. Merrick of Woodhouse Fields), Boys' under-13 200 yards handicap (in which W. Grainger beat J. James by about a yard), 200 yards handicap (three heats and a final, which T. Wheeler of Cleobury Mortimer won easily, G.J. Fifield of Wenlock being second), tent-pegging (Corporal Dickin judged by Sgt-Major Bosher to have beaten Corporal Convey), Boys' under-15 200 yards handicap (in which W. Grainger beat his elder brother John by about two yards), and a one-mile handicap (which drew a good field and was won by J. Hogg of Shrewsbury, W.H. Bache of Hughley being second and T. Scoltock of Jackfield being third).

Finally, in all its pomp and pageantry came the tilting over hurdles. Tom Rudd of Harpsford Mill had won this competition in the summer, so was the reigning Champion Tilter. The trumpet was blown in fanfare, and young George Beard the Herald proclaimed the event. Rudd then rode up in front of the grandstand and threw down his glove in a chivalric challenge that ought to have been familiar to Coubertin from the mediaeval literature of his own country. The glove was taken in turn by Corporal Dickin and D. Merrick. There followed a 'severe struggle' beneath the tilting bar, with its Greek script saying 'always to excel'. Rudd emerged, once again, the victor, Merrick second.

Rudd then rode off a small way, enabling the Ironbridge band to form up in procession and strike up:

See, the conqu'ring hero comes!

Sound the trumpets, beat the drums.

Sports prepare, the laurel bring,

Songs of triumph to him sing.

The girls strew the ground with flowers, through which Rudd's horse picked its way. Rudd dismounted in front of the grandstand and sank down before Mrs Benson. She crowned Rudd with olive leaves and exhorted him to 'let honour be your guide'. The children sang Willie's Victor's Ode, cheers were given for Mrs Benson, for Brookes and for Ralph Benson, before another round of the national anthem closed the Games.

A rather damp Pierre de Coubertin must have been relieved to regain Brookes's house, perhaps to warm himself with a reviving bath before the evening's dinner. Sixty supporters of the Games convened at the Raven under Benson's presidency and enjoyed the hospitality of Mr and Mrs Lane's 'choice spread'. Among the guests were tilter Charles Ainsworth, James Bodenham the draper who had made the sash, Brookes's colleagues Drs Mackenzie and Hart, George Meredith, Sgt-Major Bosher, Robert Hartland the ale and furniture dealer from Sheinton Street, Richard Steadman organiser of the procession, tilter John Webster, T.H. Horton, William Poyner the Spital Street baker, J. and C. Milner, Thomas Jukes junior, and

Secretary William Lawley. After grace, toasts were raised to the Queen and the President of the French Republic. The Ironbridge band played throughout. In proposing the toast to their guest of honour, Benson 'was pleased the elements could not prevent them that evening in drinking the health of Baron Coubertin in the proverbial warm, honest and heartfelt manner peculiar to the Wenlock Olympian Society. (Cheers.)

'Much credit and their thanks were due to M. Coubertin, not only for his pluck in crossing the Channel, but also for his braving the pitiless rainfall to witness their sports that day.' Benson repeated the invitation to return to the summer games, and referred 'at length' to the work Coubertin was doing in France for physical education. 'He hoped the result of this visit might be that on some future occasion they would see some Frenchmen contesting in their tilting or other equestrian sports, not for the championship of England only, but for the championship of the world – (applause)' rather as French racehorse Alicante had done that day, winning the Cambridgeshire Stakes at Newmarket.

When Coubertin rose to respond, he was greeted 'with rounds of applause' and he begged them to forgive his errors of English. He assured them that he would not 'like one of his fellow countrymen who was paying a visit to America...deliver his address in French', with someone sitting behind him directing the applause. He then admitted frankly, that when he first came to England, nine years before, 'he hated the English' for being unbeaten by Napoleon. Since then, he had 'changed his opinions'. France had now lived in peace for 20 years, during which much had been accomplished. He believed 'the best thing they could do was to give their young men physical training. (Applause.)' Coubertin announced that the Athletic Society of France had made Brookes an honorary member, and 'had also decided to give one of their gold medals to be competed for at the next festival of the Wenlock Olympian Society'.

Brookes, in answer to the toast to his health, dwelt on the national importance of 'bodily training by drill and gymnastic exercises during school life, and by athletic sports afterwards', the discussion of which (rather than Olympic Games) was, after all, the reason for the visit of their guest. 'France, as shown in the Athletic Congress held last year in Paris, has wisely come to the determination to improve the bodily development and strength of her people by gymnastic training and athletic sports. In this movement she is fortunate in having the advocacy and cooperation of a talented and energetic man, our distinguished guest...A nation's greatness, gentlemen, depends upon that of its individual citizens, who should be men of sound constitutions, and strong and well-developed frames, fitted for the active duties of life for which the Almighty intended them'. He noted that Prussia, Austria, and Sweden all offered physical training, the last two to women too.

Brookes concluded his speech by proposing a toast to their President, his wife and family, Benson responding by alluding, perhaps unfortunately, to the belief of the Duke of Wellington that Waterloo had been won on the playing fields of Eton. After the speeches came songs, including *England is England Still* and *The Rhine Wine* sung by T. W. Evans and Mr Lane respectively. The view of one press reporter present was that 'perhaps, no previous meeting of the society has been characterised by the same unanimity of thought and feeling as this one, or, at all events, never has the plea for physical training been more earnestly and eloquently advanced…Slowly, but surely, we fancy, [Dr Brookes] is seeing the results of his labours, and few will grudge him the pleasure'.

After dinner, the company moved to the WARS Reading Room above the Corn Market for a ball. Brookes would have seized the opportunity to show Coubertin the WARS library and its books contributed by British statesmen. He would have described its classes, from literacy to botany, music and art, their collections from natural to modern history, the latter including a cuirasse worn at Waterloo on display in the Reading Room, all with the aim of educating the middle and labouring classes, the better to equip them for their working life. He probably explained WARS's affiliation to the Royal Society of Arts, and told Coubertin that members had won prizes nationally in art.

Brookes would have taken out the WOS Minute Bookes and shown the visitor his letters from Wyse about the 1859 Zappas Games in Athens, and his letters from Gennadius about reviving the Olympic Games, so that athletes might compete internationally. He proudly showed off the evidence that he had of the exchange of prizes between himself and Kings Otto and George I of the Hellenes. He must have shown Coubertin the cutting from the *Clio* newspaper to prove that he had sympathetic support for the revival of international Olympic Games in Greece itself. Coubertin at this time, though, was more interested in the subject of the benefits of PE to nationhood, and the reform of education, and so probably listened with diplomatic patience, perhaps suggested by his description afterwards of Brookes's Olympic correspondence as 'voluminous'.

It is tantalising to visualise these two men enfolded in cigar smoke, sitting up into the small hours, and to imagine what they might have discussed. For Coubertin the old man was living history. He would surely have enjoyed Brookes's tales of 'walking the Paris hospitals' in 1829–30, and his first-hand account of the 'trois glorieuses' days of July 1830 when Paris had erupted into revolution. Brookes no doubt shared with Coubertin the sheer disbelief of his contemporaries when he first mooted the possibility of staging games in Wenlock. It had been, quite literally (given the word's Latin root) ludicrous. As pre-arranged they must have discussed the necessity of introducing PE in schools, and no doubt Coubertin would have asked Brookes to enlarge on his theme of the contribution of degeneracy to France's defeat in 1871.

Brookes must have learnt from Coubertin, with a tinge of envy, of the promise of his Athletic Association – recalling his thwarted hopes for the NOA. With their shared concern for France's future, perhaps they discussed Jules Simon (whom Brookes had quoted) and his work, possibly causing Coubertin to reflect that in Brookes he had found another aged mentor rather like Simon. Brookes must have been intrigued to learn of the spread of sport through the American College system. What might Brookes have given for Coubertin's youth? What might he have achieved, had the growing opportunities for worldwide travel been available to him?

Turning to Coubertin's onward destinations, Brookes would have supplied background (and perhaps introductory letters) on athletics and gymnastics in Birmingham. Of Rugby, he could have supplied a sketch of Thomas Hughes, the author of *Tom Brown*, who had sat on Brookes's NOA Games committee for Wenlock in 1874. Arnold, Brookes and Coubertin shared humanist views on the importance of the individual within the industrial economy. Thomas Arnold was concerned for the conditions of the poor. Thomas Hughes and his fellow Christian Socialists had founded Working Men's Colleges in London, as Brookes had in Wenlock, which fostered sport among the working classes. Coubertin himself would champion labourers' universities – 'universités ouvrières' – in the 1920s.

The following morning, Brookes stood on the platform at Much Wenlock Station and watched the steam from Coubertin's departing train surge between the gold and bronze autumn leaves of Linden Walk. He must have seen in its dispersal, hope that the last of his wishes, for international athletics competition in Greece, might finally force its way through adverse circumstance and objection. Coubertin, in the position of unifier of French athletic societies, at the age of only 27, with his connections in America, had so many opportunities to take this forward, opportunities for which Brookes would have longed at the same age. Coubertin might yet do so, if Brookes had enthused him sufficiently on the subject. Might Coubertin prove to be Brookes's Hermes, his wing-footed messenger?

It is hard to believe, if he afterwards took a stroll along Linden Walk and looked over the Field, that there was no conscious awareness in Brookes's mind of passing a baton to the younger generation. Coubertin was only four years older than Willie had been when they brought home his body to that station. That Coubertin's visit would result in Olympic Games he obviously could not have been sure, particularly given Coubertin's greater interest in educational reform. But he had surely tried to impress upon Coubertin his ambition in this sphere. Advancing age must have made him want to perpetuate his own life's work. Younger men on the NPRS committee with Brookes, men with greater energy and positions of influence, were now inching forward his dream of PE in elementary schools. In Coubertin had he found a man to take forward, in parallel, his Olympian dream?

Of the impressions of Wenlock with which Coubertin returned to Paris, there survives his account called 'Les Jeux Olympiques à Much Wenlock' published in his *Revue Athlétique* of Christmas Day 1890. This is worth dwelling upon for the pointers that it offers to the elements of Brookes's games that Coubertin took away with him from Wenlock along with his 'arc de triomphe'. After opening with the sheer unlikelihood of a town in rural Shropshire being responsible for reviving the Olympic Games, Coubertin goes on to say how, 50 years before, when Brookes began his games, those around him had been surprised by the importance that he attached to physical education. Many must have wondered what influence beyond his own country practice, Brookes's propaganda could have.

Coubertin searches for an explanation for Britain's rediscovery of athleticism and credits Kingsley and his muscular Christians with reinvesting the word with something more than brute strength. Brookes, of course had invested athletics with the same idea through the inclusion of tilting in 1858, just as muscular Christianity had taken hold. Coubertin observes how in the 1850s *The Times* announced the results of university sports in Britain in a couple of lines hidden in a corner of the newspaper; today, around the world, groups gather to hear who won the Boat Race, following with all the interest that they formerly brought to the results of battles for power. Today the most keenly-sought news is that of athletic sports at Queen's Club (home of the Oxford v Cambridge match since 1877) or baseball matches in New York or Chicago. Some have struggled against it, but have drowned in the rising tide of enthusiasm for athletics.

Coubertin says that trying to trace back a single line of pedigree for the movement would be futile, for at certain times, ideas spread round the world and propagate like 'véritables épidémies' – an interesting use of a medical metaphor – several men having worked simultaneously in different places towards the same goal. This is how he sees the development of the movement in England, although that at Much Wenlock he admits to be one of the more interesting thanks to its air of poetry and its 'parfum d'antiquité'. He attributes Brookes's endeavour to studying medicine in Paris and feeling the mysterious influence of Hellenic civilisation on humanity, an influence he believed particularly appealing to the British nature.

Coubertin explains that in some respects, 'l'antiquité ne suffisait pas au Dr Brookes', antiquity was not enough for Brookes, as it did not include the notion of honour. Thus he came to introduce tilting, the costumes and the presentation of the laurel crown by a lady to a kneeling knight. Coubertin noted the long procession through the town, the children singing hymns and strewing flowers, the banners and garlands of greenery in the streets, the herald in costume at the head of the procession, and the mounted tilters. He describes the ground with its cricket pitch and tennis lawns, the grandstands, the swimming pool and the green for dancing. Coubertin thought the specimen trees exceptionally beautiful. He lists the illustrious figures to whom these had been dedicated before observing that his own was therefore not in bad company. In the next breath, he was too modest to relay Brookes's generous comments about himself. In short, he wanted to convey of Brookes 'qu'il connaît la France, qu'il la comprend et qu'il l'aime,' – that he knows France, understands her and loves her.

Of the running races and other sports at Wenlock, already known in France, he would say nothing, but he writes about the equestrian competitions at length, both the tilting, and the Yeomanry's tent-pegging. He then describes the dinner and ball in the Society's Reading Room. Its surroundings reminded one that the Society concerned itself with the mind as much as the muscles. He believes it would be hard to find a borough as progressive and generous as Wenlock, its advantages visible from the moment that you set foot in the station, (more like a delightful cottage) surrounded with flowers and shrubs (plate 24). He appears to have had a tour of the Guildhall, the 'Hôtel de Ville'. Coubertin observes that few athletic associations could have a more beautiful games field than the Wenlock Olympian Society.

Sport, he believes, where it had overflowed from England to the rest of the world had not taken the appearance that Brookes had given it in Wenlock. Modern sport rests on the principles of the past which are just as true and noble today as they were in the gymnasia of Athens, but the form is modern – cricket, football, rowing, gymnastics, fencing – in other words appropriate for the 1890s. He tells of Brookes's efforts to spread olympic games (Coubertin does not use capital letters) first at the Crystal Palace, then Birmingham and Shrewsbury. He sees some merit in this, giving participants a chance to come together and have more impact. But almost immediately the enthusiasm for physical exercise burst forth irresistibly, and there was no need to invoke memories of Greece and to look for encouragement in the past. ('On n'eut pas besoin d'invoquer les souvenirs de la Grèce et de chercher des encouragements dans le passé.') Sport was loved for its own sake.

A yet more audacious attempt occurred in Greece. Brookes wrote to the King of the Hellenes and did so well that His Majesty gave a magnificent cup for the Wenlock Games [in fact Shrewsbury NOA] and favoured the re-establishment at Athens of olympic games. But, Coubertin wrote, patronage is not everything. The Greeks took part in one games and left off. Coubertin had seen, he says, the results of the competitions and the names of the laureates. Since then, one has never heard talk of olympic games in Athens.

In closing his piece, Coubertin again dwells upon Brookes's prophetic words at the Crystal Palace about the nation falling if men give up manly sports for the effeminate pastimes of the drawing room, words upon which Coubertin believed one should meditate 'religieusement'. He believes that the expansion of England and her prodigious progress over 40 years had as their sole cause the love of her sons for 'les exercices fortifiants du gymnase, les jeux virils et les sports de plein air qui donnent la santé et la vie' – the strengthening exercises of gymnastics, virile games and outdoor sports, which bestow health and life.

It can therefore be seen that it was not the athletic events that Coubertin took away with him, for these were already familiar in France, and are dismissed in this account in one short phrase of an eight-page article. At the most fundamental level Coubertin sensed the ancient Greek ethos beneath Brookes's work, that of bringing the importance of the physical into line with the intellectual and spiritual person. He also seems to have found the juxtaposition of agricultural Much Wenlock with civilised classical Athens as irresistible as it was uncomfortable and this may have helped it to settle deep and irrepressibly within Coubertin. He seeks to dismiss it, just as he did Grousset's suggestion of national Olympic Games for France, preferring the modern form of sport. Yet something evidently takes root here for Coubertin that grows to become undeniable.

Secondly, Coubertin is surprisingly reluctant to credit Brookes with any part in the muscular Christianity movement. Certainly, a day's annual sports in Shropshire started seven years before Hughes' novel, stood for little next to the breadth of enthusiasm whipped up by *Tom Brown's Schooldays,* Kingsley's *Westward Ho!* or the public school movement. Yet while playing down Brookes's contribution, Coubertin appears to mock those around Brookes for not realising the effect that Brookes could have beyond his own rural medical practice, as demonstrated by the publication of an article about the Wenlock Games in a French journal. This confused ambivalence about Brookes's contribution is an early manifestation of Coubertin's later side-lining of Brookes in the Olympic story.

Coubertin is undeniably charmed by Wenlock's games. He acknowledges, almost against his will, that it has something that sets it apart from the other contemporary moves towards athleticism in England. Some of this appeal may be striking because it was in contrast to what was happening elsewhere. Coubertin claims that the principles underlying all sport are the same, and that Brookes's games were different only because of their antique form. But there were differences here beyond form. In Wenlock, Brookes had started games for every grade of man. In a sunlit field, lords competed with labourers, shopkeepers shut up for chivalry, and country boys contended for a crown. The very fact that the event took place at all was a victory for its community; that it was seeing success without being a city, and without the platform of being a school or university was a triumph.

Elsewhere at this time, the gentleman versus the player, the professional versus the amateur, the élite versus the everyman had become the natural order of sport – to come out on top was the motive. There was a jockeying for primacy, an unattractive exclusivity, an elbowing aside. Brookes had always reached beyond the din for inclusivity in excellence, and he might just have distilled it from the purity of the Shropshire hills and given it form in the relative stillness and smallness of the Wenlock endeavour. Honour, not honours, was his guide.

Brookes's love of the Hellenic people and their culture Coubertin attributes to his study of medicine in Paris, completely overlooking Brookes's months in Padua where he was more likely to have felt closest to the Greek struggle for identity in 1830–31. But Coubertin was in no way wide of the mark when he said that Brookes knew and loved France. Brookes cared deeply for her, and for all that she stood for as she struggled with herself in the 19th century.

Principles aside, the physical aspects of Wenlock's Games day that Coubertin notes are also interesting when considering the future Olympic Games. He picks out for special mention the procession, the pageantry and the equestrian sports. He is particularly impressed by the quality of the games field, with the facilities, the grandstands, and the specimen trees. Alongside these he mentions the beauty of the station building and planting, the dinner, with its formality contrasting with impromptu renditions of 'for he's a jolly good fellow', and the ball. In short, the form and framework of the day are all singled out, and very little of the athletic content. He also notes, when looking at the bookshelves of the WARS Reading Room, that in Wenlock, the mind is as important as the body.

Seven years later, Coubertin returned to his memories of the Wenlock Olympian Games in a memorial essay about Brookes, published in the *American Review of Reviews* January–July 1897, entitled 'A Typical Englishman: Dr William P. Brookes of Wenlock in Shropshire'. In this, he refers once again to the procession and the pageantry, Linden Field, its facilities and trees. He says of Much Wenlock itself 'you almost feel as if you had been there before and had made friends with the people'. There was 'something peaceful and soothing about Wenlock that one notices at once; everybody seems satisfied with his own lot; everything looks clean and neat'.

At the annual meeting of the Wenlock Olympian Society in early February 1891, Ralph Benson read aloud Coubertin's account of his visit to their Games. Afterwards, Brookes wrote to Coubertin informing him that he had been elected an honorary member and inviting him to return to their Whit Tuesday meeting in 1891. Coubertin returned the favour. The *Wellington Journal* of 14 March 1891 reported that Brookes had been elected 'Membre d'Honneur' of the USFSA 'in consideration of his distinguished services in the cause of physical education and athletic exercises', an honour conferred upon only 16 people in Europe and America at the time.

Coubertin wrote to Brookes on 26 April 1891 regretting that there was no chance he could be at the Whit Tuesday Games in Wenlock 'for we have on Whit Monday an International Meeting here in Paris' and their own national Championship from 14 May until 4 June, which would end with the Paris colleges' four-oared races on the Seine. Coubertin's letter was buoyant with news of a 40-minute visit from the President to their games the week before, and the inclusion in his union by now, of 27 athletic associations. He ended by informing Brookes that he would send a golden medal, to 'be given as a prize at your next festival'. On a personal note, he ended 'Remember me, please, to your daughter & grand daughter. I am most thankful for their kind "Souvenir".'

The 1891 Wenlock Olympian Games were held on 19 May in fine weather 'but for an occasional shower of rain and hail'. The highlight, as ever, was the hurdle tilting, 'there being much speculation as to whether T. Rudd would be again able to carry off the championship for the third year'. This year there was a gold medal from France at stake. Rudd's gauntlet was picked up by Charles M. Farmer and D. Merrick. Rudd's hat trick was thwarted by Farmer who won 'amid the greatest enthusiasm and applause of his friends, who were very numerous'. He was presented with the Coubertin medal, believed to be the only medal that the Baron personally bestowed. Three cheers were raised for Coubertin.

For much of 1891–92, Brookes was preoccupied with retirement from his Wenlock medical practice after 60 years, and with furthering the cause of PE in schools through the NPRS, with whose members he continued to maintain a correspondence. He would leave his practice in the hands of the 36-year-old Allan Mackenzie. He had been born in Morayshire, Scotland, had qualified at Edinburgh in 1885, passed his MD (Durham) in 1890 and the same year married Fanny Taylor from Burleigh near Wellington. Brookes could now step down and focus his attention on the NPRS and PE in schools. At the 1892 Games it was suggested by Benson that a subscription be raised 'to ask the doctor to sit for his portrait, which will be placed in the Town Hall' in recognition of his services as the doctor to Wenlock and of his work for physical education.

In September 1892, Brookes attended once again the St George's and Oakengates Athletic sports which attracted between 6,000 and 7,000 spectators. Brookes was described in the speeches as having 'done more to foster and keep alive the Olympian games than any man in England.' Brookes was pleased to hear the allusion to the Greek games. In his reply, Brookes said (as he had in 1881) that 'If he lived long enough he hoped to go and witness an international festival at Athens, or upon the old spot where the Olympian games were started. (Applause.)'

This is intriguing, for just two months later, on 25 November 1892, Coubertin was to propose the revival of the Olympic Games at a meeting at the Sorbonne, Paris. Brookes had written to Coubertin several times in the first half of 1892. Coubertin did not reply until 20 July, blaming the amount of business he now had. Yet even when he did finally write, Coubertin never mentioned his intention to revive the Olympic Games, although it was already in his mind. We know this because Coubertin wrote the very next day in a letter to Andrew Dickson White at Cornell University, in the United States,

'I have come to the conclusion that if the Olympian Games were started anew & held every four years as in the old times, it would be a great benefit to modern athletism. You know all about the gigantic work done at Olympia by the German archeologists & the beautiful results of it. I am sure the question of the reestablishment of the Olympian Games (wh. has already been thought of in Athens as well as in England) would be discussed with great sympathy by both the athletic & the learned men'.

Despite this allusion to Brookes, there is no evidence that Coubertin told Brookes about the plan before his speech in November 1892. So we must conclude that Brookes's comment at St George's in September was merely the latest expression of his dream.

Coubertin, buzzing with plans for international fixtures of all kinds, told Brookes in his 20 July letter that his USFSA now incorporated fully 62 societies and 7,000 individual members – 'two years ago we had but seven societies & 800 members! The year has been a splendid one all round! Athletics have made an enormous progress & our men have improved enough to be able to win three championship races out of seven at our last international meeting when some of the best English athletes (cyclists & runners) were present…The only trouble we have is with reference to professionalism as in country towns money prizes are given very often for bicycle races in which our men are sometimes tempted to compete. Of course we don't allow it.'

'I am delighted to hear that my golden oak is growing all right & I only wish I could go & see it & answer your very kind invitation.

'I remember very secretly the days I spent with you at Wenlock…. Remember me if you please to Miss Brookes & your grand daughter'.

This letter did mention his plan for an eight day festival in Paris from 20–27 November 'to commemorate the foundation of the Union five years ago'. He continued, 'Then we are going to have new grounds at Levallois near Paris.' It was at this Festival two years and one month after his Wenlock visit (he backdated the formation of his society, or as he put it used 'an amended birth certificate' to make the date fit) that Coubertin first proposed a revival of the Olympic Games. The date was not all he manipulated for the occasion. As he wrote, 'was it the fifth anniversary of the USFSA we were celebrating? Not at all. The baby had been surreptitiously changed…I had decided to end my talk in sensational fashion with the announcement of the resolution to bring about an early revival of the Olympic Games. The time had come to take the plunge!'

Coubertin ended his November 1892 speech with an impassioned plea to those present to help him 'to pursue and realize…this grandiose and beneficent project; namely, the re-establishment of the Olympic Games.' Coubertin had tried to anticipate the likely objections to his proposal, but he received instead applause, albeit empty applause for him. 'Everyone wished me great success but no one had really understood. It was a period of total, absolute lack of comprehension that was about to start. And it was to last a long time'. Brookes, patient for 40 years, (or 30 counting from the Zappas Games) could have told him that.

Coubertin did not want some kind of grand Greek fancy dress display, but many of the ensuing comments were titillatingly concerned with whether the games would be competed for in the nude, requiring women to be barred, as at the original Games. Instead Coubertin sought, he said, 'to separate the soul, the essence, the principle…from the ancient forms that had enveloped it'. Then, blithely forgetting Dr Brookes and Wenlock, the Crystal Palace, Birmingham, and Athens 1859, he continued that this essence had 'during the last fifteen hundred years…fallen into oblivion. This placed me in a lonely position, very difficult to endure'. Here was Coubertin, the lonely campaigner trying to bring the enlightenment of the Olympic flame to a benighted world.

In the face of this disconcerting and disappointing response, Coubertin, who had hoped that his announcement would create a groundswell of support that would propel him towards an international congress to organise the event, had to resort to further 'deception. In the files of the USFSA…there lay a project for an International Congress to settle the question of amateurism…for me, the planned Congress had above all the importance of providing me with an invaluable screen'. In Spring 1893, he drew up a programme for an 1894 Congress to discuss amateurism. The programme had, after seven items on amateurism, as its eighth and final item 'Of the possibility of reviving the Olympic Games – Under what conditions could they be revived'. Ten months later, at the beginning of 1894, this had been altered by the addition of two further articles:

'IX. – conditions governing competitors. – Sports represented. – Organisation, frequency, etc.

X. – Nomination of an International Committee responsible for preparing the revival.'

The whole meeting was furthermore now divided into two parts, one 'Amateurism and professionalism' and the second 'Olympic Games'.

In the intervening 10 months, Coubertin went once again to America. There, in Autumn 1893 he toured the universities and sports clubs. Despite a warm welcome, 'nowhere did the idea for the revival of the Olympic Games meet with the enthusiasm it deserved. My kind friend [Professor at Princeton] William Sloane alone was wildly enthusiastic about the project'. From others it met only 'very warm conversation, sincere interest, but an obvious feeling of inevitable failure'. Sloane, Coubertin and Charles Herbert, Secretary of Britain's AAA, were the three men that forged the International Olympic Committee the following year. Coubertin tried to whip up support in London too in February 1894. At a dinner organised by Sir John Astley he met only 'a mere handful of somewhat inert guests'.

Coubertin's final act of 'deception' around the 1894 Congress was to rename it at the last minute. The letterhead became 'Congress for the Revival of the Olympic Games', relegating the discussion of amateurism. He showed a genius for showmanship, too, despite his protestations about throwing off the old forms, by including in the opening session, the first choral performance of the Hymn to Apollo. The words for this had been found on a tablet in the ruins of Delphi in 1893, and Gabriel Fauré had set them to music for the Congress. It was a masterstroke in focusing the support of the delegates. Coubertin described the atmosphere in the hall at the Sorbonne. 'A subtle feeling of emotion spread through the auditorium as if the antique eurhythmy were coming to us from the distant past. In this way, Hellenism infiltrated into the whole vast hall. From this moment, the Congress was destined to succeed. I knew that now, whether consciously or not, no one would vote against the revival of the Olympic Games'. This is indeed what was unanimously proclaimed at the last session on 23 June 1894, at which the International Olympic Committee was formed, to stage its first modern Olympic Games in Athens in 1896.

Brookes should have been at the Sorbonne Congress in June 1894. He received an invitation, and was listed on the programme as an Honorary Member of the IOC, but attendance was beyond him. He had been obliged to miss the 1893 Games at Wenlock after an accident in which he broke his leg and damaged his ankle. Brookes wrote to Coubertin a week after the Games, on 30 May 1893, enclosing a few leaves from his oak which was then of 'lovely appearance' and in 'flourishing condition', unlike the doctor. He joked about his enforced absence from his own games, being reduced to the status of 'a limping instead of an Olympian member' of the Society. He recalled fondly his happy days in Paris as a student. 'I shall shortly enter upon my 85th year, and am beginning to think that my zealous but ineffectual labours for the good of my country are fast coming to a close.'

In this letter, Brookes further expressed to Coubertin his belief that international athletic competitions might supply an alternative to war. He reiterated his opinion about French physical degeneracy being a factor in her defeat by Prussia, and expressed support for Coubertin's work. Of his own efforts to get PE into schools 'we are still the 'unready saxon' difficult to move unless tempted by mercenary considerations'. Unbelievably, though, Brookes did not mention the proposed Olympic revival that Coubertin had suggested six months earlier at the November 1892 Union Anniversary event. The only possible explanation is that Brookes was still unaware of Coubertin's intention to do so.

Why had Coubertin not shared his great dream with Brookes, if only to make the old man happy, or at least out of courtesy? And if Coubertin was experiencing such a dark night of loneliness in conjuring up support for his idea, it is curious to wonder why he did not recruit Brookes to the cause? He believed that the Wenlock Society understood best the true Olympian traditions, so Brookes could have given him real moral support. To draw Brookes in would have been, besides potentially enormously helpful to Coubertin, a compassionate gesture, as it would have given the crocked-up Brookes a real purpose to write letters and drum up support for a cause about which he had felt so passionately for so long. Perhaps Coubertin did not want to trouble the elderly Brookes. Perhaps he wanted not to be influenced by earlier attempts at Olympic revival. Perhaps Coubertin was fearful of losing control (and credit for the idea) to the elder statesman. Perhaps Coubertin was fearful that cutting Brookes in might upset the AAA, whose Hon. Sec. Charles Herbert was to contribute to the success of the 1894 Congress.

At some point between May 1893 and 1894, Brookes became aware of the proposed Congress at the Sorbonne to discuss the revival of the Olympic Games (the invitations went out after mid-January 1894). At the May 1894 Wenlock Olympian Games, it was noted that Brookes was displaying 'his wonted marvellous activity…but he was compelled to confess the weakness which deterred him joining in the procession through the streets in the morning.' Time was not on his side, rather like the herald's 'old grey pony that had done duty for more than two decades', but had gone missing from the 1892 Wenlock procession.

At the 1894 Wenlock Games, a month before the Paris Congress, the *Shrewsbury Chronicle's* reporter noted (in a description that sounds like an Olympic Torch relay – not a feature of Games until 1936) that 'The Doctor's zeal [for athletics] has been carried to the Continent and having kindled it in others, he has returned to England to learn in due course of its spread among the princes of various European nations, where, at present, the furtherance of athletics is becoming one of the 'burning' questions of the day.' Does this suggest that Brookes might have been taken to the Continent for his health that Spring – an intriguing possibility? The speeches at Wenlock focused more on Brookes's success in the campaign for PE than on the possibility of the revival of the Olympic Games.

Brookes received the Congress 'circular' from Coubertin and, as he wrote to Coubertin on 22 May, 'called a meeting of the members of the Wenlock Olympian Society…to consider the various propositions…

'Many of which they will be satisfied to leave to the decision of the Congress. In one, however, you will, I feel assured, have their considerable concurrence, viz. the establishment of an international Olympian Association and the arrangement that such gatherings shall be held in rotation in or near the capitals of all nations joining in the movement. This has long been a cherished idea of mine so far as making Greece the centre but the plan of your Congress, embracing as it does all nations, is a really superb one, and deserving of the liberal support of all nations. It should, however, be carried out with as little delay as possible because, as my experience convinces me, success is most likely to be secured by prompt and energetic action during the period of enthusiasm. You will not regret acting upon my advice and may rely upon my warm advocacy of your movement in all quarters where I have influence.'

Lyde Benson presided over the Reading Room meeting. Brookes read the Congress programme, although he stated that it was for the discussion of Amateurism and Professionalism in Athletics, so he was not aware of Coubertin's new title. The meeting was unanimously in favour of amateurs only being allowed to compete. They believed that the revival of the Olympic Games, 'will be one of the grandest and most beneficial institutions of modern days, as it will tend to increase the bodily and mental vigour of the people and to promote a friendly feeling and intercourse between the different nations of the earth.'

They also suggested the adoption of a Greek or Latin motto and that 'suggestions should be requested for a superior International medal.' Brookes relayed the outcome of the meeting to Coubertin and wished him well. He also wrote directly to the Greek Prime Minister Charilaos Trikoupis (son of the Greek Envoy in London to whom Brookes had written when he had sent Queen Amalia's belt clasp in 1860) warmly recommending the revival proposal, but Trikoupis was to become a leading opponent of Coubertin's Olympic plans.

After the Congress, Brookes received the journal of the newly-formed International Olympic Committee headed with its Latin motto, 'Citius – Fortius – Altius' [sic]. It informed its readers that the first Games would be held in Athens in 1896, news which must have brought Brookes enormous joy. Dimitrios Vikelas, appointed first President of the IOC (who would end up organising much of the Games after Coubertin's focus shifted to his new marriage and another book) reassured the Congress that Athens might not be the most modern city, but it would welcome all who came. Athens was growing and there were plenty of hotels, cafés, restaurants and theatres. The palace of industry (Zappeion), the Academy, the University, and the Parnassus literary society would open their vast beautiful rooms to celebrate the re-establishment of the Olympic Games.

How Brookes must have yearned to attend Athens. Coubertin wrote with news of his proposed marriage in December 1894, to which Brookes responded on 11 December 1894, the day of his brother Andrew's death. He felt that Greece should be glad to be honoured with holding the first games of the revival, and expressed his confidence in Coubertin to organise a splendid international institution. Once again he wished that he were younger. 'I hope, however, that I shall live long enough to rejoice in the success of your patriotic and philanthropic undertaking.' Ever practical, he advised Coubertin to get wealthy Greeks in England to contribute to the costs of the Games.

At the next Wenlock Olympian Games in June 1895, in 'simply perfect' weather, Brookes drove in the procession in a carriage alongside Lyde Benson, Brookes's constant supporter. The 'King of Wenlock' must have looked rather like the Queen and Empress – about the same height, but 10 years older, white haired, and widowed. Certainly his passing would symbolise for the town, the passing of an era, just as it would for the nation when the Queen died in 1901. Brookes, born in the jubilee year of George III, now planted an oak dedicated to the infant son of the Duke and Duchess of York – the future Edward VIII. Afterwards, Brookes read an address to the Hon George Forester whose uncle, along with the seventh Duke of Rutland, had so publicly demonstrated his support for Brookes 45 years earlier at their first Games.

In seconding three cheers for Brookes, Jasper More made the point that 'it was mainly through the efforts of Dr Brookes that the Olympian games were to be renewed at Athens next year, and afterwards at Paris and London. It was a question for them to consider whether Wenlock should be represented on the occasion at Athens.' In the event, no one from Wenlock attended the 1896 Olympic Games, and very few from Britain as a whole. Brookes, sadly, was not there. The doctor, aged 86, surrendered to the Fates at his home in Wilmore Street, at 6.50am on Tuesday 10 December 1895, just 17 weeks short of the first IOC's Olympic Games.

A muffled peal was rung for three days and William Penny Brookes was buried on Friday 13 December. WOS members were well represented, and among his bearers was Charley Weale who, with his wife also sent a wreath. The *Shrewsbury Chronicle* said that 'never was there a less selfish man, or one who so ungrudgingly and cheerfully devoted himself to public service.' The *Wellington Journal* recalled that Brookes 'always had a cheerful word for everyone', and that 'he had devoted more time to the service of others than most men, and had striven with untiring zeal, amid great discouragement, to improve the environment by which he and his neighbours were surrounded'. Allan Mackenzie wrote that for the labouring classes 'he had lived a life of incessant toil, day and night. They always looked to him as their guide and friend'. Others, in discussing an appropriate memorial to Brookes said that he 'was always a sincere and true friend to the poor, and helped them in every way which lay in his power'.

To-day, the road all runners come,
Shoulder-high we bring you home,
And set you at your threshold down
Townsman of a stiller town.
A.E. Housman

Epilogue

'Be still, be still, my soul; it is but for a season;
Let us endure an hour and see injustice done.'
A.E. Housman, *A Shropshire Lad*

'I saw it and I marvelled', recalled Dimitrios Vikelas of first seeing the Panathenaic Stadium in Athens, restored for the 1896 Olympic Games. Vikelas arrived in Athens from Paris on 3 March. Seeing what had been achieved, the sense that the event would finally take place was really driven home. A rifle range and velodrome had been constructed, the fencing would take place in the Zappeion, there were tennis courts and a cricket pitch near the ruins of the ancient temple of Zeus. Rowing was planned to take place in the Bay of Phaleron south of Athens, and swimming in Piraeus.

But would anybody come to compete? There was antagonism between the French and the Germans, the latter eventually sending a team of 19 men, mostly gymnasts. France mustered as many, mostly cyclists or fencers. Eight Hungarians attended as a team, Ferenc Kemény, a founder of the IOC, being strongly dedicated to the new Olympic movement. Across the Atlantic, William Sloane had organised a small group of athletes from Princeton University, and Boston Athletic Club had also formed a team. The 13 Americans arrived the night before the Games, though Sloane himself did not attend. Most of the other countries, including Switzerland, Austria, Bulgaria, Sweden and Denmark sent individuals.

Britain did not send a team. Only five Englishmen made the journey to Athens, all as individuals, without formal affiliation to a club, far less a nation. Happenstance and the empire increased it. Australian distance runner Edwin Flack was claimed for Britain, and Irishman John Boland entered the tennis for Britain and won. Frederick Keeping and Edward Battell of the British Embassy in Athens entered the bicycle races, though there was the now predictable debate over whether they were in fact professionals, as they worked for their living. Had Brookes been alive and fit enough to influence events, he would no doubt have ensured that a group, however small, competed.

There may have been indifference about competing, but among the Greek spectators, there was no hesitation. An estimated 40,000 to 70,000 spectators attended on the opening day, 25 March (Greek independence day by their Julian calendar)/6 April. The day before, Easter Sunday in the Greek Orthodox church, had been wet, and Wenlock weather was to persist for much of the games. However, after cloudy skies for the speeches, the sun came out. The Olympic hymn was sung and 21 contestants lined up for the heats of the 100m dash, the first event, from England, France, Germany, Hungary, Greece and the USA.

In the track and field, Greek hopes were pinned on the fifth day's new event, the marathon (not an ancient Games event). The runners set out from Marathon to run to Athens. To the thrill of the 70,000 strong home crowd, the first runner into the stadium was its own Spyros Louis, who, to overflowing joy, completed his lap and crossed the line first (plate 27). The stadium erupted. Spyros was helped to the dressing room by two of the Greek princes. In the ensuing press coverage, he was described variously as a farmer, herdsman or donkey boy – a serendipitous echo of the agricultural origins of the Wenlock Olympian Society.

At the presentation ceremony, on 3/15 April the winners were given olive crowns made from branches cut from the grove of Zeus in Olympia, along with a silver medal just as had been given at the 1859 Games. Oxford student, George Robertson presented King George with an ode in the style of Pindar (whose words appeared on Wenlock's silver medal). Each victor was summoned by a herald to receive his medal and olive crown from King George, Spyros receiving the loudest cheer. A parade of victors concluded the event, and Athens celebrated all night.

The IOC's Athens Olympic Games were a great success, prompting calls for all future games to be staged there. They moved on to Paris in 1900 and to St Louis in 1904, though both events were calamitously organised and overshadowed by the international fairs to which they were appended. In 1906 Athens staged intercalated (halfway between two Olympic) Games that helped to revive popular support for the movement. Rome should have hosted the Games in 1908, but financial difficulties caused their transfer to London at White City. The White City Games took time to capture the public's imagination, and once underway, were marred by disputes between the Americans and the British. The most outspoken critic was James Sullivan, President of Amateur Athletic Union of America founded in 1888, aspiring to become the governing body of sport in America (like Brookes with the NOA).

By the time of the 1908 London Games, the US press was characterising the Games as a battle between the scrapping, plucky young nation versus the decadent snobbish old country. Positions hardened when, in the opening ceremony, the only flag not dipped to the royal box was the Stars and Stripes. There were rows at the games over everything – the lodgings, the draws for heats, the pit for the pole in the vaulting, the boots of the Liverpool police team in the tug of war, fouling in the 400m, and most famously the marathon victory of Italian Dorando Pietri. He was helped over the line and declared the winner until disqualified after objections. American Jimmy Hayes became the victor, but Pietri remained the darling of the crowd.

It was an ill-tempered Olympics, but one that galvanised British athletics. Sullivan returned to the USA with 13 out of a possible 23 of the most prestigious track and field victories, and crowed 'Athletically speaking it was the most remarkable event in the world's history...the American athletes just swept England off the athletic map.' It was the beginning of the end of English aristocratic languor in sport – one of many things the leisured class was having to let go at this time: its country houses, land, family jewels and portraits (which, like the medals, often headed west over the Atlantic), its Parliamentary seats, and county control.

Although Brookes would not have welcomed the tone of Sullivan's words, there are some intriguing parallels between the two men. Sullivan emerged as a leader in athletics just as the middle classes in the United States were becoming concerned about the effects of their young nation's astonishing growth and industrialisation. Thanks largely to immigration, the United States was becoming the greatest economic power in the world, outstripping Britain. But the realisation was dawning that prosperity was being achieved at a huge cost to the regimented workers coralled into the new cities. The small-town, rural community that had formerly stood at the moral heart of America was being superseded. Good honest exercise seemed to offer salvation from the moral degeneracy that was threatened by urbanisation, and athletic clubs an alternative community to which to belong within the anonymous industrialised landscape inhabited by people of diverse ethnic cultures.

In other words, America was at a similar stage in the cycle of growth to that of Shropshire and of Britain a century before, and Sullivan was a man of Brookes's stamp. He was driven by an almost evangelical belief in sport as a way of improving society, and, besides forming the AAUA, was to become a successful campaigner for playgrounds and sporting facilities. Another century on, and the growing nations of India and China are poised to surge ahead of the United States, concluding another cycle. As their workers flee the countryside for the growing cities, it seems pertinent to wonder what the implications might be for their quality of life and for sport in those countries?

It is also worth reflecting that Brookes began his Olympian Class in 1850, at the moment when the balance of British population distribution tilted away from rural areas into urban. In 2008, according to the United Nations, for the first time in world history, the population worldwide was evenly split between urban centres and the countryside. The part that sport might play in the rapidly growing urban agglomerations could have interesting implications for the growth of the Olympic movement, which already outstrips any other 'world' sporting event, having 216 participating nations.

In considering these overarching issues, concern must be expressed at the pressures on athletes of their professional status, introduced (after years of uncomfortable fudge of the issue) after the 1988 Olympic Games. A fear of the effects of the ubiquitous 'rage of gain' partly inspired Brookes to begin his Games. His definition of amateur status rested on the notion of 'fair play' and arose in opposition to the corruption of professional runners, for whom the potential for financial gain proved too strong to resist. Those pressures abound in the present age of immense broadcasting payments and lucrative sponsorship income for Olympic victors (and for the Games themselves). The practice of doping is one symptom. Claims of match fixing, where athletes perform to order for a share of betting winnings, takes athletics back to the pedestrianism of a century and a half ago. The management of corrupt practice must be one of the IOC's leading preoccupations if the popularity of the Games is to survive.

William Penny Brookes was never mentioned in conjunction with the events of 1896 in Greece. That year, his old correspondent, Joannes Gennadius, wrote an article about the revival of the Olympic Games. Gennadius credited France and Coubertin with the endeavour. This, despite receiving sustained encouragement from Brookes between 1877 and 1893 to re-establish Olympic Games in Greece (as Gennadius had acknowledged with gratitude), organising himself (on behalf of the King of the Hellenes) the purchase and delivery of the silver cup for the National Olympian Games at Shrewsbury in 1877, and putting Brookes in touch with Parasyrakes prior to the appearance of the 1881 article in *Clio* announcing Brookes's attempts to revive the ancient Games in Greece.

Perhaps an English journal might have mentioned him? *The Field* looked promising, beginning an article of 4 April 1896 'As a matter of fact, the revival originated outside Greece, and, if it were possible to search to the actual fountain head, we should find the keen desire that is being shown in France to foster athletic pursuits to be the real *fons et origo*...the influence of the United Kingdom and the United States, who, so far, dominate athletics, has not been brought into play.' Lord Desborough, who as Chairman of the British Olympic Association organised the London Olympic Games of 1908, wrote, in the *Daily Telegraph,* 'It is characteristic of France, that 'mother of ideas,' that a Frenchman should have first given permanent form and substance to their revival.' Brookes's role was recalled by 'Olympian' writing in the Shropshire newspaper in 1909. He recalled of Coubertin's 1890 visit to Much Wenlock that 'the International Olympian Games were discussed', and felt sure that Coubertin 'would be the first to acknowledge that injustice has been done to Dr Brookes's memory.'

As late as 5 March 2007, as Britain prepared to host the 2012 Games, during a meeting of the Parliamentary Committee of Public Accounts, the MP for the Ludlow constituency within which Much Wenlock is today located, Philip Dunne, asked Jonathan Stephens, Permanent Secretary and Accounting Officer of the Department for Culture, Media and Sport, 'Which individual, from which country, do you regard as the person who was the inspiration of the modern Olympic movement?'.

'Baron Pierre de Coubertin'.

'Have you ever heard of Dr William Penny Brookes?'

'No,' was Stephens's reply.

'...Dr Penny Brookes was the inspiration for Baron de Coubertin...I am disappointed, to say the least,' said Dunne, 'that that has not yet sunk in at the Department responsible for delivering London 2012.' Dunne sought and received an assurance that Brookes's involvement would 'be part of all your literature to promote London 2012'. The naming of one of the Olympic mascots 'Wenlock' was one result (plate 30). In Dunne, Brookes had at last found a champion who also sat on the London Organising Committee of the Olympic Games.

Coubertin was painfully familiar with being sidelined and denied the credit for Olympic endeavour. At Athens in 1896, he had been piqued by the lack of credit given to him for the revival of the Games. In 1900, he had the Paris Olympic Games wrested from his control by the organisers of the world exhibition to which the Games were appended. He did not even attend St Louis in 1904 when, again, the world exhibition, not the IOC, organised the Games. In this light, it is interesting to turn again to his article 'A Typical Englishman: Dr William P. Brookes of Wenlock in Shropshire' of early 1897 – the first time that Coubertin wrote about Brookes after his death, and the first time since Olympic Games had been organised by the IOC.

The article has several strands: Brookes the man, the revival of athletic sport in Britain, Wenlock and its Olympian Games, Brookes's Greek contacts and 'local patriotism' in

Britain. Of the revival of athletic sport, Coubertin notes that in Germany and in Sweden it was undertaken from military and medical motives respectively. 'In England things went quite another way'. He describes 18th-century degeneracy overthrown by Kingsley and Arnold's muscular Christianity, which conquered Oxbridge before taking the United States and France, with the 'Latin nations…following rapidly', plus Belgium, Hungary, Bohemia and Switzerland. 'International meetings have thus been made possible…But such meetings are of an essentially modern character; the games are modern; modern are the rules, the dress and the prizes. In Wenlock only something of the past has survived: it is safe to say that the Wenlock people alone have preserved and followed the true Olympian traditions.'

Coubertin's analysis of the Wenlock Olympian Games picks out for particular notice, the 'award of prizes for literary compositions and artistic works' which complete 'the classic parallel' nowhere else attempted. He notes that to achieve this, Brookes 'persevered, brought patience, personal tact and untiring energy to bear upon his apparently hopeless task'. Besides the intellectual prizes, Coubertin again focuses on the procession and pageantry at Much Wenlock. 'No modern athletes ever walked down to the ground where the games and sports were to take place amid such displaying of etiquette and stateliness as did the Wenlock youth going to their "Olympian field" at the opening of the annual festival.' The beauties of Linden Field, its facilities and its tree-planting are all mentioned.

Once again, the athletic sports 'had no special character except the tent-pegging…and the tilting at the ring', with its homage to mediaeval chivalry and the elevated role of women. At the ancient games, 'no woman had ever been allowed into the Greek stadium. This injury to the beauty and charm of the fair sex the old gentleman resented deeply. Not feeling satisfied with giving the ladies the best seats at the Wenlock festival, he had forced upon his countrymen the queer custom of having the champion tilter crowned with laurels by a lady.' Coubertin found the blend of ancient, mediaeval and modern 'strange'. Yet, Coubertin had himself written in 1894 that sport could only produce good moral effects if it were 'founded upon disinterestedness, loyalty, and chivalric sentiment'.

It is in Coubertin's account of Brookes's Greek contacts and local patriotism that his unease can really be sensed. Coubertin says that 'Brookes had hoped to see the 'Olympian festivals' succeed not only in Shropshire but in the rest of England. Several were held under the same regulations in Birmingham, Shrewsbury and Wellington. But no regular movement was started'. Notably, he omits the London NOA Games, despite having quoted from Brookes's 1866 speech there himself, in 1889. He describes Brookes's contact with Queen Amalia in 1860, and King George's cup for the Shrewsbury NOA Games in 1877, but omits the 1859 Zappas Games and Brookes's aspiration for the NOA Games to be international.

'Dr Brookes even endeavoured to promote a festival in Athens…But the proposal was declined by the Greek government. A festival of this kind could hardly be planned as long as the Paris Congress had not met to reorganize and revive the Olympian games on a permanent and broader scale. Dr Brookes lived long enough to see this work done, and stood on that occasion among our most hearty supporters' – a supporter but not a leader.

In his last section on local patriotism, Coubertin quotes Caesar's opinion 'that the first rank in a small village was to be preferred to the second one in a big city'. He tells how in modern times, the city has become everything to most nations, yet 'the Anglo-Saxon race alone has succeeded in keeping up the two feelings', for the home town and for the city upon whose stage the individual might act. This local patriotism, 'a modest and noble desire to beautify a spot dearer to him than any other in the world, or to improve the condition of a community of which he still feels himself a member', Coubertin describes as the 'corner-stone' of the British empire (move over Arnold). 'This (local patriotism) is the way Dr W.P. Brookes did love Wenlock and the Wenlock people. He did not care for immortality and was a practical philanthropist. He believed in every man taking care of those near to him and leaving others to do the same. If progress can be reached by a shorter road, there exists no safer one'.

Coubertin was evidently a fan of Brookes, 'my oldest friend, because he had just completed his 82nd year when I made his acquaintance and visited him in his little kingdom of Wenlock'. By implication Coubertin brackets Brookes with the 'recognized leaders of the movement in favour of athletic exercises and outdoor sports'. Coubertin describes that package received from Brookes before the 1889 Congress, 'which I should have deemed to work of a very young man owing to the enthusiastic and boyish brightness of the style and conclusions, had not the writer taken care to insist on the fact that he had been at work for fifty [40] years'.

Coubertin was particularly struck that 'repeated failure has not embittered his mind nor weakened his confidence in the goodness of his cause'. From the contents of that package, 'I inferred that Wenlock must be a queer and charming little place, and Dr Brookes a very popular man in Wenlock, and so it was.' When he finally met Brookes in the 'merry' and oddly familiar town, he was impressed. He describes Brookes's 'quiet and equitable philosophy, his refined manners, his everlasting good humor, and above all, his favorite theories on the importance of bodily training'. He credits Much Wenlock's appearance to 'Dr Brookes's work and Dr Brookes's spirit. I suppose the Wenlock people don't know all that they owe him.'

Despite the generous admiration of Wenlock's role, and its unique contribution to athletic games, there hangs about his praise for Brookes as a figure, a 'parfum' of damning with faint praise. Coubertin somehow builds up Brookes, only to keep him firmly in his place – Wenlock. His endeavours beyond the borough – 'no regular movement was started', and in Greece 'a festival of this kind could hardly be planned' – apparently counted for nothing. There is very much a sense that it needed Coubertin to recognise the unique spirit of Wenlock and transfer it to the world stage. For this is what, essentially, Coubertin did. Until 1890, for Coubertin sporting events were modern in form, and antiquity had no place in them. Between 22 October 1890 in Wenlock and 21 July 1892, that completely changed. No wonder Brookes was a 'most hearty supporter'. Yet Coubertin makes Brookes no leader but instead, a big fish in a small pond, with no place on the world stage. Coubertin grants him first place in Wenlock, but none in Athens.

Brookes might have been forgotten in Athens in 1896, but at the May Wenlock Olympian Games, 'The familiar figure of the venerable doctor was greatly missed'. The procession formed up and the band led it off, but it fell silent while the procession marched past his home. At the

Field, William Roberts was the starter, Thomas Barnett and Charles Ainsworth were among the judges, and William Lawley was Secretary 'with credit to himself and profit to the society'. Richard Webster won the tilting and a set of silver knives and forks from the Hon. Mrs G. Forester, whom Lord Wenlock thanked for her kindness.

Although the Field looked 'if possible, more beautiful than ever' and the events were competed for as keenly as usual, it was undeniable, as the President Lyde Benson acknowledged from the Grandstand (plate 25), that 'something is lacking, something is wanting today. My friends, there is not a Wenlock man or woman, scarcely, I think, a Wenlock child, but could tell us what is wanting today. We want our dear old doctor back again. (Loud applause) Yes, for the very first time since he established this society we miss him – and miss him sorely from our annual festival.

'But shall we dare to mourn when we remember that he lived long enough to know the complete and glorious triumph of that cause which, throughout his long and useful life, he had ever held next his heart? Unprompted, unaided, nay more under what would have been to you or me heartbreaking discouragement, he was the first to advocate with all the energy of his strenuous nature that attention to physical training which has now won national and international recognition in our amended Education Code and in the revival of the Athenian games'.

There was heated disagreement in Wenlock over an appropriate memorial to Brookes. The suggestions included gates at the entrance to Linden Field, installing coloured glass in the Brookes window in Holy Trinity, or a clock, but in the end, two memorial tablets were made, the larger inserted at the west end of Holy Trinity, almost opposite his house, and another smaller on the front elevation of the Corn Exchange. Perhaps most fitting was the re-naming of Much Wenlock's secondary school, overlooking Linden Field, 'William Brookes School' in 1970. It is a 'Coubertin School', and as such sends representatives to an International Youth Forum held in a different world city every two years.

More disturbing for the Society than the wrangling over Brookes's memorial were the tragic events of 1897–98. William Lawley, then in his early fifties, had a breakdown and violently attacked his wife. He was taken to Coton Hill Asylum in Staffordshire, released to relatives in Manchester but returned a year later and cut Helen Lawley's throat in their home next door but one to Adeline Brookes, in May 1898. The events that precipitated this tragedy are not clear, but Lawley appears to have been a man over-burdened with responsibilities. Apart from running his own printing and stationery business, and being Secretary and Treasurer combined of WOS 1883–88, then Secretary alone, he was the Registrar of births, marriages, and deaths, Assistant Overseer of the Poor Rate, and Proprietor of the Gas Works. It has been suggested that, after purchasing the Gas Works in 1890, he became anxious that he had paid too much for them.

On close inspection, there is some evidence of instability before this. He was inexplicably absent from the Games in 1891, by which time the dual roles that he held had been split once more, F. Serjeant becoming Treasurer. On 27 March that year, he had failed to attend the meeting at the Raven, having 'informed several of the committee he would have no more to do with their society,' and a deputation was dispatched to meet him. At the annual meeting at the end of April 1892, Brookes proposed a vote of thanks to Lawley as Secretary. He expressly said that 'he wished to tell them that Mr Lawley recently made an excellent proposal with regard to the games ground, which had the effect of saving many valuable plants, and also diminishing the cost of keeping the ground in order, as well as being a great improvement,' which could be interpreted as a sensitive gesture by a doctor who recognised a man under strain.

Despite losing the two men who, since 1880 had run the Society, the members rallied, and the Wenlock Olympian Games continued until World War One. The war memorial at Holy Trinity, to the other side of the west door from that to Brookes, includes several names familiar to the Society – Herbert, Charles and Dennis Nevett, William Hill, Daniel and Henry Sankey, Charles Owen ('a keen athlete having competed at Wenlock Games') and a William Roberts. Particularly pertinent, though, is that of Cecil Bodenham. Cecil was the youngest child of Alderman James Bodenham the draper and WOS committee-member who donated the tilter's sash. Cecil was educated in Wenlock, where, turning seven in 1895, he was of the first generation nationally to benefit from PE at school (though Much Wenlock had included it by 1871). By 1905 James Bodenham had shut his shop, resigned from the Town Council and retired to Weston-super-Mare. Cecil went to Liverpool to work, appropriately given his background, at Owen Owen, the department store.

When war broke out, Cecil joined the 1st/9th battalion of the King's (Liverpool Regiment), and was killed on 12 August 1916, during the Battle of the Somme. His battalion lost 52 men that day, and by the end of it they were back where they had started. Having no known grave, he is commemorated on Thiepval Memorial. His obituary noted that Cecil Bodenham 'was a keen sportsman and was Hon. Sec. of the firm's Sports Club'. This Shropshire Lad had taken the message of the Wenlock Olympian Society to his work in Liverpool, and in a life too short, had managed to spread it abroad. He was the embodiment of Brookes's injunction to 'Sow a single seed of a rare plant in the most secluded spot and if the soil and other conditions are favourable to its germination, it will grow up and bear other seed, and, in time, produce plants sufficient to cover the length and breadth of the land.'

No Olympic bid today is considered without discussion of its 'legacy', so it seems appropriate to consider that of the Wenlock Olympian Games, and of William Penny Brookes. The extent to which the Games that Coubertin saw at Wenlock influenced him has been the subject of evaluation since the contribution of Wenlock was rediscovered. From the previous chapter, it will be seen that Coubertin did not believe that he had been much influenced by the track and field events that he saw on that wet autumn day at Wenlock. Certainly, it would be hard to claim that the 200 yards handicap and the one-mile (the only adult track events that Coubertin actually saw) had any influence. Coubertin said that by this time athletics were widespread, and by the 1880s and 1890s, they had indeed spread throughout north America, parts of Europe and pockets of empire.

What Coubertin could not see from his perspective, though, was just how little organised sport there had been when Brookes first led his procession to Wenlock Racecourse in 1850. Pedestrianism was thriving then, certainly, but the Society was ahead of its time in organising a meeting of so many different events over two days. Only at Highland Games in Scotland could something similar be witnessed. The influence of the Wenlock Olympian Games as a municipal rather than collegiate undertaking was unparalleled and encouraged the establishment of other clubs, as acknowledged in contemporary press coverage.

Brookes also did what he could with only the postal service and newspapers at his disposal, to establish links with other men of similar interests – Hulley in Liverpool, Hubbard in Birmingham and Ravenstein in London in particular, and Oliver and Alexander at Moseley and Birchfield Harriers. Brookes was an important figure, and the Wenlock Olympian Games an important fixture, in the coalescence of an athletic and gymnastic circle in the third quarter of the century. Though Wenlock's Games were subsequently overtaken in standards and in size, as they were bound to be in urban centres with much larger populations of young men seeking recreation, they were unique in England when they were begun. Wenlock's Games occupy a significant place in British sporting history, at a time when where Britain led, the world followed. It seems appropriate that the Crystal Palace cricket ground where the NOA Games of 1866 were held, later became (by serendipity, not design) Britain's National Athletics Stadium.

Although Coubertin saw only two track events in October 1890, from 1850–95 the programme at the Wenlock Olympian Games included the following, which all (bar pole climbing, quoits and bowls) are, or have been, Olympic sports (at varying distances): footraces including walking and steeplechases, hurdles, high jump, standing high jump, long jump, standing long jump, pole climbing, pole leaping (vaulting), archery, quoits, hammer, throwing the stone or shot, pentathlon, bicycle races, football, cricket, bowls, boxing (once only), javelin/throwing the Assegai (spear), gymnastics and tug of war. The national games in which Brookes was involved also incorporated rowing and swimming.

Besides the limited track and field events of October 1890, Coubertin saw tilting at the ring and tent-pegging (first demonstrated in 1882 and included in autumn 1890 and 1892 only). Although as a sport tilting was an eccentric inclusion that owed much to Strutt's *Sports and Pastimes*, the skill demanded of the riders in the tilting ought to justify its place as a forerunner of equestrian events in the modern Games. Coubertin was probably influenced by this. Although not part of the 1896 Athens Games, show jumping was introduced at the Paris Games of 1900, and extended at Stockholm in 1912.

Far more influential on Coubertin were the structure of the programme and the pageantry of the Wenlock Olympian Games. The procession through the streets with the band, children and flowers, the herald, the symbols of the sports carried aloft on wands, the flags and banners, the Cavalry in uniforms, the arches of greenery with mottos, the closure of businesses to give support, the tree-planting, the attendance of dignitaries, the speeches, the spirit of international exchange in the warmth with which Coubertin was welcomed, the playing of the national anthem, the throwing down of the gauntlet, the crowning by a woman of the victor on bended knee – all of these elements unquestionably lodged in Coubertin's imagination and are reflected still in the opening and closing ceremonies, and in the presentation of the medals at the modern Olympic Games. The correspondent for the *Birmingham Daily Post* noted of the first IOC Olympics in Athens that 'it would not be heresy to say that more attention is given to pageantry than to athletics'.

The modern Olympic medals themselves might also have been influenced by the exquisite craftsmanship in the Nike medal by Hunt & Roskell, and the two grades in which they were made for Wenlock. The medals at the first IOC Olympics were silver for first place and bronze for second. The summer games medal designs have almost always depicted Nike. Coubertin was struck by Wenlock's use of Greek slogans on the tilting post (and sometimes in floral decorations). He had been dismissive of classical trappings, but Wenlock caused him to reflect that modern sports could be successfully combined with ancient elements, indeed they might lend ballast to a new endeavour, as his commission of Fauré's Delphic Hymn for the Sorbonne congress of 1894, acknowledges. He saw the impact that it had on its audience. Similarly, Brookes urged Coubertin to adopt a Latin motto for the revived Olympic Games as he had for the Wenlock, Shropshire and National Olympian Games. Coubertin's first journal after the Congress was headed 'Citius Fortius Altius' (today the motto is 'citius, altius, fortius' – faster, higher, stronger) supplied by Henri Didon, a Dominican priest and teacher who, like Coubertin had travelled in England to study physical education.

The upgrading of the transport infrastructure is a feature of any host city's preparations today. This is paralleled by Brookes's bringing of the railway to Much Wenlock, and the location of the passenger station close to the gates of the Linden Field. The Field itself was repeatedly admired by Coubertin, with its dual tracks for equestrianism and running, special enclosure for field events, bowls, tennis and cricket, swimming tank, bandstand, grandstands and trees. The Wenlock Games newspaper reports broke new ground in 'gymnical' reporting, and attempts to capture the action. References to 'Quarry Corner' or 'Station Corner' sound surprisingly modern. The 1867 photograph of the Wenlock Olympian Games is believed to be one of the earliest ever photographic images of a sporting event. Wenlock broke new ground in all these spheres.

Wenlock's inclusion of cultural events, and the award of prizes for poetry, painting, and recitation also struck Coubertin, and are part of its legacy. Brookes took this element from the ancient Games. He always promoted the fitness of the whole person, body, mind and spirit. Coubertin took this to heart and in 1906 convened an advisory conference to 'study the way in which art and literature could be included in the celebration of the modern Olympiads'. In 1912, at Stockholm, Coubertin introduced competitions in architecture, sculpture, painting, literature and music. (Coubertin himself, using a pseudonym, won gold that year for literature [poetry] in a curious reminder of young Willie Brookes at Wenlock.) This survives today in the cultural Olympics that are an often overlooked element of the Games in each country, in which all aspects of culture are celebrated in the years running up to the Games.

Interestingly, Brookes credited Coubertin with the 'superb' idea of moving the Olympic Games around every four years, after the initial games at Athens in 1896. Brookes had always dreamed of seeing the games revived in Greece, and never considered that international games might take place elsewhere. This was quite an oversight, given that Brookes had himself chosen peripatetic venues for his Shropshire and National Olympian Games in the 1860s, moving from London to Birmingham, to Wellington, to Shrewsbury, and having aspired to move to Southampton, Norwich, Liverpool, and Bristol besides. Brookes had intended by this means to infect each location with enthusiasm for sport.

Beneath the superficial appearances of the modern Olympic Games, lie further ties between Wenlock and Athens in 1896, and no doubt more remain to be uncovered. In particular, the correspondent for the *Birmingham Daily Post* was national and international champion weightlifter Edward Lawrence Levy, Chairman of BAC, who sent home daily dispatches. Levy went to Athens intending to compete. After a dispute, he withdrew and instead served as a member of the International Weightlifting Jury alongside Prince George of Greece. In 1887, Levy had been, at Brookes's invitation, a handicapper at the Wenlock Olympian Games. After Athens 1896, Levy would serve on the organising Committee of the 1908 London Olympic Games.

There was a further feed-through from Brookes's work on the National Physical Recreation Society to the British Olympic Association (the National Olympic Committee). From 1902, the President and Treasurer of the NPRS were members of the British Olympic Association, and the NPRS was a founding body of the BOA in 1905. When the IOC visited London in 1904, the committee that welcomed them included the three British IOC members (Howard Vincent, Courcy de Laffan and Charles Herbert), but among the six others were Herbert Gladstone, Arthur Kinnaird, and W.G. Grace, the first two being members with Brookes of the NPRS committee and Grace, representing cricket, but having also competed at the 1866 NOA Games. Furthermore, the NOA's founding articles formed the framework for the International Olympic Charter. The NPRS was still meeting in 1908 and offered a major prize at the London Olympic Games. Lord Desborough, who organised the 1908 Games as Chairman of the BOA (1905–13), was a member of the 'Souls', a group of society intellectuals and politicians who were given their name by Brookes's correspondent Lord Charles Beresford, twice WOS President.

The most direct legacy of the Wenlock Olympian Games would be in the participation of Wenlock medal winners at the Olympics. It has happened twice, so far. In 1923, Harold Langley of Birmingham's Sparkhill Harriers took part in the 67th Wenlock Olympian Games (plate 28). About 3,000 spectators saw him win the Pentathlon. The *Shrewsbury Chronicle* lauded this 'fine all rounded athlete, for whom a great future can be predicted'. The following year, Langley was part of the British team at the Paris *Chariots of Fire* Olympics, along with Harold Abrahams and Eric Liddell. He was not placed in Paris, but, in true Wenlock spirit, went on to give service as a Field Judge at the post-war London 'austerity' Olympics of 1948.

The other medal-winner to have taken part in both Games is Alison Williamson (plate 29). In 1981, at the age of 10, Williamson, from Church Stretton near Much Wenlock, won a silver medal in her archery competition at Wenlock. Archery had been included in the early Wenlock Olympian Games, and in the 19th century was one sport in which it was acceptable for women to participate (though they did not at Wenlock in Brookes's day). The women of the leisured classes enjoyed participating in 'bow meetings' at country houses.

As a result, some of the earliest women competitors in the modern Olympic Games were archers, at St Louis in 1904 (women had first competed in tennis at Paris in 1900). In 1992, Williamson was seventh at the Olympic Games in Barcelona (where she also broke two British records); in 1996 she was 10th at Atlanta; in 2000 she was ninth at Sydney. In 2004, though, a century on from those first women archers in St Louis, Williamson went to the Athens Games and there won a bronze medal. Alison Williamson thus became the first competitor to win medals at both the Wenlock Olympian Games, and at the Olympic Games. That she should have done so in Greece was surely the culmination of Brookes's dream. Her medal-winning performance came just as Brookes's contribution was becoming widely accepted.

Among Wenlock's most remarkable legacies, though, is its Games which continue to be staged annually (www.wenlock-olympian-society.org.uk). There were pauses during the 20th century, during the World Wars, and again from the 1950s until 1977. They were revived that year (the Queen's Silver Jubilee) by Much Wenlock's Mayor Norman Wood, a former PE teacher at William Brookes School. Today the Games stretch over five days in early July. The competitions include archery, athletics, bowls, badminton, clay pigeon shooting, cricket, equestrianism, fencing, five-a-side football, golf, a seven-mile road race, tennis, triathlon and volleyball. In 2010 winning athletics competitors attended from the following clubs: Birchfield Harriers, Coventry Godiva, Wrexham AC, Bridgnorth AC, Telford AC, Birmingham Running & Triathlon, Blackpool Wyre & Fylde, Cannock & Staffs, Shrewsbury Athletics Club, Wolverhampton & Bilston, Charnwood AC, Sutton & District, Oswestry Olympians, Halesowen AC, Dudley & Stourbridge Harriers, Sale Harriers and Wakefield Harriers. The Society also stages festivals of Live Arts in March and Rock Music in November. Year-round the Society supports a thriving athletics club of over 40 members, a bowling and a fencing club. The Society also uses its limited funds to help charitable sporting endeavours in the local vicinity. Its other aim is to preserve the ideals of Dr William Penny Brookes.

Complementary to the breadth of Brookes's Olympic legacy, is the depth of his long campaign to win Physical Education for all children in elementary schools in Britain, a cause about which he was 'singularly ardent'. Lawrence Levy called Brookes the 'Pioneer of Physical Education for the Masses'. It is a cruel irony that Brookes has no living descendants. Neither of his two surviving grandchildren, Arthur and Gertrude Great Rex married. Yet, in one sense, Brookes has an unknowable line of descent in any of us that might be living because children that had PE in school were better able to throw off the effects of illness, poverty or war, as a result of being physically fitter. Less dramatically, participants at all levels would surely testify to the confidence, pleasure and friendships that sport, begun at school, has given them.

The form of PE has undergone significant change in Britain over the 20th century, but two hours per week of Physical Education remains, at the start of the 21st century, a compulsory national curriculum subject in primary schools (ages five to 11) although time spent getting to facilities and changing reduces this. Growing obesity among children (one in five of primary school leavers) is a cause for concern, though debate continues about whether this is due more to diet, to exercise, or both. The need that Brookes early expressed to sustain participation in exercise after school years, indeed right through life, is now widely understood, if imperfectly observed.

There can be little doubt that Pierre de Coubertin was the right moving spirit to draw together the various strands that resulted in the formation of the IOC in Paris in 1894. Coubertin was born in France at the time when her need to redefine herself was pressing, and when education, as practised both in Britain and the United States of America, was perceived to be part of the solution. Coubertin was fortunate to have government support for his research into sport on both sides of the Atlantic, and fortunate to have the leisure to pursue it. He was also fortunate that athletics, transport and communications had reached the stage of development that they had by the 1880s, rendering international participation a truly practical proposition (something beyond Brookes, though not for want of ambition). The Greek nation was stable enough too, to accept the responsibility.

International Olympic Games were also in step with the rising spirit of globalisation at this time. Worldwide movements like the International Red Cross (1863) had sprung up, and a movement for peaceful internationalism in opposition to aggressive nationalism was gaining ground. Coubertin felt strongly that, while nationally sport was a useful preparation for life, internationally it provided opportunities for cultural exchange between young people that might reduce prejudice and promote mutual understanding. Brookes had of course experienced the benefits of this for himself, and his inclusion on the committee for the 1874 NOA Games in Much Wenlock of Leonhard Schmitz (until that year Principal of London International College) suggests that Brookes had long seen international athletic competition as a channel for promoting understanding among the young.

Part of the genius of Coubertin in his twenties was his willingness to listen to those older than him and to learn from their experience. Therefore he truly built on the experience of those who had gone before him, and thereby achieved the remarkable things that he did. Coubertin also had the necessary dash to push ahead with his dream of Olympic revival once it had formed in his mind. Brookes was supportive of his endeavour once he knew about it, and he recognised, as seen through his repeatedly expressed wish that he were 20 years younger, that he was born too soon.

Besides in so many ways inspiring Coubertin in his Olympic endeavour, I would go further and suggest that Brookes might equally have inspired Coubertin in another aspect of his life's work. In the 1920s, Coubertin was to publish a *Mémoire concernant l'instruction supérieure des travailleurs manuels et l'organisation des universités Ouvrières* – regarding the further education of manual workers and the organisation of labourers' universities. He acknowledged the influence of Toynbee Hall in Whitechapel, London, but I would suggest that the Wenlock Agricultural Reading Society that he saw in 1890 might also have influenced Coubertin in his work for labouring men. This was an objective close to Coubertin's heart, but it has been eclipsed by the light from the Olympic torch. In the Bureau International du Travail (BIT) and its Director Albert Thomas, Coubertin found a partner to take this dream forward, though not as quickly as Coubertin would have wished. Might Coubertin also have recalled at moments of frustration, his praise in 1897, for Brookes's ability not to become embittered during his long campaign for the introduction of PE into schools?

In summary, it can be said that the achievements of the Wenlock Olympian Society, and Dr William Penny Brookes in showing the way to sport for all classes, in education and nationwide athletic competition in Britain, and in reviving international Olympic Games with the aspiration of fostering greater understanding internationally, are profoundly significant. Others predated Brookes in holding sporting events that made reference to the Olympic Games: Robert Dover at Chipping Campden (from 1612), Johann Bernhard Basedow at Dessau from

1774, Gustav Johan Schartau's Olympic Union of the 1830s which started games at Ramlösa, Sweden, the Olympic Club of (then) Lower Canada in 1844. Brookes was possibly influenced by the Necton Guild of Norfolk (1817–26).

However, the claim of Wenlock over these societies to be the legitimate forerunner of the Olympic movement are threefold:

The Wenlock Olympian Society was among the earliest sustained clubs of its kind, and was uniquely extended into a county, and then a national organisation, so fostering sporting links nationwide;

Brookes made contact with the Greek people directly, urging them to revive their ancient Games, including sending a prize to the 1859 Zappas Games in Athens (before Coubertin was born);

Pierre de Coubertin travelled to Wenlock at Brookes's invitation and was significantly influenced by the ethos and the form of the event that he saw. Brookes was a founding Honorary Member of the IOC.

To extend credit to Brookes and to the Wenlock Olympian Society should in no sense, though, be at the cost to Coubertin of his extraordinary achievement. The surviving correspondence between Coubertin and Brookes is warm, the younger man happy to be a disciple of the remarkable 'oldest friend' that he found in Brookes who, in return was delighted to pass his Olympic baton to the younger man (though the relay was not an Olympic sport until 1912). Brookes's love of France and its people was deeply seated. Brookes would not for one moment have begrudged Coubertin his title of Rénovateur. Over a century after they began, the Olympic laurels are now so many and so heavy that they require more than two men to carry them.

But let us not make the same mistake in bringing Brookes to the podium that was made by crediting Coubertin alone. Brookes could not have made the Wenlock Olympian Society succeed by the sheer force of his considerable will. Countless others laid turf, delivered sheep hurdles, printed posters, parked phaetons, manned bazaar stalls, made arches of greenery, donated climbing poles, knocked in posts and took gate money. Every year, as thousands poured into their town and there was money to be made, Wenlock shuttered up and went to the field to support its doctor in a gesture far-removed from the commercialism of the modern Olympics. And they are still giving, in the spirit of the original Games. If, as the quadrennial juggernaut looms into view, you should struggle to find the soul of the Olympic Games, I recommend a trip to Much Wenlock during the Games in early July. There you will see competitive club-level sport at its friendliest and best. There is no more authentic place in which to seek the modern Olympic spirit. As Coubertin acknowledged in 1890, 'The Wenlock people alone have preserved and followed the true Olympian traditions'.

THE *BORN OUT OF WENLOCK* WALK

(Directions are in italics)

Please note that from 1500m the walk includes two sets of steps, However, the Bull Ring (1900m) can be reached by returning up Sheinton Street, and the churchyard (2000m) is accessible from Wilmore Street, avoiding the steps.

Museum: As you leave the museum, to your left is the black and white Guildhall. It is from there that Brookes set out with his little procession to the first Games in 1850, past where you are standing. *Follow his route by turning right out of the Museum.* Across the road you can see the George and Dragon pub, run by the Yates family who also owned the hair dresser's next door. Thomas Yates the hair dresser was top scoring batsman in the cricket at the first Games in 1850. *Straight on.*

50m: Corn Exchange. This was built in 1852–53 for the Wenlock Agricultural Reading Society (from which the Olympian Society separated in 1860). The arcade beneath was for trading grain, Much Wenlock being a strongly agricultural area. A fund-raising Grand Fancy Bazaar was held upstairs in October 1856 to raise money to extend the building to the back. On the first day, 800 people visited. The latest plough and harrows were on display in the arcade, as well as a washing machine, which was the admiration of the ladies. Upstairs was the Reading Room where Coubertin attended a ball after the Games in October 1890. Today the Reading Room houses the Town Council. *Walk beneath the arcade and through the passage to the right to have a look at the back of the building if you wish (the busts visible in the top window were used in WARS drawing classes) but return to the front to continue.*

100m: Reynald's Mansion – this lovely building was a butcher's shop in Brookes's day. The half-timbered building marked 'Bank', ahead on the other side was the Falcon Inn. The landlord was George Wheeler whose ostler, Richard Felton, excelled at the quoits and hit a bull's eye in the archery in 1851. Wheeler's daughter also helped supply the refreshments at the 1856 bazaar at the Corn Exchange. The stone premises opposite the Falcon housed the workshop of Thomas Edwards the wheelwright and timber dealer, who in 1858 made the tilting bar and lances.

MUCH WENLOCK c.1900

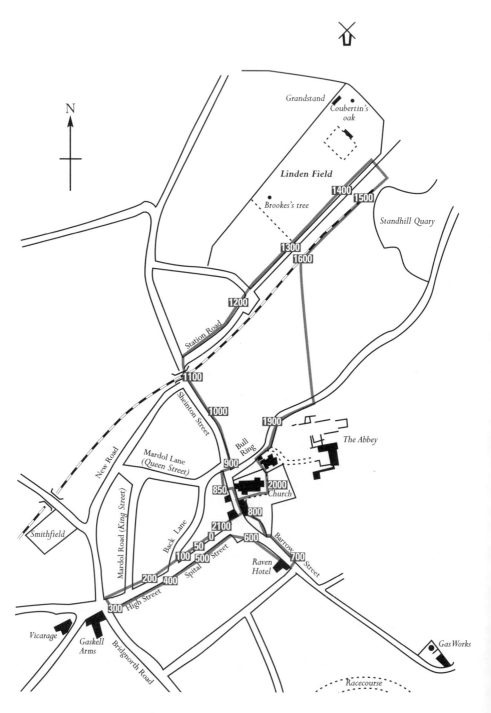

N

Grandstand

Coubertin's oak

Linden Field

1400
1500

Standhill Quary

Brookes's tree

1300
1600

1200

Station Road

1100

Shenton Street

1000

1900

The Abbey

New Road

Mardol Lane (Queen Street)

Bull Ring

900

Mardol Road (King Street)

850

2000 Church

Smithfield

Back Lane

800

2100

Spital Street

0

50

100 500

600

Barrow Street

700

Raven Hotel

200 400

High Street

300

Vicarage

Gaskell Arms

Bridgnorth Road

Gas Works

Racecourse

Just in front of you is the turning right into Back Lane. The old sewer known as 'Schittebrok' that had run down the High Street in front of you since the 14th century turned here down Back Lane and ran behind Brookes's house. Recognising the health hazard that it represented (his father had died of typhoid fever in 1830) Brookes had it covered over. *Cross over Back Lane and go straight on.*

The other side of Back Lane is Ashfield Hall, another half-timbered building. It was between this house and the Fox that Brookes was assaulted in 1863 by James Beddoes and Charles Weale, who suspected the doctor of having an affair with Weale's wife Lucy. The affair caused a scandal when Brookes brought Beddoes to court. After the assault, Brookes staggered on to the street here, was again attacked, took refuge in a cottage opposite, and then went to retired currier, Joseph Amphlett's house a little further up, for a reviving ale.

200m: The Fox Inn was often decorated on Games Days with attractive floral arches, for example in 1859, when John Cooper the landlord had strung from the stable to a cottage opposite 'a triumphant arch decorated with rosettes, ribbons, and banners suspended'. Next to the Fox is a former farmhouse – one of several in central Much Wenlock in the 19th century, and beyond that, the house with the door high up in the roof-line is the former seed-merchant's premises.

Pause before crossing King Street. In front of you, at the top of the High Street behind trees, stands the former vicarage. Revd William H. Wayne, the vicar from 1842 lived there until his death in 1872. It was Wayne who clashed with Brookes in 1860, claiming that the Olympian Class was not and ought not to be part of the Reading Society. This caused the Olympic Society to break away from WARS.

You can also see from here the Gaskell Arms Hotel, where, particularly while Mrs Frances Rhoden was landlady, Olympian Society meetings and dinners were held. It was at a meeting here on 31 March 1868 that Brookes read out the first of his petitions asking Parliament to provide PE in primary schools, stating that 'it would be a great advantage were a short time devoted each day to some light gymnastic exercises'.

Today's busy junction in front of the Gaskell Arms was from 1868 the place where Thomas Jukes formed up the mounted procession to the Games Field every year, the tilters in their coloured silks, the fife and drum band, and children carrying tokens of the Games, and baskets of flowers, the competitors and officials. Brookes sometimes spoke from the steps before the procession set off down the High Street behind you.

Cross over to the other side of the High Street.

300m: The corner of the High Street and the Bridgnorth road. It was up this road alongside the Gaskell Arms (then the Wynnstay Arms) that Brookes's first little procession turned in 1850 on its way to the racecourse. It was also at the top of the bank that William Lawley, the WOS Secretary, raced for a wager in 1862. He lost to 'the Star' of Bridgnorth, but it was a good-humoured race and they all took the route you are about to, back down the High Street to the George and Dragon.

Turn and walk back up the High Street towards the museum.

400m: The houses on the right here were in 1861, the homes of a saddler, horse breaker, agricultural labourers, cattle dealer, carpenter, bricklayer, shoemaker and tailor among others.

In 1851, lodging here in the house of widow Sarah Griffiths were Edwin Yardley and Esther Smith, aged 26 and 25, who were soon to marry. He was the Olympian Class's first Treasurer and later Secretary of the Olympian Society. Esther's work decorating the streets on Games days won praise from the newspapers.

The black and white Talbot Inn was where the marriage of Isabella Brookes to Charles Great Rex in October 1863 was celebrated with dinner followed by a public dance for 150, which 'kept up till a late hour'. Landlord Francis Moreton was Treasurer of WOS in 1872 and spoke at the dedication of the Wellingtonia tree on Linden Field to Brookes that year. 'About 25 years ago,' he recalled, 'we could scarcely muster 100 persons to witness our games, but now we can command thousands.' *Straight on.*

500m: You have a better view of the Corn Exchange from this side of the street. The front was illuminated by gas with three stars and 'VR' for Queen Victoria, in 1856. Note the plaque on the front, added as a memorial to Brookes after his death, also WARS's motto 'Facere laetas segetes' – to produce joyful harvests. The imposing stone building further on, dated 1878 was built as a bank, and between there and the end of the street was poor quality housing. The Post Office on your side of the street was in Brookes's day Mr Atkinson's, the Chemist, and the George and Dragon is beyond that. The first ever Wenlock long-jump winner was John Bright, the assistant at the hairdresser, today the last shop on the right-hand side.

As you approach the T junction at the end of the street, the shop next to the Guildhall was formerly Bodenham's the draper's (see plate 3). James Bodenham supplied the yellow sash for the winning tilter, embroidered 'Honour, my guide'.

Turn right at the T junction, cutting across the open space with the clock, into Barrow Street.

600m: Pierre de Coubertin would have come up this street in 1890, after his wet afternoon at the Wenlock Olympian Games, for dinner at the Raven, ahead. Just before you get there, on the right, the house with bow windows either side of the door is the former Plough Inn. Its landlord in 1871 was William Roberts, Wenlock's great hurdler who also high- and long-jumped (18ft 4in in 1861). Next to that is the former butcher's shop adjacent to the Raven. Thomas Everall, landlord at the Raven in 1880 when he assaulted his wife's lover and was sent to prison, ran the shop as well as the hotel.

The Raven remains a fine hotel today. Numerous Olympian Society meetings were held here, as was the dinner in Coubertin's honour, in 1890. The reporter present that evening observed that 'Slowly, but surely, we fancy, [Dr Brookes] is seeing the results of his labours, and few will grudge him the pleasure'. If you walk on to the end of the Raven where St Mary's Lane comes in from the right, you can see in the distance on the other side of the road, a cowl over a front door. That was the former Royal Oak pub to which William Roberts had moved from the Plough, by 1881. Beyond that on the left is the former Gas Works that Brookes helped to promote from 1856. *Cross over the road for a good view of the Raven. (Compare with plate 7)*

700m: Another Raven landlord (c.1841–71) was Robert Hartland who sat on the Olympian Society committee. Under him, the Raven was noted for its floral decorations on Games days. For the 10th Games in 1859, 'a grand arch was erected…to Mr Share's residence opposite handsomely gilded and flowered, with the day's motto, 'Welcome to Wenlock's Merry Sports'.

The house behind you was in 1851 the Wenlock Academy whose servant, John Hickman won the £1 prize offered by Lord John Manners at the first ever Games.

Walk back along Barrow Street towards the museum and before you reach the former Bodenham's, fork right over the cobbles by the black and white cottage, on to Church Walk, which gives a good view of the Church porch and graveyard. The graves that you can see in the distance to the right with blue ironwork are those of the Brookes family. At the far end of the row of houses on your left is the black and white Guildhall. The entrance is via the passage underneath it (where there is also illustrated an election poster listing Brookes as a supporter of Liberal candidate R. Jasper More, MP for Shropshire South in 1865–68).

The Guildhall was built in 1540 and Brookes refurbished the interior panelling and furnishings at his own cost, in 1848. This is where Brookes attended the Petty Sessions (on which he more usually sat as a borough magistrate) when he brought charges against James Beddoes for the assault on him in the High Street in 1863.

In the bushes to the left of the path here you will find a memorial to novelist Mary Webb (1881–1927). Her father, George Meredith sat on the WOS committee after they moved here in 1882, occasionally chairing meetings. He was at the Coubertin dinner, too, in 1890. Mary Webb's novels paint vivid pictures of Much Wenlock in the late 19th century.

If you would like to go and look at the graves now, do, though you will walk past them on your way back from Linden Field. If not, fork left passing out of the churchyard on to Wilmore Street. Cross the street.

850m: 7 Wilmore Street was Brookes's lifelong home – he was born (1809) and died here (1895). This was also the location of his medical practice. On the few occasions that he could not attend the Games, the procession would stop here. In 1884, when he had broken his arm, he addressed the procession from the steps; in 1893, when he had broken his leg, he leaned out of a window and waved. At the first Games after his death, in 1896, the band fell silent as the procession passed. Next door is the former printing premises of William Lawley, Secretary of the Society from 1880. When the Reading Society was first formed, this was the lending library until the Corn Exchange was built. Next door (right as you look – see plate 2) was the Lawleys' home. William Lawley's wife, Helen hailed from the (former) Stork Hotel on the end of the row. *Cross Wilmore Street to the house on the corner diagonally opposite.*

900m: It was from the Lawleys' house that 14-year-old Violet tried to drag her dying mother in 1898 after Lawley, who had suffered a breakdown, had cut her throat. Trying to reach Dr Mackenzie's house in the Bull Ring, Violet got only as far as the Schoolmaster Francis Danks's house (No. 4) here on the corner where they were taken inside, and Helen Lawley died. The police from the Station next door apprehended Lawley immediately. *Do not go down the Bull Ring, but continue along Wilmore Street into Sheinton Street, following the route of the Olympian Games's processions.*

On the left, almost opposite the former Police Station is the former ale and porter dealership of Robert E. Hartland (No. 5), and opposite that the former glass display window of Cecil Tart the butcher's (No. 58 – he may have emigrated to Canada in 1909). These two shops were especially noted for the floral display strung between them on Games days. In 1888 it was 'considerably enhanced by the charming display of plants upon the ledge of Mr Hartland's shop front.' *Go straight on.*

1,000m: At this point you are almost opposite one of the few surviving original gas lights installed by the company that Brookes helped to found (it might be partially obscured by a road sign). As you might guess from the size of the houses here, this street's inhabitants were not wealthy. They included laundresses and washerwomen, charwomen, agricultural and railway labourers, a bricklayer, a mole-catcher, a sizable Irish population (especially from Co. Mayo) in 1851, tailors and dressmakers, a cap maker, and shoemakers. The inhabitants of the row of almshouses on the right, included in 1861 two blind ladies. *Continue along Sheinton Street to the junction.*

1,100m: The wall on the right here is all that remains of the former bridge that carried the railway across the road. High up, left and right, you can see stones with inscriptions, explained on the information board nearby. The coping stone (right) was laid by Lt-Col. Herbert Edwardes when he came to the Games on a disastrously wet day in August 1860. He wished for 'Success to this railroad! and strength to this bridge. May money pass over it heavily, time lightly, and men and women safely.' The bridge was a popular vantage point for watching the procession. The train first brought spectators to the Games in 1861, across this bridge, stopping on the other side of Sheinton Street from here, at the future Goods Yard. The supreme tilter, Charles Ainsworth's auctioneer's market was also beyond the Yard on the aptly named Smithfield Road. *Beyond the wall, turn right into Station Road.*

Station Road was built at a cost of £150 *c.*1860, as the approach to the station (now a private house) and it runs parallel to the former line. *Either walk up the pavement, or climb the steps to the right and walk along the former line as far as the station.* Brookes was a Director of the Wenlock and Severn Junction Railway company that brought the line to Much Wenlock, and his younger brother Andrew was its Chairman. The station was begun by the end of September 1864. The line (which was extended to Craven Arms) was run by Great Western Railways from 1863 until the last train passed along this line on 21 July 1962.

1,200m: *Pause at the Station.* It was here that Coubertin first set foot in Much Wenlock and felt immediately at home. He described the station as more like a cottage. Brookes ensured that opposite the platform, across the line, a rockery and trees were planted for waiting passengers to enjoy. (see plate 24) On the main eaves of the house can be seen from the road the town's logo, the letters 'WEN' within a lock. *Go straight on through the gates in front of you.* This is the entrance to Linden Field, where the Games were held, and now the strategic location of the station becomes clear. Over these gates was raised an arch of evergreens and dahlias in October 1890, saying 'Welcome to Baron Pierre de Coubertin, and prosperity to France'. So touched was Coubertin that he asked if he might take it with him. *Walk straight along the path ahead.*

1,300m: Straight in front of you an avenue of lime trees leads into the distance. Those to the right (42) were planted in a single row by Brookes and his Olympian Society colleagues, Thomas Jukes, Henry Price, Thomas Evans, Thomas Edwards (the wheelwright), George Wheeler of the Falcon, Thomas Jukes junior and Edward Stroud the schoolmaster, on 30 October 1869, the year after Brookes's son had died. Originally the limes led to Linden Field (Linden means lime), which did not extend right back to the Gates in Brookes's day. The tall, single Wellingtonia tree off to the left, near the school, is Brookes's tree, planted by the schoolchildren for him in 1872.

Brookes hoped it would become an 'emblem of a great movement'. It is visible in the background of plate 5 by the white tent. You can clearly see the recently-rebuilt William Brookes School beyond. *Walk straight along the avenue.*

1,400m: The former railway line is running to your right. In front of you to the left on the skyline is the old windmill tower, which gave its name to Windmill Field, the former name of Linden Field. The rising bank overlooking the field was where most of the spectators sat, and it was a picture on sunny Games days (see plate 6). Linden Field was gifted to the town on the silver jubilee of King George V and Queen Mary in 1935 by Mrs Mary Ward in memory of the Gaskell family, and it is today referred to as the Gaskell Recreation Ground (as well as Linden Field).

The Bowling Club enclosure is ahead. The clubhouse is the former temporary railway station at the Goods Yard – early recycling. The dances on Games day took place within the enclosure. In May 1872 a bowling match was contested the day after the Games when it was noted that 'the ground after being danced upon by the gay and festive couples of the day before, was not in the best condition'. The hedge was formed by 200 laurels – appropriate for the Games – donated by Thomas Jukes and planted the same day as the limes, with a cedar at each corner (now gone, see plate 26).

The grass running track ran round the perimeter of the field. In Brookes's day, the runners would have been coming towards you – they ran in a clockwise direction at that time. The clump of trees to your left as you walk includes an oak planted for the King of the Hellenes, George I, who sent a silver cup for Brookes's 1877 NOA Games at Shrewsbury. King George was the grandfather of HRH Prince Philip, the Duke of Edinburgh. The finishing line was in front of the grandstand, which stood beyond the bowling club on the rising ground at other side of the field. *If you want to, walk round behind the Bowling Green pavilion (which is where the tennis courts and archery butts were formerly located).* The trees at the far end of the field were mostly planted on games days between 1875 and 1895 for royalty and supporters of the Society's work. They include oaks for Queen Victoria, and the Prince of Wales (later Edward VII, both planted in 1887), Coubertin's Golden Oak (1890, plaque at the foot), and a 'noble sea-green pine' for Lord Beresford (1889).

Back on the Linden Walk, cross the former railway line and go through the kissing gate.

1,500m: From here you can see how low Much Wenlock sits in its landscape – it is almost hidden from view. You go uphill in any direction when you leave the town. The church tower would have stood out even more when it had a spire, as it did in Brookes's day (removed in 1933). Below the field to your left is the former Priory (which can be visited) whose landholdings determined the boundary of Wenlock Borough (created in 1468) the largest non-county borough by acreage in England. *Walk straight ahead down the path.*

1,600m: The path is about to cross the field diagonally towards the Priory. It was in this field called Cutler's Yard, somewhere below the station, that Brookes's daughter Maria (deputising for Andrew Brookes's seven-year-old son Alfred who was to die the following year) cut the first sod of the railway line on Monday 26 March 1860. She 'placed it in the barrow, ran it along the plank, and tilted it a short distance in the field, which task was done amid hearty cheering.' The railway would enable competitors to come to the Wenlock Olympian Games from much further afield, including London, Liverpool, Gateshead, Manchester and Birmingham. *Go through the kissing gate near the Priory at the bottom of the bank and turn right.*

1,900m: You are now in the Bull Ring, so-called from the days when the oxen stood in the streets to be sold at cattle fairs. The house to the right of the 1,900m marker, 'The Priory', was the home of solicitor Roger Blakeway (and afterwards of Brookes's partner Dr Allan Mackenzie) and it was in Blakeway's cellar that the pig took cover during the only ever pig chase (1858). The stone tower is a former gatehouse for Wenlock Abbey. To the left of it is Much Wenlock's National School built in 1848 and today called Priory Hall. It was one of the first schools in Britain to include gymnastic exercises for the children. In 1871, Brookes measured the boys to plot their progress, the results proving that children that did gymnastics instead of merely drill showed greater development, particularly in expansion of the chest. Between 1861 and 1878, the school was 'unsurpassed by any known to HM Inspector'. *Turn left off the Bull Ring and up the side of Priory Hall, up a flight of steps and into the churchyard.* The walled yard that you are leaving, in which the school was built, was a former ball court for games.

2,000m: You are again in the churchyard. The large cross to the left marks the Gaskell family graves. They had a home at the Abbey, reached through the little gate beyond (private). As you turn at the corner of the church, you can see the coloured ironwork of the Brookes family graves incorporating an olive crown. To the left of the path is that of William Penny Brookes and his wife Jane, and their daughters Maria and Adeline (the latter was the only child of five to survive her father). To the right of the path is the grave of William Penny Brookes's sons John and William, his parents William and Mary, his sister Mary, his brother John, his daughter Isabella Great Rex and her son Talbot. Brookes's son, William drowned aged 23 while studying as a highly-promising post-graduate medic at Christ Church, Oxford (plate 14).

Holy Trinity is entered at the far (the west) end. Inside the church, Brookes's memorial is immediately to the right of the west door through which you enter. To the other side of the door is the war memorial that includes the name of Cecil Bodenham, son of the draper James Bodenham who supplied the sash for the champion tilter, and Charles Owen who competed at the Wenlock Olympian Games. Also at the west end of the church, further along and partly obscured by the wooden partition, is the clear-glass memorial window that Brookes and his brother installed to the memory of their parents. The windows along the south side are to the memory of Revd Henry Wayne. This is the church where in 1863, Brookes's daughter Isabella married Wayne's curate, Charles Great Rex. A red carpet was laid from the Brookes's house opposite, and 500 people watched Isabella and her five bridesmaids walk to church, little girls strewing flowers under her feet. *Walk left up Wilmore Street and you will be back at the Museum.*

2,100m: You have returned to the Museum, within which you will find many artefacts connected with the Wenlock Olympian Games. These include the tilting lances and the die for the Nike medal that was specially commissioned by the Society in 1861, when it began to move away from cash prizes to medals.

ATHLETES' BIOGRAPHIES

This is a list of competitors at Wenlock Olympian Games, Shropshire Olympian Games, and National Olympian Association Games covering 1850–95. It has been compiled from the WOS Minute Books and from newspaper reports of the Games in the hope of providing as much information as possible about some early competitors from clubs in the midlands and the north for whom little data may remain. It is as exhaustive as possible, but inevitably some gaps may remain. There may also be errors in typesetting and recording, which are indicated where they are suspected.

WOS Wenlock Olympian Society Games annually 1850–95

SOG Shropshire Olympian Games

     1861 Wellington, Shropshire

     1862 Much Wenlock

     1863 Much Wenlock

     1864 Shrewsbury

NOA National Olympian Association Games

     1866 Crystal Palace, London

     1867 Birmingham

     1868 Wellington, Shropshire

     1874 Much Wenlock

     1877 Shrewsbury

     1883 Hadley, near Wellington 'in conjunction with' the NOA

AAC Amateur Athletic Club

BAC Birmingham Athletic Club

GGS German Gymnastic Society of London (membership predominantly English)

Manchester AGC Manchester Athenaeum Gymnastic Club

G. Ace of Swansea BC second in heat of one-mile bicycle handicap NOA Hadley.

J. Adams of GGS second boxing, heavyweight NOA London.

Thomas Adney second 200yd foot race 1852 (1851 census aged 21 living in Sheinton Street, Much Wenlock with his widowed father Benjamin aged 60).

Benjamin Ainsworth winner half-mile flat race and second in local quarter-mile flat race at WOS 1878; second dead heat in 200yd local flat race WOS 1879 with J. Bache and fourth in local half-mile flat race.

Charles E. Ainsworth winner tilting over hurdles, beating eight, WOS 1875, and second in hurdle tilting in 1876 – referred to as of Weston. Winner tilting at Bewdley Regatta, August 1876; second flat tilting WOS 1877; second hurdle tilting NOA Shrewsbury; second flat tilting and wins hurdle tilting WOS 1878; winner hurdle tilting and is described as 'very popular winner' of Spoonhill and is crowned by Viscountess Petersham 1881. He joins the WOS committee in 1882 in place of F.B. Harrison. Winner hurdle tilting WOS 1882 and crowned again by Countess of Harrington. 1883 WOS he is second in flat tilting and wins hurdle tilting for third time in a row. Competes hurdle tilting NOA Hadley; joint second flat tilting and winner of the hurdle tilting WOS 1884. In latter he took three rings in succession which was 'unprecedented'. Fourth win in succession and seventh win overall. Withdraws for a bit, then again WOS 1887, 'of Spoonhill' he wins flat tilting 'most popular', and the hurdle tilting. Auctioneer in Much Wenlock, married to Selina E. by 1891, with daughters Florence A. aged six and Nellie aged three.

H.C. Ainsworth of Claverley second in flat tilting WOS 1892; WOS 1893, an H.E. Ainsworth (error?) wins after over an hour – of Claverley and aged about 17 'certainly had by far the best command of his horse'. Very popular hurdle tilting winner WOS 1893 six competed in all. Winner hurdle tilting WOS 1894 after securing the ring three times out of four (no flat tilting this year). At the end of the 1895 WOS, Mr H.E. Ainsworth gave a very clever exhibition of bare-back horse riding and swordsmanship that is greatly admired.

Joel Ainsworth of Spoonhill Farm, son of the President (aged 19 in 1861) winner tilting WOS 1859.

William Ainsworth of Upper Spoonhill Farm – pony bolted, which disqualified him from tilting WOS 1860. Winner tilting after 40 minutes WOS 1868. W. Ainsworth praised for boxing WOS 1869. He is on the committee in 1871. Possibly chairman at the dinner 1871 when he describes Lord Forester as the earliest, most constant and most liberal supporter of the society.

W.T. Ainsworth winner flat tilting WOS 1881 including beating Viscount Petersham. Same year second in hurdle tilting, sharing it with R. Webster; 1882 – he is described as of Bourton; second in flat tilting WOS 1882. He and Harrington display tent-pegging in 1882; Winner hurdle tilting WOS 1885 – noted he had been attending the games for 21 years; described as 'of Hempton' and second in flat tilting and hurdle tilting WOS 1887. Winner hurdle tilting (only five competitors) WOS 1888.

W. Akehurst of Small Heath, winner one-mile handicap WOS 1895 22 entries.

James Allen BAC fourth in running high leap WOS 1871, and joint second with Clement in running long leap; fourth in hammer WOS 1871.

A. Anderson (Southampton AC) third half-mile flat race against clock, run in squads (2 min 34 sec) NOA London.

John Anderton of BAC second in running high leap, and ditto running long leap, and took part in 200yd foot race, WOS 1872. The same year he wins the General Competition (Pentathlon), leaving Oldfield second; WOS 1873 he is second in running high leap, ditto in running long leap, ditto in 200yd foot hurdle race. In later life he wrote pantomimes for the Prince of Wales Theatre, Birmingham, including *Ye Old Brum and Ye New*.

Arthur Angell of Winchester fourth running long leap, second vaulting NOA London.

Corporal Anslow winner of sword tilting by the D Troop Shropshire Yeomanry NOA Hadley.

J. Anslow of Ironbridge second in 200yd handicap WOS 1892.

A.C. Auster of SBC second in one-mile bicycle handicap, third three-mile bicycle handicap NOA Hadley.

John Austin of BAC third in hurdle race NOA Birmingham.

W. Bach of Birmingham winner one-mile bicycle handicap WOS 1887.

J. Bache joint second with B. Ainsworth in 200yd local flat race WOS 1879 in a dead heat.

W.H. Bache of Hughley third in half-mile race and second one-mile foot race WOS 1885. Winner half-mile handicap WOS 1887; second in one-mile handicap WOS 1888. Winner half-mile handicap WOS 1890; second in half-mile handicap 1893 – close and exciting finish with Meredith.

A. Badger of Wolverhampton – second half-mile foot race WOS 1851; 1851 census has Alfred aged 22 of Montrose Street a shoemaker, brother of below.

Benjamin Badger of Wolverhampton winner 1854 half-mile race; 1851 census has him as older brother of above. Special mention at prize giving in 1855 to him or brother.

E.V. Bailey of Birmingham, second under-17 half-mile flat race NOA Birmingham.

C.W. Baldwin of Birchfield Harriers third in heat one-mile bicycle handicap NOA Hadley.

J.E. Balls of Norwich Gymnasium, winner of a General Prize for merit NOA Birmingham.

Thomas Barnett of Wenlock wins General Competition 'cleverly' WOS 1868. Third in running high leap, second in running long leap 1869 WOS. Winner the Zulu contest when first held at WOS amateur sports September 1879.

A.T. Barney of King Edward's School, Birmingham second under-14 100yd flat race, climbed 57ft, NOA Birmingham.

H. Bate of Birmingham winner two-mile flat race WOS 1884.

Bates (no initial given) second under-13 120yd handicap WOS 1890.

G.Z. Binley of Birmingham ('a bad') third in half-mile steeplechase, winner of two-mile walking match (22 mins) NOA Wellington.

Birbeck (no initial) of Coalport; Winner second and third heats 200yd foot race WOS 1851.

Birch (no initial) of Shrewsbury winner two-mile bicycle race WOS 1882.

J. Bishop of Oxenbold (younger brother of below) winner hurdle tilting WOS 1895 (six competitors).

W. Bishop of Oxenbold (older brother of above) second flat tilting WOS 1886; third hurdle tilting WOS 1887; second flat tilting and ditto hurdle tilting WOS 1888; third flat and hurdle tilting at WOS 1889.

William Bishop of Fairfield CC, Bury winner half-mile flat race and one-mile ditto, WOS 1877.

H. Bithell of Longville winner flat tilting WOS 1895.

O.J. Blet of BAC second 200yd flat race WOS 1878.

E. Blockley of Gloucester Gymnastic Society competed WOS 1869 150yd hurdles but was shut out by the crowd on the course.

J. Blunt of Kinver second in one-mile handicap WOS 1893. Ditto WOS 1894.

C. Board of Ironbridge winner, half-mile and one-mile handicaps WOS 1894.

E.G. Boor of London AC third two-mile race NOA London.

William Bourne of Broseley won the donkey race in 1857; 1861 census aged 53 Blacksmith and Publican of the Three Horse Shoes, High Street, Broseley. His wife, Mary aged 55 was a 'Pork Pie maker'.

G. Bott won 200yd handicap as a boy against the men WOS 1890.

Henry Bowdler third under-14s 100yd foot race WOS 1866. Third 100yd under-10s WOS 1868; second 200yd flat race for boys WOS 1871.

J.C. Bowdler second to Oare in the one-mile foot race WOS 1865. John Bowdler is a close second to

George Palmer one-mile foot race WOS 1866. Described as 'of Shrewsbury'. John Bowdler is second in half-mile hurdles over 10 flights WOS 1867. Second in quarter-mile race NOA Wellington.

R.E. Bowdler winner 120yd boys' race WOS 1885.

Joseph Bowen of Wellington broke his leg in the 150yd hurdles (8 flights) NOA Wellington. One J. Bowen disqualified from two-mile walking race NOA Much Wenlock.

C.F.G. Boyes of Wolverhampton third one-mile bicycle handicap WOS 1888 'a capital race'. Came to grief with F.F. Sharpe in the one-mile bicycle handicap WOS 1891, not in the top results; second in the three-mile bicycle race – slow and tedious race – WOS 1891; second in one-mile bicycle handicap and ditto three-mile bicycle handicap WOS 1895.

H. Bracegirdle of Warrington second in pole leaping (9ft 10in) NOA Shrewsbury.

W. Bradley of Wellington fourth in two-mile bicycle handicap WOS 1886.

William Braithwaite of Meadowley champion tilter WOS 1873. At the same games, he also wins the 120yd hurdles for farmers. NOA Much Wenlock has 'a narrow escape' in hurdle tilting 'his horse stumbling at the sharp turn near the winning post, brought its rider head foremost to the ground, where he lay prostrate for a moment or two, the horse galloping off the field towards the station, where he was secured'. Winner flat tilting at the Manchester games August 1876. WOS 1877 second in hurdle tilting to J. Webster; same year wins flat tilting. Winner tilting over hurdles NOA Shrewsbury and has to crown himself, (described as 'of Droitwich'). Winner hurdle tilting WOS 1879. Winner hurdle tilting 1880 when he is described as being of Elmley Lovett, Worcestershire; second hurdle tilting NOA Hadley.

J. Brewty of London AC third 100yd flat race, third 176yd flat race, NOA London.

P.A. Brindley of Leeds, second running high leap (64in), winner running long leap (17ft 9in), second standing high leap (4ft 7in) NOA Birmingham.

Bromwich of Wenlock winner quarter-mile foot race WOS 1869.

Henry William Brooke of GGS, London second high leap (5ft 2in), second running long leap, second standing long leap (8ft 9in), first half-mile flat race run against clock in squads (2 min 32 sec), first half-mile steeple chase (4 min 40 sec), third climbing (135ft) and winner (with Landsberger) of highest honours, NOA London. Competes in General Competition at WOS 1869. Wins running high leap, is third in putting a 32lb shot, wins running long leap. He wins running high leap at 5ft 3in 'very nearly his own height', WOS 1870, and the General Competition over Clement. Wins running high leap WOS 1871, fourth in running long leap, second in foot hurdle race, and is ineligible to win General Competition this time; second in 150yd hurdles WOS 1871. Died in London on 2 January 1929.

Broomfield wins 200yd flat race WOS 1882.

Brown of Wolverhampton races in WOS October games 1861 in one-mile hurdles.

A. Brown winner under-12 120yd race WOS 1884.

D.H. Brownfield of Stoke winner of both running high leap, and 120yd hurdles over 10 flights WOS 1882.

T. Burd of Ironbridge winner boxing at WOS 1869.

H. Butler of Wenlock third in putting the weight (33ft 5in) NOA Shrewsbury.

H. Cadwallader of Shrewsbury winner 120yd boys' handicap WOS 1895.

J. Calder of Worcester winner one-mile bicycle handicap WOS 1891.

J. Carver of Wellington second in half-mile flat race WOS 1883.

G.H. Case of Bridgnorth third in two-mile bicycle race WOS 1882.

C. Cave of Shrewsbury winner half-mile race and second two-mile flat race WOS 1884.

J.H. Chadwick of Kidderminster second in 440yd flat race WOS 1883.

J.G. Chamberlain of King Edward's School, Birmingham climbed 57ft NOA Birmingham.

R. Chambers of Speedwell BC, Birmingham won two-mile bicycle race and the one-mile bicycle race WOS 1883; third in heat of one-mile bicycle handicap (off scratch) NOA Hadley; second in two-mile bicycle race and winner one-mile bicycle race WOS 1884.

E. Charlton beat eight to win half-mile foot race 'in splendid style' WOS amateur 1867. Winner one-mile foot race after poor start, and also the General Prize. 'His running was the talk of the ground' at the amateur autumn WOS 1867.

J.G. Chidlaw BAC third in half-mile flat race WOS 1877.

J. Childs Broadstone winner of half-mile handicap, and of one-mile handicap – 'a capital race throughout' – WOS 1891.

Thomas Childe, Wenlock second in the half-mile race for amateurs and second in the General Competition WOS; second in the amateurs' General Competition too WOS 1868. (Sometimes spelt with -e and sometimes without).

Childs of Broseley won one-mile hurdles WOS 1870.

Childe of Broseley third in one-mile hurdles WOS 1871. T. Childs, Ruabon wins one-mile hurdles WOS 1875, but is second to Finch in the one-mile flat race.

W. Clarke of Oswestry second in hammer and ditto in putting 32lb shot WOS 1872.

William Clayton of Wenlock winner flat tilting WOS 1870, beating all three Webster boys of Stanway. He therefore won handsome silver goblet presented by R. Jasper More of Linley. Competes in flat tilting WOS 1881.

G. Cleeton wins WOS 1882 half-mile flat race for locals, and second in one-mile flat race.

Robert Clement of GGS London winner 200yd foot race as well as 150yd foot hurdles, easily WOS 1870. In 1870 he also contested the General Competition against Brooke, but Brooke won. Third in running high leap WOS 1871, and joint second running long leap with Allen. Wins hammer WOS 1871. Wins WOS 1871 General Competition against four others, getting the first class medal.

James Cleobury of Broseley is third in half-mile flat race WOS 1883.

F.C. Cobden of Hoarley Grange wins throwing Assegai when first held at WOS 1879. He is vice-President for WOS from later in 1879.

Edward Cocks of Shipton won flat tilting NOA Much Wenlock.

W.J. Coleridge, Shrewsbury winner half-mile handicap and ditto one-mile handicap at WOS 1886.

W.G. Collett of AAC, London second 176yd flat race NOA London.

T. Collins of City AAC, London third 440yd hurdle race (over 20 flights), second half-mile steeplechase NOA London.

J. Cook of Bromsgrove second in half-mile handicap and second in one-mile handicap WOS 1895.

H. Cookson of Shrewsbury winner of his heat in quarter-mile handicap NOA Shrewsbury.

A. Cooper of Bridgnorth won half-mile over six hurdles for farmers or farmers' sons only, at WOS October 1861. He is in the contentious 1862 hurdles race with White vaulting. 1863 Archibald Cooper wins one-mile foot race 'with great ease'. Also competes in high running leap at SOG 1864. At same games wins wide running leap, having cleared 16ft 5in. Wins one-mile hurdles at WOS October 1864, but loses running high leap to Roberts. In a meeting 1878 about the petition, Archibald Cooper is said to be of Wrexham.

C.M. Cooper of GGS joint-winner with Landsberger of climbing (146ft) NOA London.

W.H. Cooper, Birmingham third in three-mile bicycle race WOS 1877, described as 'plucky...quite a lad...much applauded by the spectators'; third the same year in one-mile bicycle race.

C. Cope (same as below?) joint-third (dead heat with Denison) 440yd handicap NOA Hadley.

J.C. Cope of Oakengates second in 440yd race and winner one-mile flat race WOS 1884; 'of St George's' wins half-mile race WOS 1885; second in half-mile handicap and ditto one-mile handicap WOS 1886. Joined Birchfield Harriers in 1887. Winner one-mile handicap WOS 1888. Winner half-mile handicap and third in one-mile handicap, described as AAA Champion two-mile steeplechase 1888, 'a well-known local runner' WOS 1889; second half-mile handicap WOS 1890.

C.G.B. Corbett of MAGC second in standing high jump (3ft 10in) NOA Wellington.

G.W. Corbett, Wellington second in three-mile Bicycle race WOS 1877 and same year second in one-mile bicycle race.

W.H. Corbett of Oakengates second half-mile handicap, and winner of one-mile handicap at WOS 1889.

Charles Corfield of WOS second in half-mile race open to Shropshire men only NOA Shrewsbury; second in half-mile flat race and third in quarter-mile ditto WOS 1878; prominent in amateur WOS Sept 1879; comes second in 220yd local flat race 1881 (20 ran).

Edward G.S. Corser of Hereford second in two-mile flat race (he 'ran a splendid 'waiting' race'), first half-mile flat race (1 min 48½ sec 'Good time, as all must admit'), second in one-mile flat race NOA Much Wenlock. Becomes Solicitor in Shrewsbury. Acts as starter at NOA Shrewsbury.

Edward Cox of Wenlock wins under-14 100yd foot race WOS 1865.

Cresswell equal second in flat tilting WOS 1893.

J. Critchley of Kidderminster second in one-mile flat race WOS 1884.

C.B. Cross of BAC second in Pentathlon and second in one-mile hurdles WOS 1878. Winner Pentathlon and Pole Leaping (6ft 6in) WOS 1879.

H. Crossley, Stoke Victoria Athletic Club second in 100yd race, second in 120yd hurdles, winner of broad jump (19ft 7in) and winner ('very easily' in 65 1/5 sec) of quarter-mile hurdles at NOA Shrewsbury.

Sidney Crowley of MAGC winner of fencing NOA Wellington. Winner of single stick NOA Much Wenlock.

F.H. Dalton Coventry third half-mile handicap WOS 1887.

E.C. Danbury, Marsh Brook second in High Leap and winner 200yd flat race WOS 1885.

W. Darlington of Moseley Harriers winner one-mile handicap (36 2/5sec) NOA Hadley; third in one-mile flat race WOS 1883.

A.N. Davies of USFC, Shrewsbury second in quarter-mile handicap NOA Shrewsbury.

C. Davies, Corporal of Tedstall winner Victoria Cross Race WOS 1894; third in Victoria Cross Race WOS 1895.

Clement Davies of BAC winner standing high jump (4ft 3in), joint-winner (with T.W. Jones and Sproston) of high jump (4ft 11in) NOA Wellington. Founding Secretary and later President of BAC until 1886.

J. Davies of Beulah Football Club second in heat of 120yd hurdles NOA Shrewsbury.

H. Davies of Chester fourth in one-mile handicap NOA Shrewsbury.

T. Davies of Wenlock winner 120yd boys handicap WOS 1893. Winner 120yd boys' handicap WOS 1894.

W. Davies winner under-13 120yd handicap WOS 1890.

W. Denison of Civil Service AC second in heat 120yd handicap, joint-third (dead heat with Cope) 440yd handicap NOA Hadley.

J. Denning, Shrewsbury winner of one-mile flat race NOA Much Wenlock.

C.L. Devis of Birmingham Gymnastic Society second in running high leap WOS 1871; also wins running long leap; second in the General Competition WOS 1871.

W.R. Deykin of Birmingham second in single stick NOA Much Wenlock.

J. Dowding of Leominster wins the two-mile bicycle handicap race WOS 1881.

H. Downes of Wall is third in one-mile hurdles at WOS 1877.

Isaiah Downes of Eaton-under-Heywood is second in quarter-mile hurdles for farmers NOA Much Wenlock.

Thomas Downing of Shrewsbury won the under-18s quarter-mile flat race at SOG 1864.

F.F. Downward of Shrewsbury School Boat Club won half-mile handicap open to Shropshire men only (2 min 10 sec – 'had the race entirely in his own hands') and the one-mile handicap ('by four or five yards' in 4 min 42 2/5 sec) at NOA Shrewsbury.

W.H. Drayton of Pengwern Boat Club second in heat of 100yd flat race NOA Shrewsbury.

J.E. Duckworth of Haslingden AC, winner running high leap (65in), second running long leap (17ft 2in), winner 100yd flat race (10½ secs), winner 200yd race (20½ secs), winner hurdles (32 secs), winner standing high leap (4ft 8in) NOA Birmingham.

E. Dutfield Winner 440yd flat race and third 120yd hurdles (over 10 flights) WOS 1882.

G.E. Dutfield of Moseley Harriers joint-second (with H. Price – Dutfield won run-off) 120yd handicap NOA Hadley.

A.E. East of BAC winner (in 61sec) of quarter-mile race and of heavy-weight boxing, NOA Wellington.

John Edmonds second in half-mile steeplechase NOA Birmingham; third quarter-mile race NOA Wellington.

E.J. Edwards of Bourton Cricket Club third in heat of 100yd flat race NOA Shrewsbury.

E.W. Edwards of BAC wins 120yd hurdles, second in Pentathlon ('his achievements were much admired'), joint-winner (with Wylie) high jump (5ft 1in), second in broad jump (18ft 4in), winner of pole leaping (10ft), at NOA Shrewsbury. Granted a walk-over in the pole leaping, and wins 120yd hurdles at WOS 1878.

J.M.S. Edwards of Bourton Cricket Club second in Shropshire under-18s quarter-mile race NOA Shrewsbury.

W.H. Edwards of BAC second in half-mile flat race WOS 1877.

J.G. Elliot of GGS first running long leap NOA London (17ft 2in); second 100yd flat race, second in hurdle race, winner of a prize for general merit, NOA Birmingham.

T.G. Elliott (error for above?) of GGS, London third half-mile steeplechase NOA London.

John Ellis of Chester wins the quarter-mile flat race at SOG in 1864 – but not much competition.

C.G. Emery of AAC, London first 100yd flat race (10½ secs), second 440yd hurdles (20 flights) to W.G. Grace, medal-winner boxing, light-weight, NOA London.

E.G. Emery of AAC, London first 176yd flat race (18¼ secs) NOA London.

Fred d'Escofet of BAC winner Pentathlon WOS 1881.

R. d'Escofet of BAC winner high jump, clearing 5ft, and second in pole jump, failing at 9ft, WOS 1889.

R.G. Evans of Jackfield second in 200yd handicap WOS 1891.

T. Evans second in 120yd boys handicap WOS 1893.

Thomas Evans second in under-14 100yd foot race WOS 1866.

Daniel Everall of Leighton second in the tilting SOG 1864. Also competed in tilting at WOS 1866.

S. Everall third in under-12 200yd WOS 1882; 'of Broseley' second under-15 200yd race WOS 1884.

Thomas P. Everall wins hammer throwing 45ft 3in autumn amateur WOS 1867; and again in 1870 61ft 2in; second in hammer WOS 1871. WOS Secretary and Treasurer 1875–79.

G. Everett third 120yd handicap under-13s WOS 1890.

Charles Farmer of Newton second in high jump WOS 1888.

Edward Marston Farmer won hurdle tilting WOS 1891, beating off T. Rudd who had hoped for a hat-trick. Won Coubertin medal – great enthusiasm and applause of his friends. Ties for second in hurdle tilting in WOS 1893; third as Trooper Farmer in the Victoria Cross Race and third in the Umbrella and Cigar Race WOS 1894.

W. Feast of Redditch third in three-mile bicycle handicap WOS 1893.

J. Fellows of Birmingham second boys' 10lb shot-put (26ft 6in), second boys' running high leap (4ft 4in), second boys' running long leap (13ft 1½in), second boys' throwing the cricket ball (63yd 2ft) NOA Birmingham.

Charles Felton of Long-Lane second in tilting over hurdles (winning a 'handsome hunting whip, elaborately mounted in silver') NOA Wellington.

Richard Felton of Wenlock winner of quoits WOS 1850 and 1851. Also won archery WOS 1851 games with a bull's eye.

F. Felton third in 200yd flat race WOS 1878; third in half-mile flat handicap, and second (of two) in 120yd hurdles WOS 1879.

John Fennel of Coalport wins running long leap and standing long leap at WOS 1866. J. Fennell won standing long leap WOS 1867.

J. Fieldhouse, Birmingham came second in first ever bicycle race three-mile WOS 1876.

E. Finch of Stanton won one-mile foot race WOS 1869. Edward Finch of Rushbury wins the one-mile steeplechase WOS 1870. E. Finch of Walls Bank, second in one-mile hurdles WOS 1871, and wins one-mile flat foot race same year. Edward Finch of Rushbury wins one-mile flat foot race 1872. WOS 1873 he wins one-mile flat race; NOA Much Wenlock third in two-mile flat race – he dashed off with 'a long lead for three out of the eight laps'; 1875 WOS he wins one-mile flat race, beating Childs. Competes in one-mile flat race WOS 1877 but not placed. Finch of Rushbury is third in one-mile handicap NOA, Shrewsbury. Edward Finch WOS second in half-mile flat race WOS 1878; WOS 1879 third in one-mile hurdle race.

G.J. Firfield of Wenlock winner 120yd handicap WOS 1890.

Warren FitzWarren Esq Vice-President and President of Amateur sports in 1869, the 20th games. Won the newly-introduced General Competition (Nike medal) WOS 1868. Winner long jump (17ft 4in) NOA Wellington. Enters General Competition WOS 1869, against H.W. Brooke of London. He is second in running high leap WOS 1869. In the chair at the dinner at the Raven WOS 1869.

William Fletcher of BAC joint-second (with Watt) in pole leaping (8ft 5in) NOA Birmingham.

H.N. Flewker of Wolverhampton second in 120yd handicap and ditto 200yd handicap WOS 1887.

Gerard Fowler of BAC wins Pentathlon WOS 1876 – first time it is so called.

Sarah France won the sewing WOS 1857.

French see Tench.

C.W. Gainham of London winner of half-mile handicap 22 entrants 'capital race' WOS 1895.

H. Garrathy, Shrewsbury, second in 120yd handicap WOS 1888.

E.B. Garrett of Shrewsbury winner 120yd handicap and third in 200yd handicap WOS 1895.

H.W. Gaskell second in one-mile flat handicap WOS 1879.

J. George of Wellington second in boxing NOA Wellington.

George Geyden of Birmingham second in quarter-mile flat race NOA Much Wenlock.

S. Gittens of Baschurch second in one-mile handicap WOS 1890.

J.W. Goldsworthy, Hereford wins two-mile walking race NOA Much Wenlock.

F.W. Gollings of Ironbridge wins 120yd handicap and 200yd handicap WOS 1893 in 13 seconds and 23 seconds respectively.

J. Gollings of Broseley; won 150yd hurdles over 10 flights WOS 1869.

I. Goodridge, Wenlock second in pole leaping WOS 1883.

A. Gough of Broseley wins one-mile handicap WOS 1893.

W. Gough of Shrewsbury wins pole leaping WOS 1882. Joint winner of pole jump with E.C. Pritchard WOS 1887 at 9ft 10in (see below).

W.H. Gough, Crewe wins pole leaping WOS 1885. W.H. Gough of Brownsover, Rugby second in pole jump and second in the high jump at WOS 1886; second in the pole jump WOS 1888.

W.G. Grace of Bristol first 440yd hurdles (over 20 flights – 1min 10 secs) NOA London.

Andrew Grainger of Wellington won 150yd hurdles (eight flights) after only competitor (Bowen) broke his leg, won mile race, won half-mile steeplechase NOA Wellington. Won one-mile professional hurdles for Salopians at WOS 1869 'a most hollow affair'.

J. Grainger wins under-12 120yd handicap WOS 1886.

William Grainger competed in tilting WOS 1866. Won running long leap WOS 1868. Quarter-mile open flat foot race competitor WOS 1871.

W. Grainger winner 200yd handicap under-15s (local) WOS 1890; second in under-15s 120yd handicap WOS 1891; second in 120yd boys' handicap WOS 1892.

Green of Bilston winner of boxing NOA Wellington.

W. Green of Birmingham third one-mile handicap WOS 1887.

William Gregory wins first ever tilting match WOS 1858. Victor at thrilling tilting match WOS 1865 – formerly lived in Wenlock but now in Birmingham. Winner tilting WOS 1867, beating F. Tench to second. Competes for tilting WOS autumn amateur games 1867.

George Griffiths of Wellington: wins half-mile hurdles at SOG 1864, and also at WOS 1864, beating John Kite of Bridgnorth. Wins quarter-mile flat race WOS 1865, beating Kite. George and William Griffiths of Wellington contest one-mile over 7 hurdles WOS 1866 and George won, but objection was taken that one of them had gone round instead of over the hurdles! Second in one-mile hurdles over 15 flights, to William Jones of Shrewsbury WOS 1867. Griffiths second to Roberts in hurdles WOS 1868. Winner quarter-mile race NOA Wellington.

R. Griffiths of Ketley winner of middleweight boxing NOA Wellington; second in boxing WOS 1869.

H. Grimstone of Manchester AGC won hammer throwing WOS 1872, and ditto throwing a 32lb shot. At WOS 1873 he wins putting 32lb shot.

Grobes of Oswestry won one-mile hurdles WOS 1872 'a splendid race'.

E.H. Guest of West Bromwich, third in one-mile bicycle race WOS 1882.

F.G. Hale of Worcester winner one-mile bicycle handicap and second in the three-mile bicycle handicap WOS 1894.

C.A. Halmer of Moseley Harriers wins two-mile bicycle handicap WOS 1879 – exciting finish with Worthington.

H. Hampton of Wellington third in one-mile hurdle WOS 1870.

A. Harley of Wenlock third under-15 200yd race WOS 1884.

C.E.R. Harley of Broseley second in 120yd handicap and second in 200yd handicap WOS 1895.

H. Harley of Wenlock second under-12 120yd race WOS 1884.

John Hargreaves of Manchester AGC wins running high leap WOS 1873.

F. Harris of Worcester second one-mile bicycle handicap 'devoid of incident or interest' WOS 1891.

M. Harris of Hadley wins one-mile foot hurdles WOS 1871. Disqualified from one-mile flat foot race 1871. He is defeated by Grobes into second in one-mile hurdles WOS 1872.

S. Harris of BAC competed 200yd foot race and running long leap WOS 1872.

F.B. Harrison of Barrow third in 200yd flat race WOS 1877 in 'a brilliantly contested race'; same year competed but not placed in half-mile flat race; third 100yd race NOA Shrewsbury, when he is described as of Willey Wanderers (cricket club). WOS autumn 1877 he is starter and Secretary, and addresses the amateurs at the end. WOS 1878 wins 200yd flat race 'easily' and 'in splendid style', and local quarter-mile flat race; 1878 he is President again of amateur WOS, with F. Sarjeant as his sec. He is handicapper of local races in 1880 games. By 1882, he 'has left the neighbourhood'.

H. Harrison of Oakengates second in 200yd flat race WOS 1882; second in a dead heat with Holt 200yd flat race WOS 1882.

H. Hartjen of GGS winner of fencing NOA London.

J.R. Hartley of GGS winner 36lb shot-put (30ft) NOA London; joint-winner (with Landsberger) of throwing the spear, winner of a general prize for merit at NOA Birmingham.

J.R. Hayes of Whitchurch winner 120yd handicap and winner of 200yd handicap WOS 1891.

Phillimore Haynes of Wricton third in quarter-mile hurdles for farmers NOA Much Wenlock.

C. Hazenwood of Manchester Athletic Club second in half-mile handicap (running off scratch), wins quarter-mile handicap (52 3/5 sec) NOA Shrewsbury.

C.A. Heath of King Edward's School, Birmingham second under-17 100yd flat race NOA Birmingham.

G. Henderson of Liverpool AC first in vaulting (6ft 6½in), first wrestling, Cumberland style, first in sabre and bayonet exercise, NOA London.

W.E. Henn of Dudley second in two-mile bicycle race handicap WOS 1881.

G.A. Henson of Edgbaston in crash with man crossing course WOS 1892 but remounted and came a good third, and second in the three-mile bicycle handicap the same games; second in one-mile bicycle handicap and winner three-mile bicycle handicap WOS 1894 – by now of Coventry.

J.C. Heynes of Cardington winner flat tilting WOS 1892.

John Hickman won Lord John Manners' £1 prize at the first-ever games 1850. Competed in the half-mile foot race WOS 1851. T. Hickman (error?) won 200yd foot race WOS 1852.

A. Higgitt, Balsall Heath second in 120yd handicap and winner 200yd handicap WOS 1894.

William Hill 'Captor of the Pig' 1858.

Hoare see Oare.

H. Hoare of Shrewsbury third in heat quarter-mile handicap NOA Shrewsbury.

Hodnet of Homer second in hammer, won half-mile foot race and second in throwing stone WOS 1868.

W. Holbrook of Shrewsbury second 120yd boys handicap WOS 1894.

H. Holland of Chester wins half-mile flat race at SOG 1864.

John Hollis won blindfold wheelbarrow race 1854.

C.A. Holt, All Saints' Football Club, Shrewsbury wins 100yd race (11 sec) at NOA Shrewsbury. Wins 200yd local flat race and 200yd flat handicap at WOS 1879; 1882 WOS third in 200yd flat race and second in 200yd flat race in a dead heat with Harrison.

A. Hood of Speedwell BC winner by 5yd of one-mile bicycle handicap (3min 15sec), second to H.H. Smith three-mile bicycle handicap (a 'splendid race from start to finish') NOA Hadley.

H. Hopton of Wenlock second running high jump WOS 1884.

H.J. Horsfall of Birmingham climbed 57ft NOA Birmingham.

A. Horton of Wolverhampton second in half-mile and two-mile bicycle handicaps WOS 1889.

Hotz joint-winner (with Landsberger) of wrestling NOA Birmingham.

R. Houghton of Wellington won pole leaping (cleared 9ft), and running high leap at WOS 1883.

A. Hughes, Shrewsbury second in 200yd handicap WOS 1889.

Lucy Hughes second in knitting WOS 1857.

W. Hulson of Wellington second 200yd race WOS 1884.

G.J. Humpherson of Bewdley second in 120yd handicap WOS 1891.

William Humphreys of Wellington was the only competitor in the boys' high leap, 'jumped very nearly his own height – 4ft. 1in. and was, as he deserved to be, warmly applauded', NOA Wellington. Won under-14 foot race WOS 1869.

E. Humphreys of Southampton AC second half-mile flat race, second mile race, first two-mile race NOA London.

Rowland Hunt of Boreatton third in heat of 120yd hurdles NOA Shrewsbury; 1892 President of WOS.

John Husbands of Clunbury second in 150yd foot hurdles WOS 1870.

Thomas Iddens 1868 WOS second in running high leap for amateurs and second in throwing cricket ball.

A. Ihlemann of GGS, second in javelin, third 36lb shot-put (29ft), joint-winner (with G. Henderson) wrestling, catch as catch can NOA London.

Inglis of Manchester opponent of G.W. Renshaw in gymnastic competition ('seldom have we seen professionals acquit themselves better') NOA Much Wenlock.

C.S. Jackson, Hereford second in two-mile walking race NOA Much Wenlock.

H. James of Southampton AC third mile race NOA London.

Sarah James, of Much Wenlock recited 374 lines without any mistake WOS 1854. She also got first prize for her writing WOS 1854.

W. James of Birchfield Harriers, winner one-mile flat race, and one-mile hurdles WOS 1882; 1883 WOS winner one-mile flat race; fourth in one-mile flat race NOA Hadley.

Thomas Jeffries of Birmingham winner boys' running long leap (13ft 9in), winner throwing the cricket ball (65yd 2ft) NOA Birmingham. NOA Much Wenlock (by which time he is of BAC) General Competition winner high leap (5ft 6in), third in shot-put (left+right=34ft 6in) third in long leap (in which he had 'an extraordinary jump' of 21ft disallowed 'by putting his hands to the ground'), joint-second in a dead-heat with Wilding in quarter-mile race, unplaced in rope climb, so third overall.

T. Jervis of Wenlock fell in the hurdle tilting and dislocated his shoulder, but it was quickly reset WOS 1876. He had been second in the flat tilting.

G. Jinks of Sparkbrook second in half-mile handicap WOS 1894.

M.E. Jobling of Northumberland Cricket Club second 200yd race, winner half-mile race (2 min 15 sec), winner of mile race (by three yards in 4 min 47½ sec), winner half-mile steeplechase (by three yards in 2 min 28 sec) NOA Birmingham.

W. Johnson of Rushbury tied for first in flat tilting WOS 1872 with R Webster and second in the hurdle tilting, beaten by Webster the same year. WOS 1873 second in hurdle tilting to William Braithwaite; second in the flat tilting NOA Much Wenlock.

Bromley Jones of Buildwas winner of tilting SOG Wellington taking ring three times. Also won at WOS autumn 1861. Won tilting SOG Much Wenlock 1862. As such he was given the bronze medal of the Liverpool Athletics Club.

C.H. Jones of Kidderminster winner 440yd race WOS 1884.

E.J. Jones of Robertsford equal third in flat tilting WOS 1888.

J. Jones of Shrewsbury second in half-mile steeplechase NOA Wellington.

James Jones (as above?) of Wenlock fourth in half-mile flat race NOA Much Wenlock.

R.W. Jones of Robertsford winner 200yd handicap (22 seconds) 'a good race' WOS 1888.

R.W. Jones of Shrewsbury second 440yd handicap WOS 1886.

S. Jones of Grinshill second in half-mile handicap and second in one-mile handicap WOS 1892.

Thomas W. Jones of BAC joint-winner (with C. Davies and Sproston) high jump (4ft 11in), second two-mile walking match, NOA Wellington. For many years a Judge for WOS.

W. Jones of Shrewsbury third one-mile handicap WOS 1890.

Edward Jukes of Coates Farm, Much Wenlock winner tilting NOA Birmingham.

Thomas Jukes/Juckes of Coates Farm, Much Wenlock winner under-14s race WOS 1854. Third donkey race WOS 1857; second in the first ever tilting at the ring WOS 1858; WOS 1859 T. Jukes Junior of Coates Farm third in pony tilting, 'the somewhat rustic-looking and rather shy young champion'. Winner WOS 1861 when only two competed. Winner tilting SOG 1864, and WOS Oct same year. Winner tilting NOA Birmingham. T. Juckes and Thomas Edward Juckes both compete in tilting at the autumn amateur WOS 1867. T.E. Juckes won. T. Juckes competed flat tilting WOS 1869. Thomas Jukes gave the 200 laurels to enclose the bowling green in 1869, and T.E. Jukes helped to plant them. T. Jukes treated them all to dinner at the Stork at the end of their work. Mr Jukes of the Coates is presented in 1871 with a coloured photo in a gilt frame of the Queen of Beauty 1867 crowning the tilter in a gilt frame 'as a mark of their respect and gratitude for his untiring exertions in furtherance of the success of the Society'. Mr Jukes was the starter 1871 and organised the procession. He is given high praise at the dinner as one of earliest competitors in the tilting matches; 1888 Mr T. Jukes still marshalling the procession 'in his own inimitable way'; 1890 40th WOS games he is described as 'one of the most ardent supporters of these games ever since they were started, and for over 30 years has marshalled the processions, which have always been one of the principal features of the anniversaries'. May be gentleman in white suit with beard to left of pony in plate 12.

J.W. Keeling of Birmingham third General Competition WOS 1875, and first 200yd foot race.

J.A. Keenan of Shrewsbury third two-mile bicycle handicap WOS 1888. Possibly the same man listed as A. Keenan of Shrewsbury second one-mile bicycle handicap WOS 1889 'poor field'.

J.H. Ketley of King Edward's School, Birmingham second in sack racing NOA Birmingham.

George Kidson of Wenlock winner hammer WOS 1866 but immediately upstaged by a throw by William Mitchell, visiting dignitary from Manchester. **Kitson** second in hammer and winner stone throwing WOS 1867. Kitson winner hammer WOS 1868.

A. King of Thames Rowing Club, London third half-mile flat race NOA London.

Charles King of Newcastle competed in running long leap WOS 1872.

John Kite of Boar's Head, Morville second pony tilting 1859; second 400yd foot race SOG Wellington; second half-mile foot race at Wenlock autumn games 1861 – close race, for farm labourers only. Second to George Griffiths of Wellington half-mile hurdles WOS October 1864; second to Griffiths again in quarter-mile flat race. Winner half-mile hurdles over 14 flights WOS 1865 – by then described as of Bridgnorth. Winner half-mile hurdles over 10 flights WOS 1867.

W. Kite second under-15 200yd race WOS 1885 (27 secs).

George Kynaston beat six to win under-10s foot race WOS 1867.

Samuel Langford of Wenlock winner under-14s foot race WOS 1867; second in quarter-mile handicap WOS 1870; WOS 1873 second in the half-mile flat race for labourers; third in half-mile flat race NOA Much Wenlock.

Hugo Landsberger of GGS second 36lb shot-put (29ft 5in), joint-winner with C.M. Cooper climbing (146ft), second wrestling, catch as catch can, winner (with Brooke) of highest honours, NOA London. Winner climbing (138ft), joint-winner (with Hartley) of throwing the spear, joint-winner with Hotz of wrestling, and winner of the General Prize for merit and awarded a Wenlock medal, NOA Birmingham; second 36lb shot-put NOA Wellington.

G. Latham of St George's, winner 120yd boys' handicap WOS 1892.

G. Lauser of GGS third High Leap NOA London.

Henry Lawley (brother of below) winner under-14s foot race WOS 1850. Winner jingling WOS 1855, archery WOS 1859. By 1871 he is Railway Station Master at Longwood, Yorkshire, until at least 1881.

William Lawley (brother of above) runs for money (loses) on the open heath on the Bridgnorth road 1862. Winner amateurs' General Competition WOS 1868. Winner 100yd at NOA Wellington but disqualified for having competed for money. Winner hammer WOS 1869; second hammer WOS 1870 to Everall; third hammer WOS 1871. Judge WOS 1872; third hammer WOS 1872. Sings glees at the dinner 1872. Started but retired from 100yd flat race NOA Much Wenlock. Wins high praise as WOS Secretary, 1881; 1888 referee and Secretary; 1892 wins praise from Brookes for his suggestions for care of Field. Suffers a breakdown 1897–98. Prints many of WOS programmes.

H. Leeke of Holbrooke Hall, Derby winner 16lb hammer-throwing (76ft 2in) NOA Birmingham.

Sgt W. Leighton second in Gimcrack Race, and his team won tug of war WOS 1895.

J. Leslie of Shrewsbury third in one-mile foot race WOS 1885.

F. Lewis of King Edward's School, Birmingham, second under-14 200yd flat race NOA Birmingham.

F. Lloyd of Shropshire SC winner of Shropshire under-18 quarter-mile race 'with great ease' (62 sec). By 1883 some question about his amateur/professional status.

William Lomas of Warrington second in one-mile hurdles, first in quarter-mile hurdles for farmers (though afterwards disqualified), second in half-mile flat race, and ditto in the quarter-mile hurdle race ('a strong runner…in our humble opinion better suited to longer than two-furlong courses') NOA Much Wenlock.

Walter Long of GGS, winner 290yd swimming (4 min 47 sec) and 870yd swimming NOA Birmingham.

W.W. Long of Cheshire winner light-weight boxing NOA Wellington.

T.H. Maddox of Ludlow winner 200yd handicap WOS 1895.

F. Male of BAC second in 120yd hurdles WOS 1878.

Edward Mapplebeck of BAC second in one mile race, winner two-mile race (10 min 58 sec) NOA Birmingham. Winner mile race NOA Wellington.

W.P. Margetson of GGS second in wrestling, Cumberland style, second in fencing, NOA London.

Marmon of Manchester winner of a General Prize for merit at NOA Birmingham.

B. Marshall of Manchester AC second in one-mile handicap at NOA Shrewsbury.

E. Marson of Wednesbury Harriers, winner of 4m flat handicap (21min 231/5 sec), but 'winner objected to', outcome unclear, NOA Hadley.

James Massey winner under-10s race WOS 1854, son of High Street bootmaker.

F. Matthewson winner three-mile bicycle handicap WOS 1895.

J. Mayhew of BAC third WOS Pentathlon 1877.

Louis McCann of BAC, winner putting 32lb shot (20ft) WOS 1876.

F. McDonald of GGS medal-winner boxing, light-weight NOA London.

A. McNeill of Birmingham winner of boys' 10lb shot-put (27ft 5in), winner under-17 half-mile flat race, NOA Birmingham.

H. McNeill of BAC winner of sack racing (by a yard and a half) NOA Birmingham.

A. McPhee of BAC second 16lb hammer-throwing (65ft 9in) NOA Birmingham; winner 36lb shot-put NOA Wellington.

J.T. Mein (Kidderminster) winner one-mile bicycle race and second in the two-mile bicycle race WOS 1882.

A. Meredith second under-15s 200yd handicap WOS 1890.

Anne Meredith second in the ladies' race for a pound of tea WOS 1851.

A.T. Meredith winner half-mile handicap – large field and heavy going WOS 1893.

D. Merrick (brother of both below) of Woodhouse Fields second flat tilting WOS 1890. Winner of flat tilting and competed in hurdle too, but not placed WOS 1891.

E. Merrick (brother of above and below) of Woodhouse Fields winner flat tilting and second in hurdle tilting WOS 1890; second hurdle tilting WOS 1890. Winner hurdle tilting 1892. Competes again in 1893, but beaten by Ainsworth; second as Trooper Merrick in the Victoria Cross Race WOS 1894; ditto Victoria Cross Race WOS 1895.

W. Merrick (brother of both above) of Woodhouse Fields equal second in the flat tilting WOS 1893 with Poole and Cresswell.

G.E. Miles of Bridgnorth second in 440yd handicap WOS 1887; third in one-mile handicap WOS 1888.

J.F. Millington, Wolverhampton second in two-mile bicycle race and second in one-mile bicycle race WOS 1883.

A.W. Milner of Birkenhead third in two-mile bicycle race WOS 1883.

R.B. Mole of Brewood, Staffordshire competed in pole vaulting against J.G. Wilson, when 10ft 4in was cleared and £5 won by both, NOA Much Wenlock.

J.S. Moore of Kidderminster third 120yd flat race and winner 200yd flat race WOS 1883; second 120yd race WOS 1884 to R.N. Jones of Ironbridge – 'splendid race'. Same year winner of 200yd race.

E. Moore of Eastwall second in the hurdle tilting WOS 1870.

H. Morgan of Bewdley second in 120yd handicap WOS 1889; third 120yd handicap WOS 1890.

F.E. Morris of Shifnal winner under-15s 120yd handicap WOS 1891.

T. Morris of Shrewsbury second in two-mile bicycle handicap WOS 1886.

Thomas Morris of Shrewsbury second in middle-weight boxing NOA Wellington.

George Morrison won drawing and also writing prizes WOS 1860.

J. Mullins of Shrewsbury winner one-mile handicap WOS 1887.

T. Murphy third in 440yd flat race WOS 1883.

A. Murray of Gobowen winner 120yd handicap and 200yd handicap WOS 1887.

Isaac Nevett climbed the 55ft high rope at the first attempt at amateur WOS 1867.

Mary Nicholas won girls' drawing WOS 1857.

Edith Nicholls won shirt-making girls WOS 1869.

Ann Nicklin winner best knitting WOS 1852.

John Nicklin third in the 60yd under-10s foot race WOS 1866.

James Nuttall of Birmingham second in one-mile flat race in autumn WOS 1864 but believed to be a professional, so not applauded.

Arthur H. Oakley of (Oakley Park) third 100yd flat race, second running long leap (18ft 8in), third 120yd hurdle race at NOA Much Wenlock.

Oare or Hoare participant in the 1862 SOG Much Wenlock contentious White hurdles race; second in one-mile hurdles to Cooper WOS 1864, and in the half-mile flat foot race 'open to farm labourers residing in the county'. He was the favourite, too. Also participates at SOG 1864. Wins one-mile foot race, beating J.C. Bowdler WOS 1865. Samuel Hoare of Bourton wins the one-mile hurdles WOS 1866. Winner one-mile foot race (five started) WOS 1867 beating George Palmer; second 1868 WOS 1mile farm labourers' race to Palmer. Second in half-mile steeplechase NOA Wellington.

S. O'Donnel of Southampton AC third one-mile race, second two-mile race NOA London.

A. William 'Tiny' Oldfield of BAC wins General Competition WOS 1873, when he kisses hand of Queen of Beauty and causes a sensation; 1874 NOA Much Wenlock General Competition third in high leap (5ft 3in) second in shot-put (left + right=36ft) second in long leap (19ft 7in) first quarter-mile race (69¼ sec) so winner overall. NOA Much Wenlock he also wins 100yd flat race (by 4yd). Probably he who is second in 200yd foot race in 1875 WOS. In 1876 he is acting as WOS judge in place of Joseph Hubbard who is ill. Wins 200yd flat race WOS 1877 'a brilliantly contested race'. By 1886 working on a cocoa plantation in British Guiana. Died of yellow fever in Birmingham in 1895.

C.B. Oldfield of BAC wins running high leap NOA Much Wenlock.

Charles Olliver of Shrewsbury third in boxing NOA Wellington.

H.M. Oliver of Birmingham second one-mile flat race WOS 1877, winner one-mile hurdles. Winner half-mile flat race WOS 1878 when described as of Moseley Harriers. He becomes handicapper for WOS open events from 1879.

R.S. Oliver is second to H.M. above in the one-mile hurdles WOS 1877.

James Onions of Wenlock second hammer WOS 1866; winner hammer and second throwing stone WOS 1867.

Arthur Onslow winner under-14 200yd foot race WOS 1870.

C. Oppirman of GGS London second half-mile flat race run against the clock, in squads (2min 33sec).

Arnold Overton of Stourbridge third flat tilting WOS 1883. Competed in hurdle tilting NOA Hadley.

Alice Owen winner sewing WOS 1871.

J. Owen of Donnington third 120yd boys' handicap WOS 1894.

David Padmore of Wolverhampton winner long jump, high jump and hurdles WOS 1854.

C. Palmer winner one-mile flat handicap WOS 1879.

George Palmer farm labourer winner half-mile foot race WOS autumn 1861; second half-mile flat race WOS Autumn 1864. Winner half-mile race for farm labourers WOS 1865. Winner one-mile foot race WOS 1866 after close run with John Bowdler of Shrewsbury. Beaten into second place in one-mile foot race WOS 1867. Winner farm labourers' race one-mile WOS 1868.

Joseph Pardoe of Shinehill near Wenlock second in tilting WOS 1868. Winner of tilting over hurdles (though he had to crown himself with olive) NOA Wellington. WOS 1872, tilting over hurdles 'thrown from his horse which bolted across the field – he was little hurt'. WOS 1873 second in 120yd hurdles for farmers.

J.R. Parr NOA Much Wenlock General Competition fourth in high leap (4ft 4in), fourth in shot-put (left+right=33ft 9in), fourth in long leap (12ft 4in), fourth in quarter-mile race but outstanding in the rope-climb, going up to 75ft twice and making a third ascent to 60ft – no second prize was awarded, so fourth overall.

Miles Parton of Ketley winner quoits WOS 1861 (coal-miner).

W. Pearce of Edgbaston second in half-mile race WOS 1884.

W. Pelly of Southampton AC second 100yd flat race NOA London.

Viscount Petersham heir to Earl of Harrington second flat tilting 1881 WOS. By 1882 he has inherited and becomes Society's President and takes part again but does not manage to take a ring. After the hurdle tilting (in which he did not participate) he and William Ainsworth enjoy tent-pegging.

G. Pheasy of Wall second in pole leaping WOS 1882.

E. Phillips of Elmsdale, Birmingham second one-mile bicycle handicap WOS 1886; third in one-mile bicycle handicap WOS 1887.

E. Phillips of Shrewsbury winner one-mile bicycle handicap WOS 1895.

Samuel Phillips of Dawley Quoit Club winner quoits WOS 1883.

Piggot of Birkenhead ran in the 200yd handicap WOS 1891 but unplaced.

T. Pitchford, Donnington Wood winner 120yd handicap WOS 1886.

S. Plant, Old Park wins 120yd handicap and is second in the 200yd WOS 1888 in 12.1 seconds. Described as of Dawley when second 120yd handicap WOS 1890.

J.M. Player of Coventry winner 120yd handicap (11 3/5sec), third in heat 440yd handicap, NOA Hadley.

W. Player of BAC third standing high jump (3ft 6in) NOA Wellington.

J. Plowman of GGS joint-winner (with G. White) of pole leaping (8ft 10in) NOA London; third running high leap (63in), third running long leap (17ft), winner pole leaping (9ft 5in) and wins a prize for General Merit, NOA Birmingham.

W.G. Poole of Shrewsbury equal second in flat tilting WOS 1893. Also that year second in the new 'humerous' Victoria Cross Race. Trooper W. Poole wins Gimcrack Race (put on boots, drink glass, light cigar etc) WOS 1895.

W.H. Poole of CTS second in heat one-mile bicycle handicap NOA Hadley.

F. Potham of Moseley Harriers second in two-mile flat race WOS 1883; second one-mile handicap, winner 440yd handicap NOA Hadley.

W. Pound of Ludlow third in half-mile handicap WOS 1895.

A. Powell of Stourport winner 120yd handicap WOS 1894.

B. Powell of Lawley Bank winner quoits WOS 1882.

E.J. Powell of Ludlow second 120yd boys handicap WOS 1895.

Richard Powell of Dawley Quoit Club second in quoits WOS 1883.

Edward Poyner of Beckbury winner high jump and hopping on one leg in 1850. Winner half-mile foot race in 1851. Winner hurdles 1851 'decidedly the best leaper, bounding over the hurdles with the agility of a stag.' Still running in 1854.

E.W. Poyner second in Pentathlon behind Cross, (only two competed) and second in one-mile hurdle race WOS 1879. Prominent in amateur WOS autumn 1879 and second in Zulu contest; second in quoits WOS 1882.

Hermon H. Poyner second in quoits WOS 1878; third in quoits WOS 1883. Master baker and confectioner with shop on Spital Street.

Poyner (no initial) wins under-14 200yd race WOS 1878.

W. Pratt of Birchfield Harriers third one-mile bicycle handicap NOA Hadley.

John A. Preece of Cressage winner flat tilting WOS 1876. Winner flat tilting 'amidst great acclamations' at NOA Shrewsbury. His mount suffered a probably fatal injury to the brisket on stumbling over a hurdle WOS 1882 yet he shared still second place with C.W. Tully.

Richard Preece of Cressage winner flat tilting WOS 1877; second in flat tilting WOS 1879; winner flat tilting WOS 1880.

H. Price of Ludlow AAC joint-second (with Dutfield – Dutfield won run-off) 120yd handicap NOA Hadley.

W. Price of Wolverhampton second 200yd race WOS 1885.

Edwin C. Pritchard of Broncroft, near Craven Arms winner pole jump 9ft 2in WOS 1886. Winner high jump WOS 1887 and same year shared first prize in pole jump with W.H. Gough of Shrewsbury – divided the prize at 9ft 10in. Winner high jump and pole jump WOS 1888; second in high jump and winner of pole jump (9ft 10in) WOS 1889.

A.H. Proctor of Shifnal winner 120yd flat race; second in 200yd flat race WOS 1883.

John Proudley, of Wellington winner 300yd race for those employed in the forge WOS 1861.

John Pugh of Buildwas – SOG Wellington horse stumbled at an early stage of tilting, fell, and rolled over him. Fortunately unhurt but disqualified; 1861 WOS autumn games won tilting on ponies and 'exhibited an expertness which would have gained for him honours in ancient Greece' and got laurels and goblet from Lady Forester.

E. Purchase of Bridgnorth FC winner putting the weight (36ft 3in) NOA Shrewsbury.

H. Purslow of Shrewsbury third in under-14 150yd flat race for Shropshire competitors NOA Shrewsbury.

C.G. Pym of AAC winner high jump (5ft 4in) NOA London.

J.C. Rathgell fourth high leap, NOA London.

A Reading of Birmingham climbed 57ft NOA Birmingham.

J.H. Reece of Wolverhampton winner three-mile bicycle handicap – slow and tedious race – WOS 1891. Same name but of Balsall Heath second in one-mile bicycle handicap and second in three-mile bicycle handicap WOS 1893.

J. Rennie of Edgbaston second in half-mile race WOS 1885.

G.W. Renshaw of Manchester climbed 57ft NOA Birmingham. G.W. Renshaw of Haslingden won the gymnastic competition at NOA Much Wenlock 'the spectators enjoyed a treat of the highest order, and it is seldom that we have seen professionals acquit themselves better'.

E. Reynolds of Wenlock third in heat Shropshire under-18s quarter-mile flat race NOA Shrewsbury.

Hubert Reynolds of BAC second in two-mile race (in 11min 10secs) NOA Birmingham.

R.S. Reynolds of Much Wenlock winner 120yd handicap WOS 1889; third in 120yd handicap WOS 1891.

J.O. Richards of Bridgnorth competed in first bicycle race WOS 1876.

J. Richards winner quoits WOS 1878.

G.T. Richardson of Wolverhampton winner one-mile bicycle handicap WOS 1891.

F.E. Roberts of Shrewsbury third Shropshire under-18s quarter-mile flat race NOA Shrewsbury.

Henry Roberts winner under-12 boys race and under-15 ditto WOS 1883.

William Roberts of Much Wenlock winner one-mile hurdles WOS 1858 and 1859. Winner 1860 too – very wet and only race to be run on the day. Winner one-mile (over 14) hurdles open to all England at SOG Wellington, and high jump ditto 5ft 2in. Winner one-mile hurdles WOS autumn 1861 and high jump and long jump (18ft 4in). Runs against White in the contentious SOG Much Wenlock 1862 Games when White vaulted the hurdles. Judgement given in his favour; winner long and high jump WOS 1863. Autumn WOS 1864 winner running long leap and running high leap, clearing 5ft 2in and beating Cooper. Winner foot hurdle race WOS 1868, beating Griffiths; third in the Steeplechase WOS 1868. Second in 150yd hurdles over 10 flights WOS 1869. Winner 150yd hurdles WOS 1871. NOA Much Wenlock second in the 120yd hurdles and described as 'the old Wenlock favourite'. Stumbled and fell in 120yd hurdles heat NOA Shrewsbury 'the first race after the storm…the ground was a mere puddle'. Acts as a starter from 1881 WOS games. Painter, Plumber and Publican. Possible date of death 1910 (see plates 11 and 26),

W.M. Robins of Dennis Park second in half-mile bicycle handicap and ditto one-mile bicycle handicap, and ditto two-mile bicycle handicap 'an exciting finish' WOS 1888. Winner half-mile, one-mile and two-mile bicycle handicaps WOS 1889. Winner half-mile bicycle handicap, third one-mile bicycle handicap and second two-mile bicycle handicap WOS 1890 (spelt Robbins).

Rochelle of Stanmore third in two-mile bicycle handicap WOS 1889.

E. Rogers of Shrewsbury winner under-14 Shropshire competitors' 150yd race NOA Shrewsbury. Objection raised that he was over age – outcome unclear.

William Rogers of Shrewsbury won steeplechase 1861 when water jump caused a lot of mirth.

F.L. Rohrback of GGS third wrestling, catch as catch can, NOA London.

Rollings of Homer second in one-mile hurdles WOS 1870; Samuel Rawlings of Homer winner labourers' flat foot race half-mile, WOS 1872.

G. Rowe, of Wenlock winner one-mile foot race WOS 1885.

B.M. Rowland of Birmingham winner 440yd handicap WOS 1886.

William Rowlands of Homer winner quarter-mile handicap WOS 1870. Same name ('a one-armed man') of Homer third in labourers' flat foot race half-mile WOS 1872; 1881 census states that he was 'Blind in one eye not from birth' – seems more consistent with his profession as a land drainer.

Sarah Rowley won children's best sewing WOS 1852.

Charles Rudd, The Downs, joint second with Petersham flat tilting WOS 1881. Winner flat tilting and equal second in hurdle tilting with Tom Rudd WOS 1885:

J. Rudd of Harpsford Mill (probably an error for T. below) winner tilting at ring over one hurdle WOS 1890.

T. Rudd, equal second with Charles Rudd in hurdle tilting WOS 1885; second in hurdle tilting WOS 1886. Winner flat tilting and third in the hurdle tilting WOS 1888, when he is of Harpsford Mill; 1889 WOS second in flat tilting and ditto hurdle tilting, both to R Webster. Had hoped for a hat-trick at the WOS 1891 games, but was beaten to the Coubertin medal by Farmer. 'Trooper Rudd' competed in tent pegging WOS 1892, and was 'undoubtedly the best tenter', but was disqualified for not performing in regimentals; second in hurdle tilting WOS 1892; winner humorous Victoria Cross Race WOS 1893. Family butcher by profession

W. Rye of King's College Rowing Club, London first half-mile flat race (2 min 13 sec), first mile race (4min 50sec) NOA London.

Thomas Sabin of Allesley, Coventry, wearing pink and white colours, winner first ever bicycle race 3 miles, WOS 1876; WOS 1877 winner bicycle race three-mile 'easily'; WOS 1877 winner one-mile bicycle race; WOS 1878 winner three-mile bicycle race and one-mile race.

Edward Sandells second running high leap and 120yd hurdles WOS 1882; WOS 1883 second in running high leap; WOS 1884 (spelt Sandalls) winner running high jump. Winner high leap WOS 1885. Winner high jump 5ft 2in WOS 1886; second high jump WOS 1887; third high jump WOS 1889. Profession, greengrocer.

Thomas Sandalls WOS 1884 Joint winner of pole leaping with H.L. Reynolds – both cleared 8ft 10in; second pole leaping WOS 1885.

Sanderson winner WOS 1864 one-mile open flat race but came in to total silence as believed to be a professional who had fixed the race.

Sankey of Homer (probably Thomas, a limestone quarryman) third in the hammer, second in the half-mile foot race and third in putting the stone WOS 1868.

G. Scoltock third 120yd boys' race WOS 1885; second in under-12 120yd handicap WOS 1886.

T. Scoltock of Jackfield second in one-mile handicap – capital race throughout – WOS 1891. Winner one-mile handicap WOS 1892.

W. Scoltock second in under-15s 200yd WOS 1882 aged 13.

A. Scruton of BAC second half-mile race NOA Birmingham.

A. Seeley GGS, London first standing long leap (9ft 6in), medal-winner boxing, light-weight NOA London.

W. Shardlow of Shrewsbury second in heat of quarter-mile handicap NOA Shrewsbury.

Frank Frehock Sharpe of Wolverhampton winner one-mile bicycle handicap and ditto two-mile bicycle handicap WOS 1886. Winner half-mile bicycle handicap and two-mile bicycle handicap, second in one-mile bicycle handicap WOS 1887. Winner (easily) half-mile bicycle handicap in one-mile 56.1 seconds and of one-mile bicycle handicap and two-mile bicycle handicap WOS 1888; second half-mile bicycle handicap, winner one-mile bicycle handicap, winner two-mile bicycle handicap WOS 1890; second in one-mile bicycle handicap, but a poor second after coming to grief with C.F.G. Boyes, WOS 1891.

S. Sharples of PGAC is joint third in Pentathlon WOS 1876.

C. Shelbrook winner under-15 200yd handicap WOS 1886.

T. Shelden second in 440yd flat race WOS 1882.

William Shepherd of Lawley Bank winner quoits NOA Much Wenlock.

Shingler winner foot hurdles WOS 1855.

W. Shingler third under-15 200yd handicap WOS 1890.

Edmund Shorthouse of BAC winner of single stick NOA Wellington.

H. Simpson of Liverpool winner high running leap and one-mile foot hurdle race over 12 hurdles, with H. Grainger of Wellington second SOG Shrewsbury. Presented with a laurel crown and medal.

J. Simpson of Liverpool (error for above?) member of the athletics society of GB second in half-mile hurdles at SOG Shrewsbury.

T.W. Simpson of Shrewsbury winner 200yd flat race WOS 1882.

John Skett winner blindfold wheelbarrow race WOS 1855. Somersaulted into hedge.

William Skett winner jingling match WOS 1852.

C.E. Skinner, Warstone second in two-mile bicycle handicap WOS 1887.

H.W. Smallwood of Streckford Hall winner under-17 100yd flat race, winner boys' high running leap (4ft 6in) NOA Birmingham.

A. Smith of Aston third two-mile bicycle race and ditto one-mile bicycle race WOS 1885.

E. Smith, Trooper of Eaton Constantine winner of Victoria Cross Race WOS 1895; third in Gimcrack Race WOS 1895. Troopers E. Smith, J. Smith, C. Tart and E. Ainsworth won the Balaclava Mêlée WOS 1895.

H.H. Smith of West Bromwich and of Speedwell BC, second in heat one-mile bicycle handicap, winner three-mile bicycle handicap ('a splendid race from start to finish…won by about six yards') NOA Hadley. Winner two-mile bicycle race and second in one-mile bicycle race WOS 1884; second in two-mile bicycle race and winner one-mile bicycle race WOS 1885.

Henry Smith winner maths WOS 1857. In 1861 is living at 6 Sheinton Street, aged 14, listed as 'Pupil Teacher'.

Job Smith of Manchester beaten into second in hurdles by William Roberts at SOG Wellington, but he won the half-mile foot race – objection over his not being native of Salop, but overturned.

W. Smith second in 120yd boys' race WOS 1885.

W.A. Smith of Pengwern BC second in heat of Shropshire under-18s quarter-mile flat race NOA Shrewsbury.

C. Smythe of Birmingham winner General Competition WOS 1875. Second in 200yd hurdles, WOS 1875.

R.H. Smythe of King Edward's School winner under-14 100yd flat race, winner under-14 200yd flat race, winner under-14 half-mile flat race, NOA Birmingham.

Snead came second in the newly introduced General Competition WOS 1868.

William Snook of Pengwern Boat Club, Shrewsbury third in heat of Shropshire under-18s quarter-mile flat race NOA Shrewsbury. Won very easily half-mile local flat race WOS 1879; 1883 WOS he is of Moseley Harriers and wins half-mile flat race and two-mile flat race. He is noted as being at the St George's Annual Athletics Sept 1884.

W. Southall winner 400yd flat race WOS 1883.

Mrs Mary Speak winner the old women's race for tea in 1851.

Susan Speak winner the knitting prize WOS 1857.

R. Spong of BAC second in General Competition WOS 1875. In 1876, when first called Pentathlon, he comes second. Winner Pentathlon WOS 1877.

Harry Sproston of BAC winner running high leap WOS 1872; second in 120yd hurdles WOS 1877. Joint-winner (with C. Davies and T.W. Jones) of high jump (4ft 11in), second mile race, second long jump (17ft 1in), winner (easily) 150yd hurdles (five flights), winner half-mile steeplechase NOA Wellington.

W. Squires second in under-12 200yd WOS 1882.

W. Stone of Walsall second 200yd handicap WOS 1890.

N. Stratton of Wolverhampton winner 440yd race WOS 1885.

U. Stratton of Compton winner 440yd handicap, and second half-mile handicap WOS 1887.

E. Taylor winner 200yd flat race for Wenlock National School boys WOS 1871.

W. Taylor of Wolverhampton competed WOS 1851 in half-mile race.

William Tench – a lad who succeeded in carrying off a ring in the adult tilting WOS 1866. A great popular success with the crowd. Back at WOS in 1867 called **French** in the papers, and comes second 'small boy on a small pony'. Second in tilting NOA Birmingham 1867; second in tilting amateur WOS autumn 1867. Competes in tilting WOS 1868 –came to grief over a hurdle but was unhurt.

W. Tennant of Birchfield Harriers, second in 440yd handicap NOA Hadley.

Charles Thomas winner pony tilting WOS 1859.

H.T. Thomas of Hereford 'namesake of the old bone-setter' winner 120yd hurdle race (17¼ sec) NOA Much Wenlock.

H.V. Thomas of Hereford second in 200yd foot race WOS 1872, wins the same in 1873. Winner quarter-mile hurdle race, and quarter-mile flat race (56¼ sec) NOA Much Wenlock.

John Thomas, Sergeant of Police Station, Much Wenlock second in 100yd flat race NOA Much Wenlock (also on duty).

Richard Thomas of Shrewsbury winner steeplechase half-mile WOS 1867.

W. Thomas of Manchester third in climbing (84ft) NOA Birmingham.

T. Thornton prominent in amateur WOS autumn 1879. Winner hurdles WOS 1881; second in one-mile flat race WOS 1883.

W.M. Tilley of Liverpool second in running high leap NOA Much Wenlock.

Mary Titley second in sewing WOS 1857.

F.W. Todd of GWRCC, London third in half-mile handicap, third in quarter-mile handicap NOA Shrewsbury.

W. Travers of Wolverhampton winner one-mile bicycle handicap and three-mile bicycle handicap WOS 1892.

G. Trefield second in under-15 200yd handicap WOS 1886.

Trench third in 120yd boys handicap though only about 11 years of age and won his heat in a most plucky manner WOS 1893.

R. Trow of Bradmore winner one-mile bicycle handicap and three-mile bicycle ditto WOS 1893.

Richard Trow of Homer winner 400yd foot race for quarrymen and lime-burners WOS 1866.

W.H. Tuke of BAC second in fencing and second in single stick NOA Wellington.

C.W. Tully winner flat tilting and joint second hurdle tilting WOS 1882.

Charles T. Tulley of Sheinton second in flat tilting WOS 1877; winner flat tilting 1883.

F. J. Turnbull of Bridgnorth winner 220yd local flat race (20 ran) WOS 1881; 1882 WOS is second in half-mile local flat race. Winner 120yd race and third in 440yd race WOS 1885.

H. P. Turnbull fell in two-mile bicycle race of 1885 without injury, 'except the total collapse of his bicycle'. 1886 he is 'of Bridgnorth' and third in one-mile bicycle handicap and ditto two-mile bicycle handicap WOS.

George Turner of Shrewsbury is third in one-mile flat race NOA Much Wenlock. One G Turner listed 'Wenlock' is third in one-mile handicap WOS 1886; second one-mile handicap WOS 1887; second one-mile handicap WOS 1889.

J. W. Turner of Shrewsbury second 440yd race WOS 1885.

T. Turner of Wenlock winner half-mile foot race at amateur WOS autumn 1861.

W. Tyler winner under-15s 200yd race WOS 1885.

William Tyler of GGS winner 116yd swimming (1min 45sec), second 290yd swimming, second 870yd swimming, NOA Birmingham.

Edward Udal fourth in two-mile flat race NOA Much Wenlock.

T. Wace of Honourable Artillery Company second sabre and bayonet exercise NOA London.

Henry J. Wadlow third in 200yd flat race for Wenlock National School boys WOS 1871; same year is second in writing and in arithmetic. Son of Harriet Wadlow the Hotelkeeper at the Raven, Barrow Street. Later head teacher of the National School at Eyam and at the School House Winterbourne, Gloucestershire.

Jesse Wadlow of Patton Farm second in flat tilting and second hurdle tilting WOS 1895. Assistant Master at Stourpaine School, Dorset for 10 years before returning to Patton to take on the farm tenancy from his mother in 1905. A forward-looking farmer – a trait for which Patton Farm was renowned, a previous tenant having been Evan Davies a great friend of Brookes, who founded the Wenlock Farmers' Club. Jesse died in 1956.

J. Wainwright of Ludlow third in half-mile handicap WOS 1890.

M. Wainwright of Ludlow winner 120yd flat race WOS 1892.

S. M. Wainwright of Ludlow third 200yd handicap WOS 1890. Winner 200yd handicap and half-mile handicap WOS 1892. An S. W. Wainwright of Ludlow (error?) second in 120yd handicap, and second in 200yd handicap WOS 1893; second 200yd handicap WOS 1894.

T. Walker of Ketley second in 200yd handicap WOS 1886.

W. Walker of Shrewsbury third in 120yd boys' handicap WOS 1895.

Charles Wall of Wenlock first of six in a half-mile race for rock labourers winning £1 WOS 1865. C. Wall second in one-mile foot race WOS 1869.

E. Wall of Wenlock second in standing long leap WOS 1867.

John Wallace, Newcastle winner putting the shot (24ft 6½in) at NOA Much Wenlock.

J. O. Walters of Pengwern Boat Club second under-14 150yd race for Shropshire competitors NOA Shrewsbury.

J. E. Warburton of Haslingden winner two-mile flat race ('fast from start to finish' and he 'ran home winner by 10 yards' from Corser) and one-mile hurdles (5min 40sec – only two started) NOA Much Wenlock.

J. Ward of BAC winner Pentathlon WOS 1878.

William Ward winner boys' drawing 1857. Father a carpenter. **W Ward** winner pole leaping amateur WOS autumn 1867 (5ft 5in) and 1868.

Edwin Warder winner both writing for boys and arithmetic WOS 1869.

Warren (see Fitzwarrene).

Frederick Watkins of Broseley winner 200yd foot race WOS 1871. Competes but is beaten ditto WOS 1872.

J.E. Watkins of Shrewsbury second 120yd race WOS 1885.

J.C. Watt of BAC joint-second (with Fletcher) in pole leaping (8ft 5in) NOA Birmingham.

L. Watts of Wavertree third in two-mile bicycle race WOS 1884.

B. Weale second in half-mile flat handicap WOS 1879 (beating C.A. below).

C.A. Weale wins half-mile flat handicap 'very easily', and one-mile hurdle race handicap at WOS 1879. Profession, coachman/groom.

Henry Weale third in arithmetic WOS 1869; third in writing and winner arithmetic WOS 1871. Eventual profession, master grocer.

S.C. Weale of London Athletic Club second in quarter-mile hurdles NOA Shrewsbury.

William Weale second in Maths, second in writing and first Bible history and English history WOS 1857.

George Webster of the Downes winner tilting WOS 1866.

Edward Webster of Stanway competes in flat tilting WOS 1869 comes second to brother below. Edward wins tilting over hurdles WOS 1870.

John Webster of Stanway competes in tilting WOS 1868. Winner flat tilting WOS 1869. All three Websters, John, Edward and Richard (below) contest flat tilting WOS 1870. John and Richard second after William Clayton of Wenlock, though not clear how they shared the pair of silver spurs donated by Brookes. John winner tilting over hurdles NOA 1874. Publishes a challenge to all comers for WOS's 25th festival May 1875. Winner tilting at the Manchester Northern Counties Olympian Association for the Promotion of Physical Education June 1875. Winner hurdle tilting 1876 WOS. Winner tilting over hurdles at Manchester Aug 1876, beating Ainsworth and flat tilting, astonishing the crowd by taking the ring three times in succession, 'thus winning a very handsome carbuncle finger ring worth five guineas.' Winner hurdle tilting WOS 1877 and flat tilting WOS 1878; second in hurdle tilting WOS 1878; second flat tilting and second hurdle tilting Wenlock 1884.

Richard Webster of Stanway winner tilting over hurdles against 15 others WOS 1871. Ties with W. Johnson of Rushbury in flat tilting WOS 1872 and beats Johnson same year in the hurdle tilting. Winner flat tilting 1873; second to brother John in hurdle tilting NOA Much Wenlock. Winner flat tilting (brother John second) WOS 1875. Second in the hurdle tilting WOS 1883 behind C.E. Ainsworth WOS 1875; second in flat tilting NOA Shrewsbury. Winner flat tilting WOS 1879. Joint second in hurdle tilting WOS 1881. Second in hurdle tilting. Winner hurdle tilting NOA Hadley. Winner flat tilting WOS 1884. Ditto 1886 and 1889 when he also wins hurdle tilting.

H.W. Wellings of Shrewsbury Harriers third in 4m flat handicap NOA Hadley.

C. Wem winner under-12 200yd WOS 1882; 1883 WOS second in ditto and second in under-15 boys race.

J. Westley of BAC second 200yd flat race WOS 1877.

E. Whitcomb of Aston, winner 200yd handicap WOS 1889.

G. White (Norwich AC) third running long leap NOA London.

G. White (Southampton AC-error for above?) joint-winner of pole leaping (8ft 10in) NOA London.

Jack White The 'Gateshead Clipper', 1862 SOG Much Wenlock causes controversy by vaulting the hurdles.

E.S. Whitehead of King Edward's School, Birmingham third in sack racing NOA Birmingham.

J. Whitehouse of Birmingham winner two-mile bicycle race and second in one-mile bicycle race WOS 1885.

H. Whitlock of Birmingham third half-mile bicycle handicap, second one-mile bicycle handicap and third two-mile bicycle handicap WOS 1890.

W.J. Wilcox of Ironbridge second 120yd flat race WOS 1892.

Frederick Wilding of Hereford Football and Boat Club third in running high leap, second in General Competiiton, first in running long leap, second in putting 32lb shot WOS 1873. At NOA Much Wenlock, in General Competition, wins high jump (5ft 4in) wins shot-put (right + left 36ft 4in) second in long jump (18ft 9in) joint second in dead-heat in quarter-mile race, unplaced in climbing 75ft rope – second overall to Oldfield. Also winner of running long leap (19ft 5in) and second in putting the shot (20ft 7½in) NOA Much Wenlock; second in putting the weight (34ft 3in) at NOA Shrewsbury 1877, when he is described as of Hereford Rowing Club.

H. Wiley, Wolverhampton second in one-mile bicycle handicap WOS 1892.

Wilkinson competed in tilting WOS 1866.

E.V. Wilkinson of Birmingham winner one-mile handicap WOS 1890 in 4 mins 38 seconds.

C. Williams of Lutwyche third in half-mile handicap WOS 1894.

C.E. Williams of King Edward's School, Birmingham second under-14 half-mile flat race NOA Birmingham.

D.E. Williams of Ormskirk Athletic Club second in 200yd flat race WOS 1873.

J. Williams of GGS winner boxing, heavy-weight NOA London; second climbing (94ft) NOA Birmingham.

R.W. Williams third in one-mile bicycle race WOS 1883.

John George Wilson of Brewood, Staffordshire competed in pole vaulting against RB Mole, when 10ft 4in was cleared and £5 won by both, NOA Wenlock.

C. Wise of Leamington second 120yd handicap and winner 200yd handicap at WOS 1886.

W.E. Wood of Moseley Harriers (same as below?) third one-mile handicap, second 4 mile handicap, NOA Hadley.

W. Wood of Birmingham second half-mile handicap WOS 1891.

W. Woodhouse of Ludlow second 120yd flat race, third running high leap and 200yd flat race WOS 1883.

W.A. Worsop of GGS winner of javelin NOA London.

W.G. Worthington Manchester ABC second to Sabin in three-mile and one-mile bicycle races WOS 1878; 1879 just pipped at post by C.A. Halmer at WOS, and third in one-mile flat handicap running.

J.G. Wylie, a law student, of Shropshire Wanderers Football Club, third in heat of 100yd flat race, winner of heat quarter-mile handicap, winner Pentathlon and cup donated by King George of the Hellenes, third in 120yd hurdles, joint-winner (5ft 1in with E.W. Edwards) high jump, third in pole leaping NOA Shrewsbury.

Frank Yates second in half-mile local flat race WOS 1879; second in one-mile hurdles WOS 1882.

John Yates of Wenlock winner under-14 100yd foot race WOS 1866.

Thomas Yates of Wenlock third under-14§ 100yd foot race WOS 1865.

Appendix

Pentathlon (General Competition) Winners at the Wenlock Olympian Games

1868 – Warren Fitzwarren, The Towers, Market Drayton

1869 – Henry William Brooke, German Gymnastic Society, London

1870 – Henry William Brooke, GGS, London (ineligible for future years)

1871 – Richard Clement, German Gymnastic Society, London

1872 – John Anderton, Birmingham Athletic Club

1873 – Arthur William Oldfield, Birmingham Athletic Club

1874 – Arthur William Oldfield, Birmingham Athletic Club

1875 – C. Smythe, Birmingham Athletic Club

1876 – Gerard Fowler, Birmingham Athletic Club

1877 – A.R. Spong, Birmingham Athletic Club

1878 – J.A. Ward, Birmingham Athletic Club

1879 – C.B. Cross, Birmingham Athletic Club

1880 – *Not contended for*

1881 – Fred d'Escofet, Birmingham Athletic Club

Wenlock Olympian Society Office-Holders 1850–95

WPB: William Penny Brookes

Year	President	Secretary	Treasurer
1850	John Elmer	WPB	Edwin Yardley
1851	John Wadlow	WPB	Edwin Yardley
1852	George Moreton	Not recorded	Not recorded
1853	Francis Moreton	Not recorded	Not recorded
1854	WPB	Francis Richards	Edwin Yardley
1855	WPB	J. Cooper	J. Garner
1856	William A. James	Francis Richards	Edwin Yardley
1857	WPB	Edwin Yardley	Robert Horton
1858	Henry Phillips	Edwin Yardley	WPB
1859	Samuel Ashworth	Edwin Yardley	WPB
1860	E. Parsons	WPB	John Horton
1861	Henry Harnage	Edwin Yardley	John Horton

Year	President	Secretary	Treasurer
1862	WPB	Edwin Yardley	John Horton
1863	WPB	Edwin Yardley	John Horton
1864	WPB	J. Bill	Edwin Yardley
1865	WPB	Not recorded	Not recorded
1866	WPB	Edwin Yardley	Not recorded
1867	WPB	Mr Owens	Henry Price
1868	Henry Harnage	Edwin Yardley	Henry Price
1869	G.C.W. Forester MP	Edwin Yardley	Henry Price
1870	R.A. Benson	Edwin Yardley	WPB
1871	Col. Corbett MP	Edwin Yardley	Francis Moreton
1872	R. Jasper More	Edwin Yardley	Francis Moreton
1873	Lyde Benson	Edwin Yardley	Francis Moreton
1874	Earl of Bradford	WPB	Not recorded
1875	Lyde Benson	T.P. Everall	T.P. Everall
1876	C.T.W. Forester MP	T.P. Everall	T.P. Everall
1877	Arthur Sparrow	T.P. Everall	T.P. Everall
1878	J.E. Severne MP	T.P. Everall	T.P. Everall
1879	Sir Baldwyn Leighton MP	T.P. Everall	T.P. Everall
1880	Francis C. Bridgeman	W. Lawley	WPB
1881	Alexander H. Brown MP	W. Lawley	WPB
1882	Earl of Harrington	W. Lawley	WPB
1883	Lord John Manners	W. Lawley	W. Lawley
1884	Lord Wenlock	W. Lawley	W. Lawley
1885	Stanley Leighton MP	W. Lawley	W. Lawley
1886	Stanley Leighton MP	W. Lawley	W. Lawley
1887	Capt James Foster	W. Lawley	W. Lawley
1888	Lord Charles Beresford	W. Lawley	W. Lawley
1889	Lord Charles Beresford	W. Lawley	W. Lawley
1890	Capt Tremayne Miles	W. Lawley	W. Lawley
1891	WPB	W. Lawley	F. Serjeant
1892	Rowland Hunt	W. Lawley	F. Serjeant
1893	H.D. Greene	W. Lawley	F. Serjeant
1894	Lyde Benson	W. Lawley	F. Serjeant
1895	Hon George Forester	W. Lawley	F. Serjeant

BIBLIOGRAPHY

Manuscript Sources

Diaries of R.A. Slaney 1830–40s, Shropshire Archives, Shrewsbury

John Goulstone 'The first running tracks and Pedestrian enclosures: Notes on the Growth of Organised Athletics in early Victorian England' British Library, 1997

Minute Books of the Thames Conservancy Board, Museum of London Docklands

Minute Books 1 and 2 of the Wenlock Olympian Society

Minute Book of William Penny Brookes, Wenlock Olympian Society

National Archives FO 27/411 and 412 are the General Correspondance for France (1830) which includes dispatches from Lord Stuart de Rothesay

Newscuttings Book, Crystal Palace, Victoria & Albert Museum, London

Wilkinson Papers, Nottingham Archive DDW 135/3/9/1–50

Published Sources: Books:

A. Alexander *A Wayfarer's Log* (John Murray, London) 1919

H. Andrews *The Follies of a Victorian Athlete: William Snook (1861–1916)* (Leonie Press, Hartford) 2008

Aspin, J. *Ancient Customs, sports and pastimes of the English* (London, J. Harris, 1832)

J. Auden *Shropshire* (London, Methuen) 1912

B. Bailey *Portrait of Shropshire* (Hale, London) 1981

P. Bailey *Leisure and Class in Victorian England* (Methuen, London) 1987

D. Birley *Sport and the Making of Britain* (MUP, Manchester) 1993

D. Blaine *An encyclopaedia of rural sports* (Longman, London) 1840

E. Bland *Annals of Southport and district* (Riley, Guardian Office) 1903

M. Brettle *The Old Vicarage, Much Wenlock* (Ellingham Press, Much Wenlock) 2009

A.H. Buck *The Dawn of Modern Medicine* (Yale UP, New Haven, OUP) 1978 reprint of 1920 edition

M.C. Buer *Health, wealth, and population in the early days of the Industrial Revolution* (London, Routledge) 1926

W. Byford-Jones *Shropshire Haunts of Mary Webb* (Wilding, Shrewsbury) 1937

D. Cole *Much Wenlock Racecourse c.1733–1939* (published privately) 2008

D. Cox and B Godfrey (Ed) *Cinderellas and Packhorses: A History of the Shropshire Magistracy* (Logaston Press, Herefordshire) 2005

D. Cox 'Much Wenlock' *The Victoria History of Shropshire* Volume X (IHR, OUP) 1998

R.W. Cox *Sport in History: a bibliography 1800–1988* (MUP, Manchester) 1991

J.G. Dixon and others *Landmarks in the history of Physical Education* (Routledge & Kegan Paul, London) 1957

A. Fay *Victorian Days in England: Letters home by an American girl 1851–52* (Dog Rose Press, Ludlow) 2002

G. Finlay *History of Greece* Vol VI (Clarendon, Oxford) 1877

G. Finlay *History of the Greek Revolution* (Blackwood, Edinburgh) 1861

G.W. Fisher *Annals of Shrewsbury School* (Methven, London) 1899

H. Forrest *The Old Houses of Wenlock and Wenlock Edge their history and associations* (Wilding, Shrewsbury) 1915

M. Furbank, H. Cromarty, G. McDonald, C. Cannon *William Penny Brookes and the Olympic Connection* (Wenlock Olympian Society, Much Wenlock) 2007

J. Gale and J. Sims *Much Wenlock in Victorian Times* (Shropshire Books, Shrewsbury) 1990

C. Gamble *John Ruskin, Henry James and the Shropshire Lads* (New European Publications, London) 2008

Gazetteer & Directory of Shropshire, 1851

W.G. Grace *Cricket* (Arrowsmith, London) 1891

C.W. Hackensmith *History of Physical Education* (Harper & Row, New York) 1966

C. Haddon *The First Ever English Olimpick Games* (Hodder & Stoughton) London, 2004

B. Haley *The Healthy Body and Victorian Culture* (Harvard UP, Cambridge and London) 1978

D. Hall (Ed) *Muscular Christianity: Embodying the Victorian Age* (CUP, Cambridge) 1994

Harrod's *Directory of Shropshire* 1861

M. Herring *Shropshire* (Paul Elek, London) 1949

W. Howitt *The Rural Life of England* (Longman, London) 1838

E. Illingworth *A Short History of the Northern Counties Athletic Association 1879–1979* (NCAA, Leeds) 1979

M. Jay *The Atmosphere of Heaven* (Yale UP, London) 2010

R. Jenkins *The First London Olympics 1908* (Piatkus, London) 2008

D. Jones *Edwin Chadwick and the early Public Health movement in England* (University of Iowa, Iowa City) 1929

K. Jones *The Wenlock Branch: Wellington to Craven Arms* (Oakwood Press, Usk) 1998

Kelly's *Directory of Shropshire* 1885

Kelly's *Directory of Shropshire* 1895

Kelly's *Directory of Shropshire* 1900

W. Leighton *A Flora of Shropshire* (Davies, Shrewsbury and Van Voorst, London) 1840

E. Lawrence Levy *The History of Birmingham Athletic Club* (Hammond, Birmingham) 1898

J. Loveday *London Waterside Surveys* (Loveday, London) 1857

P. Lovesey *The Official Centenary History of the Amateur Athletic Association* (Guinness, London) 1979

J. MacAloon (Ed) *Muscular Christianity in Colonial and Post-Colonial Worlds* (Sport in the Global Society, Routledge) 2008

J. MacAloon *This Great Symbol Pierre de Coubertin and the Origins of the Modern Olympic Games* (University of Chicago Press, Chicago & London) 1981

P. McIntosh *Physical Education in England since 1800* (G. Bell & Sons, London) 1968

R. Malcolmson *Popular Recreations in English Society 1700–1850* (CUP, Cambridge) 1973

D. Manuel (Ed) *Walking the Paris Hospitals: Diary of an Edinburgh Medical Student, 1834–1835* (Wellcome Trust, London) 2004

Lindon Meadows *College Recollections and Church Experiences* (Ridgway, London) undated

Medical Directory

Medical Register

Mercer & Crocker *Directory of Shropshire* 1877

J. Norridge *Can we have our balls back, please?* (Penguin, London) 2009

W.A. Osbaldiston *The British Sportsman and Nobleman, Gentleman and Farmer's Dictionary of Recreation and Amusement* (J. Stead, London) 1792

Pigot *Directory of Shropshire* 1828–29

Pigot *Directory of Shropshire* 1835

Pigot *Directory of Shropshire* 1849

J. Pinnell *Wenlock Priory* (English Heritage, London) 1999

J. Randall *Tourists' Guide to Wenlock* (Randall, Madeley) 1875

Robson *Directory of Shropshire* 1840

G. Rogers et al *Fleet and Free: A history of Birchfield Harriers Athletic Club* (Tempus, Stroud) 2005

D. Sansone *Greek Athletics and the Genesis of sport* (Berkeley, University of California Press, London) 1988

P. Sheldon *The Life and Times of William Withering: His Work, His Legacy* (Brewin, Studley) 2004

R.A. Slaney *Essay on the Beneficial Direction of rural Expenditure* (Longman, London) 1824

Slater *Directory of Shropshire* 1856

W. Smith *Stretching their bodies: The history of physical education* (David and Charles, Newton Abbot) 1974

Social Science Meeting at Liverpool, 1858 (Partridge & Co, London) 1858

N. Spivey *The Ancient Olympics* (OUP, Oxford) 2005

R. Stevens *Medical Practice in Modern England* (Yale UP, London) 1966

J. Strutt *Glig-gamena angel-deod : Or, The sports and pastimes of the people of England 1749–1802* (T. Bensley for White & Co., London) 1810

C .Turner Thackrah *The Effects of Arts, Trades, and Professions, and of Civic States and Habits of Living, on Health and Longevity: with Suggestions for the Removal of Many of the Agents which Produce Disease and Shorten the Duration of Life* (Science History Publications, USA) 1985

E.P. Thompson *The making of the English working class* (Gollancz, London) 1963

H. Timmins *Nooks and Corners of Shropshire* (Elliot Stock, London) 1899

B. Trinder *A History of Shropshire* (Phillimore, Chichester) 1998

B. Trinder *The Industrial Revolution in Shropshire* (3rd Edition) (Phillimore, Chichester) 2000

E.A. Underwood (Ed) 'The Evolution of the General Practitioner in England' by W.J. Bishop in *Science Medicine and History, Essays in honour of Charles Singer* Vol 2 (OUP, Oxford) 1953

D. Van Dalen and B. Bennett *A World History of Physical Education* (Englewood Cliffs, Prentice Hall) 1971

Victoria County History of Shropshire (Constable/IHR, London) 1908–

S. Wassong *Pierre de Coubertin's American Studies and Their Importance for the Analysis of his early Educational Campaign* (Ergon Verlag, Wurzburg) 2002

M. Watman *History of British Athletics* Robert Hale, London, 1968

A. Wear (Ed) *Medicine in Society* (CUP, Cambridge) 1992

F. Webster *Athletics of To-day: History, Development and Training* (Warne, London) 1929

J. Wiblin *The Students' Guide to the Hospitals and Medical Institutions of Paris* (London) 1839

D. Young *The Modern Olympics* (John Hopkins University Press, Baltimore and London) 1996

Published Sources: Journals

Sport in History (Routledge, London)

The Examiner, 8 August 1830 Issue 1175

The Lancet

The Royal Gazette 7 Sept 1830

The Times

D. Anthony 'Olympic Influences' *Journal of Olympic History* 2002 September, Vol 10 no 3 pp67–70

D. Anthony 'Letters Pierre de Coubertin–William Penny Brookes' *Journal of Olympic History* 2004 May, Vol 12 no 2 pp61–64

D. Cannadine 'Theory and Practice of the English Leisure Class' *Historical Journal* 21 (June 1978)

A. Castiglioni 'The Foreign students at the school of Padua: the English Nation' *Ciba Symposia*, Vol 10 (1948–49) no 3, Nov/Dec

E. Day 'Much Wenlock Priory and Buildwas Abbey' *Transactions of the Woolhope Naturalists' Field Club* 1927

J. Dodd 'The State of Agriculture in Shropshire 1775–1825' *Transactions of the Shropshire Archaeological Society* Vol 55 1954 pp1–31

A.W.M. Driega 'Olympics before Pierre de Coubertin' *Journal of Olympic History* 1997 Summer, Vol 5 no 2 pp20–27.

R. Fenn 'Early Christianity in Herefordshire' *Transactions of the Woolhope Naturalists' Field Club* 1968

B.H. Harrison 'Religion and Recreation in Nineteenth-Century England' *Past and Present* 38 1967, pp98–125

N. McKendrick, 'Josiah Wedgwood and Factory Discipline' *Historical Journal* iv 1961 pp30–55

N.A. Parry 'Pioneers of physical education in the nineteenth century: Alexander Alexander' *History of Education Society Bulletin* 22 (Autumn 1978) pp21–38

Lord Rennell of Rodd 'Notes on certain pre-Domesday estates East of Leominster' *Transactions of the Woolhope Naturalists' Field Club*, 1969

P. Richards 'RA Slaney, the industrial town, and early Victorian social policy' *Social History* 4 1979

P.J. Toghill 'Dr W G Grace: cricketer and general practitioner' *Journal of Medical Biography* Vol 1 No. 3 August 1993

D. Watson 'Popular Athletics on Victorian Tyneside' *International Journal of the History of Sport* Vol II Dec 1994 No. 3 pp485–494

Internet:

www.ancestry.co.uk

www.cwgc.org Commonwealth War Graves Commission (Debt of Honour index)

www.british-history.ac.uk/report.aspx?compid=22199 Victoria County History: A History of the County of Middlesex: Vol 2, 1911 pp301–2 'Athletics'

www.historicaldirectories.org

www.johnhulley-olympics.co.uk for Hulley and his work in Liverpool

www.la84foundation.org

www.lemessagedecolette.fr Comite Français Pierre de Coubertin 'Coubertin et le monde du travail' (pdf) by JCL

www.liverpoolregt.co.uk for Cecil Bodenham

www.noeaa-athletics.org.uk article by Bob Phillips

www.nuts.org.uk/trackstats

www.victorianlondon.org/dickens/dickens-a.htm for GGS

PHOTOGRAPHS

List of Plates

ACKNOWLEDGEMENTS

This has been a truly fascinating subject to research. I am deeply indebted to Chris Cannon of the Wenlock Olympian Society (WOS) in particular, who patiently answered my queries despite, as Chairman and Archivist of WOS, being almost overwhelmed with responsibilities as London 2012 approached. Helen Clare Cromarty of WOS also helped me locate needles in haystacks, saving me hours of trawling through newspapers on microfilm, for which I am most grateful. On visits to Much Wenlock, Lucy and Kirk Heywood of the Raven Hotel extended a generous welcome and, frequently, a hot meal for sustenance, besides introductions to anyone they thought might be able to help with inquiries about local families.

Joy Sims, historian of Victorian Wenlock was faultlessly generous to a newcomer on her patch, sharing her knowledge and contacts and accompanying me round the town. Seldom was anyone better named; she made the project fun and lit up trips to explore. Martin Leath shared his copious research into athletics in Shropshire and his superior sporting knowledge, for which I am very grateful. Philip Wadlow kindly helped me unravel his family tree, again, saving me hours on Ancestry. My sincere thanks, too, to Katie Foster for her enthusiasm for my proposed efforts at an important stage.

Others to whom I am indebted include:

Louise Acton	Sophie Duncan	Ivor Moore
Margaret Addis	Philip Dunne	Glyn Morgan
Mary Beard	Catherine, Lady Forester	Pat Rogers
Riou Benson	Clive Freeman	Paddy and Sue Ryan
Alan Brisbourne	Christine Grieve	Shropshire Archives
Neil Carter	Mildred Harrison	Peter Thompson
Justin Coldwell	David Higman	France von Noorden
Henry Connor	Richard Holt	Ian Weightman
Briony Cooper	Anne Hughes	Edward Williams
Eleftheria Daleziou	David Lewis	Gareth Williams
Rosie Daniels	Hugh McLeod	Sue Yardley
Anna Dreda	Richard Milner	

At times this book has felt like a marathon sprint — demanding sustained hours of work over a relatively short period. To enable me to finish it, I have been blessed with great support from my family, to whom I am immeasurably indebted. Friends have also thoughtfully and generously expanded school runs into play time to extend my working day, for which I cannot adequately thank them (Ben and Louisa Collings and Marie Hudson in particular). My thanks, too, to Fiona Graham. As the deadline tightened, my husband more than once referred to the memorable words of our greatest Olympian, rower Steve Redgrave at Atlanta in 1996, muttering something like 'if I see you go anywhere near another book…' Thank you for your patience and understanding.

www.cbeale.co.uk

INDEX

For an index of competing athletes, please see also Athletes' Biographies from page 159.